To m…
Ger…
From …
Richard Spiegelberg
April 19, 1978

Richard Spiegelberg was born in 1944, and was educated at Marlborough College and New College, Oxford. On leaving Oxford with an Honours Degree in PPE, he joined the staff of The Economist Intelligence Unit in 1965. In 1967 he moved to the newly-launched *Times Business News* where he worked as an Industrial correspondent for eighteen months, and then as the editor of the Business Diary. He is now Management Editor of *The Times*.

'A timely book which describes the institutions of the City and how they work, records some of the most memorable scandals of recent years, and shows how greatly the power of the City is being extended. The writer shows what enormous and unbridled power it places in the hands of very few individuals' – *Morning Star*

'I recommend Mr Spiegelberg's book. It is thoughtful, stimulating, and about how our country is really run' – *City Press*

'A rousing attack on the City's irresponsibility' – *The Sunday Telegraph*

'Fascinating, lively' – *Manchester Evening News*

THE CITY
Power Without Accountability

RICHARD SPIEGELBERG

QUARTET BOOKS LONDON

Published by Quartet Books Limited 1973
27 Goodge Street, London W1P 1FD

First published in Great Britain by Blond & Briggs Ltd 1973

ISBN 0 704 31055 4

Printed in Great Britain by
Hunt Barnard Printing Ltd., Aylesbury, Bucks

1 The City Observed 1

2 The Institutions 25

3 The Rich Market for Corporate Finance 61

4 The American Challenge 83

5 The Clearing Banks 102

6 The Bank of England 133

7 The City Code 167

8 Insurance 203

9 How to Make a Million out of the City 221

Epilogue 243

Bibliography 248

Index 251

AUTHOR'S NOTE

A large number of people, within the City and without, have been kind enough to provide information, express views and generally to help me in the preparation of this book. I should like to thank them all. I am particularly grateful to Mr. Victor Sandelson who has helped me avoid pitfalls, and has provided constructive comments.

I am also grateful to *The Times* for giving me permission to write the book.

Mr Pat Matthews, at his own request, read that part of Chapter 9 which concerns him and made various suggestions, some of which have been incorporated.

My wife, Coralie, endured the almost intolerable birth pangs of this book and made two important contributions to it. She not only provided invaluable encouragement. She also typed it. I dedicate the book to her.

'We must not let in daylight upon magic.'
Walter Bagehot

'Unreal City,
Under the brown fog of a winter dawn,
A crowd flowed over London Bridge, so many,
I had no thought death had undone so many.
Sighs, short and infrequent, were exhaled,
And each man fixed his eyes before his feet.
Flowed up the hill and down King William Street,
To where Saint Mary Woolnoth kept the hours,
With a dead sound on the final stroke of nine.'
T. S. Eliot

1. THE CITY OBSERVED

On Thursday, 20 January 1972, the British Government announced that for the first time in nearly twenty-five years there were more than a million people unemployed in the United Kingdom. On the same day, the *Financial Times* Ordinary share index, the most commonly used yardstick for measuring stock market movements in Britain, rose to the significant point of 500, the first time in three years that it had attained such heights. The irony was bitter – the juxtaposition of headlines on the front pages of the London evening papers brought this into sharp relief. The message conveyed by this startling coincidence seemed equally poignant. The two otherwise arid statistics seemed to say a lot about how important values within a capitalist society tend to diverge. One could have accepted the coincidence in two ways. At an emotional level, it seemed to demonstrate the appalling insensitivity of stock market investors, in particular, and the City of London, in general, towards one of the worst social problems which the country has had to face for decades. From a pragmatist's viewpoint, there was no inconsistency. Companies, he would have argued, are not in business to employ large numbers of people. If they can produce as much or more with fewer men, their profits will increase (other things being equal) and this in turn will do wonders for their share prices. He would have gone on to speculate that because unemployment had gone beyond (what other people considered to be) politically acceptable levels, the pressure on Government to stimulate the economy faster would be greater. This too would be good for the stock market. I suppose one could have equally well shown the fundamental divergence of values by drawing attention to company profits and contrasted these with levels of unemployment.

There are some, admittedly vestigial, signs that corporate responsibility within industry is being recognized as not necessarily confined to the limited interests of the shareholder: that there are responsibilities towards customers, consumers, employees and the community at large which have to be discharged. The more pure and limited capitalist viewpoint is at its most trenchant and pervasive in the City.

In the political spectrum, the contrast in values, of course, is that between left- and right-wing. The City is outspokenly anti-socialist. For six years until 1970, the City was locked in almost continuous conflict with the second post-war Labour Government; a conflict which perhaps reached its most dramatic heights in the battle between Harold Wilson and Lord Cromer, Governor of the Bank of England, over the safety of the pound (see Chapter 6). City men who collaborate with the Labour Party are invariably regarded with suspicion in their own camp. Charles Villiers, whom the Labour Government appointed to run the Industrial Reorganization Corporation, decided not to return to Schroder Wagg (where he had been a director), when the Conservatives abolished the I.R.C., but went to run another merchant bank, Guinness Mahon.

There is a sort of dualism in Labour Party attitudes to the City. Wilson was never slow to castigate City speculators when the pound came under fire, yet his Government promoted merchant bankers to fulfil key public roles – Lord Melchett was chosen from Hill Samuel to head the British Steel Corporation and Villiers' predecessor at I.R.C. was Ronald Grierson, an ex-Warburgs director. More recently, in opposition, the Labour Party has committed itself formally to nationalizing the banks and the insurance companies. But it was a move regretted by the Party's leaders, and it stands little chance of finding its way on to a future legislative programme of the Labour Party. Perhaps the greatest irony is that, in spite of selective employment tax, long term capital gains tax, increased Government intervention in industry, the sterling crises and a host of other things which were introduced or happened during the Labour administration, the City not only survived but also seemed to thrive during those six years.

To suggest that at every point of contact between the City and the Conservatives there is total sympathy would be going too far. It is true that it is towards the City that many Conservative leaders look either to repose or to spend their energies when the Party is in opposition. Reginald Maudling was a director of Kleinwort Benson, the merchant bank, and at the same time became unhappily involved in an insalubrious 'off-shore' investment outfit (The Real Estate Fund of America) during his recent opposition years. Edward Heath, himself, until he became Party leader, went back to the merchant bank which formerly employed him, Brown, Shipley. And, of course, a significant number of Tory leaders have entered politics directly from the City in recent years.

Peter Walker is the most important of these. In many ways he typifies the new generation of self-made City entrepreneur. His new-style Toryism closely mirrors the sort of insensitive meritocracy that has been the hallmark of so many young financiers who have risen to prominence in recent years; the obsession with efficiency and the calculated lack of compassion that goes with it. Walker started off life in insurance, met up with an accountant, David Moate, to form a highly successful insurance broking firm called Walker Moate. From this base he spread out into unit trusts, property and finance, and met Jim Slater. But not long after his partnership with Slater had been consummated in the form of Slater Walker Securities, Walker's ambitions were diverted completely towards the political arena. The phenomenal success of Slater Walker has been far more the work of Slater than of Walker. Edward Du Cann, until he was deposed from the chairmanship of the Tory Party, was another high-ranking Conservative who trod the path from unit trusts into politics, sharing the same sort of political philosophy.

While it is true that the City welcomed the return of the Conservatives in 1970 ('Fears that capitalism was in decline seemed to vanish overnight,' said *The Economist*), its support for the Government has not been unqualified. The Government's handling of the Rolls-Royce collapse, for example, greatly angered a number of leading merchant banks. They claimed they had been misled by the Government into putting up more finance for Rolls during the last months before the crash. They thought the Government would prop up the company, willy-nilly – whereas in fact further Government aid was conditional on a favourable report from Cooper Brothers, the chartered accountants. The City had more than it had bargained for when the new Conservative Government allowed Rolls-Royce and the Mersey Docks and Harbour Board to go bust. The sight of lame ducks limping and collapsing was not such a pleasant spectacle, after all.

I have already gone far enough to be accused of treating the City as something which is homogeneous and clearly identifiable. It is nothing of the sort. In geographical terms, the City is taken to mean whatever stands between St. Paul's and the Tower of London, between the Thames and the Barbican – the 'square mile', in fact. The City is to the rest of London rather as the casbah is to other parts of an Arab city. Its streets are narrower and more populated: the activity is more purposive. As bodies bustle down Throgmorton Street or Cornhill, there is man motivated by money, the vital raw material of this complex, unwieldy process plant.

Yet between five o'clock and six o'clock in the afternoon, the huge and intricate machine grinds to a halt. 400,000 people work in the City by day, but at night the population falls to a mere 5000. Through London's commuter arteries, great chunks of the City's work-force are channelled back – to Croydon and Chelmsford, Orpington and Esher, Guildford and Gravesend, and almost all stations down the lines.

In physical appearance, the City has changed a lot in recent years. No less than a third of its buildings were affected by bomb damage during the war. The new buildings – providing twenty million square feet of the City's total seventy-seven million square feet accommodation – have rightly been described as 'monuments to the plot-ratio calculations of property men'. They are bleak and institutional.

There was a time when the City produced things. The 'plot-ratio' calculations have stopped that. As the price of square feet has soared – it has been up to £20 a square foot per annum* in parts of the City in recent years – many of the older industries have departed. The only really tangible things produced in the City nowadays are newspapers. The City's business, as a group of economists has explained, 'is almost entirely confined to the transfer of rights and titles and to taking decisions which make possible the exchange of goods and services, not only in this country but throughout the world'.

There is an unreality about the City. At the end of the day, the banking or insurance clerk may have little to show for his work, except perhaps for a few page entries in a ledger book or a pile of processed documents. He may not even have that to show. More often than not money moves around the City by word of mouth. A verbal agreement to buy this or insure that is usually all that is needed for 'the transfer of rights and titles'. The rich fabric of trust, of which the City boasts, is embodied, as if it were an eternal truth, in the Stock Exchange's motto 'My word is my bond.'

In 1967, a group of economists, exploring the labyrinthine inter-relationships in the City, carried out a survey of communications habits in the square mile. They found that during a typical working day in the City, three million telephone

* Which, as City people frequently point out, is a high price to pay for accommodating a wastepaper-basket.

calls are made (excluding inter-office calls), four and a half million letters are sent through the post and 450,000 messages are sent by private messenger. Through this mountain of paper and nexus of wires, money moves.

This then is the City as a geographical entity. It is not strictly accurate to equate it with the financial system of either London or the country as a whole. Some activities, it is true, are exclusive to the City. Nowhere else in the country is there a discount market, or a foreign exchange market, or a bullion market, or an international ship chartering market, or a comprehensive metal exchange, or a number of other commodity markets. Only Lloyd's, located in the City, can provide such a variety of specialized insurance services. But the City has no monopoly of banking, stock markets, insurance in general, and a whole host of other financial services. Decisions on huge investment trust portfolios are taken by the Scotsmen of Dundee and Edinburgh. Companies are floated on the Manchester and Birmingham stock exchanges. And the brass plates outside buildings in the main streets of St. Helier, Jersey, have more in common with Bishopsgate or Fenchurch Street than with the High Streets of British provincial towns. All that one can say with safety is that within the City there is a vast concentration of financial decision-making, affecting not only what goes on in Britain. The decision-making is international in its scope.

The City has never been at pains to justify itself. It points to the fact that its earnings from overseas are of the order of £400 million to £500 million a year – a fact, no doubt, which Mr. Wilson could ill afford to disregard. Insurance provides the bulk of the City's foreign earnings, followed by merchanting, banking and brokerage. Having said all that, the City's apologist would then go on to explain that the London Stock Exchange quotes more securities (over 3000) than any other world stock market; that the world centre for chartering ships and aeroplanes is the Baltic Exchange; that the City contains the biggest concentration of foreign banks (200-odd, no less), the largest gold market, the largest international insurance market, and some of the leading world commodity markets and that is the undisputed world centre of the Eurocurrency markets. He would add that the City is also the centre of a massive overseas banking network which spreads throughout the world and that a fifth of the world's trade is settled in sterling, much of it through the City. It is a formidable catalogue with which to confound the critics.

All this presents an imposing façade of self-confidence, something that can be found without searching too hard among City people. But the fact that the City finds that it has to justify itself in a sense indicates that behind the façade there is a certain insecurity. The City is an obvious target for criticism and there is no doubt that some of the criticism has come to touch on sensitive nerves. The City, of course, lays itself open to criticism. It is misogynic, although two-fifths of its work-force are women; it is philistine, in spite of the fact that City firms and organizations, including the municipal authorities, patronize the arts; it is still consciously composed of men who have been to the same schools and who share the same political views, the same clubs, the same hobbies and, not infrequently, the same families; and it is unashamedly self-interested, despite what the apologist may say about its contribution to the country's balance of payments.

All this, of course, would need no explaining away if the City worked, and was seen to work, efficiently, smoothly and equitably all the time. The trouble is that this is not the case. There are agonizing moments when nerves are lost, when integrity and competence are questioned and when the whole delicate construction of City values seems to be on the brink of collapsing hopelessly. There have been too many moments like this for comfort in recent years. Backed by illustrious City names, supposedly sound businesses run by supposedly zealous entrepreneurs turn out to be nothing but almost worthless entities manipulated or mismanaged by swindlers or incompetents. When an industrial company backs failure, it risks only its shareholders' money and its own reputation. When a merchant bank or a stockbroker does the same, it is the reputation of the City as a whole that is at stake – such is the nature of collective responsibility which necessarily exists in a tightly knit community of this sort.

The notion of collective responsibility is vitally important to understanding the City. The City is more than just a loose assortment of businesses connected in some rather complicated way with finance in all its ramifications. It is tightly cohesive. When a business is floated on the Stock Exchange, for example, a merchant bank or a stockbroking firm arranges for the capital to be raised, a variety of institutions, ranging from insurance companies to investment trusts, underwrite the new issue of capital, and the Stock Exchange supervises the market for the shares once the company is floated. In financing international trade, the clearing banks, the merchant banks, the discount houses and the insurance industry are similarly enmeshed together. The responsibility is spread across a wide variety of City entities. It forms a complicated web at which the centre is the Bank of England, the overseer, which is at one time the arm of Government in the City and the spokesman of the City in Whitehall.

Into the web is woven a complex inter-relationship of personalities. Multiple directorships in the City abound. Merchant bankers sit on the boards of insurance companies, investment trusts, property companies, discount houses, and clearing banks. Clearing bankers are directors of insurance companies, discount houses, merchant banks, etc. The permutations are manifold. City leaders talk frequently about how they 'wear two hats'. Sometimes, divided loyalties can be positively embarrassing, like, for example, in the summer of 1970, when the country's second largest property company, Metropolitan Estate & Property Corporation, got itself into a complex take-over situation with Hill Samuel, on the one hand, and Commercial Union, the insurance giant, on the other. Hill Samuel was the favoured partner and announced its proposed merger with M.E.P.C. at the beginning of July. The unfriendly bid of Commercial Union caused consternation. Apart from anything else, the insurance company had no less than seven merchant banks represented on its board in one form or another, including two directors of Schroder's, M.E.P.C.'s merchant bank. 'A situation of this kind,' said *The*

Times, 'was almost bound to arise when the City's merchant banks are heavily represented on the board of a company launching a take-over bid.'

The City, collectively, has come under suspicion in recent years. Unbiased observers have been asking whether all is really well within the square mile. It is probably true, as *The Economist* has put it, that 'the Wild West days of the City are long past. Hardly any massive swindles, frauds, hoaxes or gigantic market riggings enliven the scene'. But then a man can just as easily be unloaded of a small fortune in a West End club as in a saloon bar. The only difference is in the degree of subtlety and finesse.

The City is full of paradoxes. Over the last fifteen years the City authorities have taken successive steps to ensure that all shareholders in a company are treated equally: that no group of shareholders, for example, has access to privileged information without the rest of the shareholders knowing about it. Yet the City with its closely knit information network is designed (unintentionally, albeit) to generate 'inside' information. Share prices rise suddenly and mysteriously before a take-over bid is announced, yet the authorities almost invariably do nothing but turn a blind eye: or the Stock Exchange institutes an enquiry which almost inevitably shows there has been no irregularity.

There is another paradox in the scrupulous attention City experts pay to tax avoidance, of which the growth of 'offshore' funds has perhaps been the most conspicuous example. Merchant banks go to considerable lengths to secrete their clients' fortunes away to the Bahamas, Switzerland or some other tax haven. Underwriting syndicates at Lloyd's provide their members with the opportunity to avoid tax on a massive scale. Yet with their collective hands on hearts, both Lloyd's and the merchant banks unfailingly proclaim the benefits they bestow on the national economy. Again there is a paradox in the way muted self-interest lies unquestioned behind more explicit and more worthy motives. A number of City entrepreneurs in recent years have established a reputation for themselves as exponents of wider share ownership – a form, if you like, of people's capitalism. This has been the ideological basis for the unit trust movement which has grown spectacularly over the last decade. Yet in many cases unit trusts have simply been regarded as captive funds, through which a financial empire can be created, thus really advancing the limited interests of the entrepreneur himself and his coterie of associates and shareholders.

Unit trust investors may care to consider one further point. Are their interests always compatible with those of the organization investing their money? There is a practice, which is not unknown even among the more respectable investment management organizations of the City, whereby the manager of the unit-holder's funds can directly benefit at the latter's expense. Under Stock Exchange regulations, a buyer, having different accounts with a stockbroker, can postpone notifying the stockbroker the name of the account for which he is buying. In other words, the fund manager can place an order to buy shares, and wait to see what happens to the share price. A few days later, if the price has gone up, he can 'book' the shares to his own private account. If it has gone down, he books it to the account of the unit trust.

There is another point worth considering. Some of the biggest managers of investment funds (including very substantial unit trust portfolios) in the City are the merchant banks, which also have the function of raising capital for company clients. Again, it is not unknown for merchant banks – and reputable ones at that – to place some of the securities they have raised on behalf of corporate clients into the portfolios they manage. Investor clients of the merchant banks might well question whether the advice they are being sold is the most objective they could get.

The City, of course, has had its traumas in recent years. One of its most embarrassing moments was in 1957, when some of the most established names in the City came on trial for misusing advance information about a change in Bank Rate (see Chapter 6). The Tribunal which was appointed to investigate the possibility of a 'leak' in Bank Rate in fact cleared the names of all concerned but it left the outside world with a suspicion that the City did not conduct its affairs in a way quite appropriate to the second half of the twentieth century. All the old clichés, like merchant bankers on grouse moors and the 'old boy net', were amply confirmed in the Tribunal's findings.

The Bank Rate affair and another event in the same year, the bitter take-over struggle in the City for control of British Aluminium (see Chapter 3), had profound effects. Light had been shed through darkened windows, and the brief glimpse of the inside revealed not the orderly state of affairs which people had been encouraged to assume existed. These two events were important catalysts of change.

The City has changed quite spectacularly over the last ten to fifteen years. It has fast begun to shed its effete and parochial outlook and developed into a more vigorous and professional international centre. Richard Fry, the veteran financial journalist, has described how it was: 'At the end of the fifties, London seemed to have been left behind in the progress of world trade and finance, first by the overwhelming resources of the United States, and more recently by the striking economic recovery of continental Europe. As a symbol of decline, many of the ragged gaps left by war-time bombing fifteen years earlier were still untouched, with pretty weeds flowering mauve and yellow each spring among the rubble. The financial community was dominated by elderly men; seats on the Stock Exchange were sold cheaply; such was the prevailing pessimism that the sons of some bankers were training to be farmers. Tradition reigned and competition was considered respectable only within comfortably agreed limits.'

I have already alluded to some of the City's new virility symbols – its commanding position in the Eurocurrency markets, its massive concentration of foreign banks,* its contribution to the health of the national economy, and, more visibly, the new towering block housing the Stock Exchange (supposedly the symbol of modernization). All this and more, it is argued, was achieved in spite of the fact that the role of

* If you approach the City along the Strand, you cannot help noticing a large building straddling the Aldwych with the sign, First National City Bank.

sterling in the international currency and trading system has steadily declined – all this in spite of the fact that a Labour Government restricted the goose with a combination of selective employment tax, taxes discriminating against foreign earnings and restrictions on overseas investment.

To understand the renaissance, it is important to realize that there has been a generation gap in the City. For around fifteen years after the war, comparatively few intelligent young people went into the City. It offered few prospects in terms of a career. Sterling had not been made convertible with other currencies, for much of the time most of the commodity markets had not been reopened, and the general business climate was that of restrictions – the City's traditional anathema. It is understandable that in these conditions the City was introvert, insulated, effete and interesting as a place to work mainly to the incompetent sons or relatives of whoever already worked there. The authority and amateurism of the City elders were seldom questioned – indeed there was no one in the City to question them. Promotion was largely a function of death or retirement.

Towards the end of the 1950s things began to change. Commodity markets had reopened, sterling had been made freely convertible into foreign currencies, and the magical powers of the Eurodollar were becoming apparent. It was at this point that the City began to regain its pre-eminence as an international financial centre. It was also around this time that many organizations in the City slowly began to realize that the traditional skills on which they had long depended were likely to prove inadequate in years to come for the changing nature of business. It needed only such full public exposure as the Bank Rate Tribunal to ram home how riddled the City was with amateurism.

Some of the new skills the City imported deliberately. Others simply drifted in, attracted by the new climate and opportunities which were developing. The merchant banks recruited accountants, lawyers and other experts. Graduates, who hitherto had seldom been given the opportunity to make any impact on City life (at least certainly not *qua* graduates), began to find their way into clearing banks, the overseas banks, the merchant banks, the insurance companies and some of the larger stockbroking firms. The infusion of younger and more skilled people itself generated a demand for higher standards of professionalism.

Then, of course, there were the free-wheeling outsiders who entered the City as adventurers, intent on exploiting existing inefficiencies not only in the City but also in industry throughout the country as a whole. The foremost among these has been Mr Jim Slater. Slater has been the City's most prodigious success story in recent years. Now in his early forties, he commands a financial empire valued in the stock market at almost £200 million and spreading its tentacles across banking, insurance, unit trusts, property and, of course, industry. Shareholders of Slater Walker Securities, his master company, have such affection for him that they were willing to insure his life for £10 million.

As far as the City is concerned, Slater was an outsider when he went there in 1964 to 'seek his fortune', as someone described it in Dick Whittingtonese. The son of a middle-class London building contractor, Slater started off in a conventional enough way. Under the direction of his father, he studied accountancy, qualified as an accountant and answered a job advertised in a newspaper which read: 'Persons without a keen sense of economy need not apply.' It was a company with a number of subsidiaries in difficulties. Slater was taken on as a trouble-shooter, a role for which he was to prove amply suited. After two years, Slater grew restless, decided to change jobs and moved to Park Royal Vehicles, a company making buses. Seven years later Park Royal and its parent company, Associated Commercial Vehicles, were taken over by Leyland. Slater was quickly promoted and became deputy sales director, with Donald Stokes as his boss. Selling vehicles quickly proved to have less attractions for Slater than making money. With a modest £2000 worth of savings, Slater turned his eyes towards the stock market. His trick then was to buy into companies which had come on hard times and whose investment rating had not been upgraded even though the companies were out of trouble. Two companies, Bernard Wardle and Klinger Manufacturing, fitted his bill nicely - in six months he doubled his £2000. He then borrowed £8000 from his bank and converted this into £50,000 in three years.

Sooner rather than later his break with Leyland had to come. 'Every time I left the country I found I was losing touch,' he says. By the end, he claims, Leyland could not pay him enough. Slater's career in the City began in a way which has become the conventional starting point for financial entrepreneurs in a hurry. Together with Peter Walker he bought a dying company, H. Lotery, suppliers of uniforms to Her Majesty's services, whose shares had been languishing at around 1s. 6d. H. Lotery owned valuable property in the City which Slater Walker, as the company was renamed, was able to sell off at a handsome profit. Slater Walker built up a capital base by hectic share-dealing and then launched out on the take-over front. Slater's formula was quite simple. It had been tried before in the 1950s by property tycoons like Charles Clore and Harold Samuel, and it has been slavishly and enthusiastically followed by the new generation of financial entrepreneurs. It is based on the simple observation that a large number of publicly quoted companies exist whose share prices are well out of line with their asset values. Slater's first major acquisition was Crittall-Hope, a company of window-frame manufacturers whose management had paid scant regard to the niceties of maximizing the return on the assets of which they were in charge. From industry to industry - unlikely areas like rubber-processing, builders' merchants, optical equipment and gas meters - Slater and his colleagues moved like predators, taking over companies, splitting them up, putting together bits of one company and bits of another, selling off unwanted parts, and, in general, rationalizing, to use the blanket term.

And then the grand strategy suddenly changed. In a manner which has been compared with that of Napoleon, Slater hastily altered directions. Instead of Slater Walker being a holding company (or conglomerate, to use the more fashionable term) for a loose assortment of different companies in different industries, it became a bank with a portfolio of industrial investments rather than wholly owned subsidiaries. The industrial investments became captive clients of the bank. In 1969, Slater Walker bought the Ralli Bank and proceeded to hive off part of its industrial holdings, leaving a pile of cash which could be diverted to banking, insurance, property, share-dealing and any other financially attractive activity that came its way. One technique Slater has perfected with consummate skill is that of buying a sizable shareholding in a company and then selling it off to a likely bidder for that company. He made a quick profit of £1·75 million, for example, by buying eleven per cent of Cunard and selling it three months later to Trafalgar House Investments which has since taken over the ailing shipping company. Slater now regards the company as an 'investment bank', along the lines of the French *banques d'affaires* – 'an investment company,' he explains, 'with a lot of substance to back us up.'

Slater's prescription for reforming British industry corresponds very closely with new Tory thinking. In a speech in 1971 to the Institute of Directors, he outlined his views: 'We need to obtain a new relationship between management and ownership. We need more youthful representation in many of our board-rooms. We need to continue with the fundamental reform of taxation. We need a more enlightened approach to industrial relations and we need to develop a positively international approach to doing business.' He wants the Government to encourage share option schemes (enabling executives and directors to buy shares in their company cheaply), to lower direct taxation, and to alter company legislation so that it is more difficult for old men to remain directors of a company and easier for shareholders to exercise their rights.

Probably the supreme irony of Slater's career was in 1969 when he was invited by Lord Stokes to become a director of British Leyland. By that stage, Slater had become one of the largest private shareholders in British Leyland – he has since prudently sold most of his holding. At the time he joined his old company as a director, Slater Walker was making more profits than Leyland was when he left it five years previously.

The injection of new skills and new people into the City has brought about some fundamental shifts in thinking. In particular, the traditional role boundaries in the City have begun to break down. In the old days the City was composed of orderly compartments. To encroach from one sector into another was more or less unthinkable. Everyone knew his place. The new generation of outsiders, with their more limited preconceptions of what the ideal order should be, have played an important part in unwinding the dogma of separatism. Recently constructed financial empires, such as that of Jim Slater, embrace a wide spectrum of City activities. The older established financial houses have widened the range of their services beyond all previous proportions.

More interestingly, one is beginning to see the boundaries of ownership become much more blurred. Rothschild's and Samuel Montagu, for example, both merchant banks, now own part of the share capital of two stock jobbers – Wedd Durlacher (the biggest jobber) and Berger & Gosschalk respectively. Lloyds and the Midland banks have a financial interest in two merchant banks, Wm. Brandt and Samuel Montagu. Joint ventures abound between City organizations from different sectors. Insurance companies have a labyrinthine network of links with merchant banks, building societies, property companies and clearing banks in the field of unit trusts. Property is another excuse for joining hands. Lending in the Eurocurrency markets, another.

Tradition, of course, still abounds in the City. There are very clear limits to how fast the pace of change can be allowed. Nowhere was this more amply demonstrated than in 1970 when two great City pluralists, Sir Kenneth Keith of Hill Samuel and Sir Charles Hardie of the Metropolitan Estate and Property Corporation, decided to merge their respective empires to bring about what they called 'a sensational change to the structure of the City'. The idea was Bismarckian – it was to create a huge financial supermarket; 'a unit in international terms of sufficient size to enable the City to make a great impact'.

The City's reaction to the Hill Samuel/M.E.P.C. £200 million merger plan was that of outrage and indignation. In the first place, M.E.P.C.'s large institutional shareholders felt that they were unreasonably being asked to change the nature of their investment from that of a property company to that of a financial conglomerate. It was the traditional City separatist view. One of M.E.P.C.'s stockbrokers, J. and A. Scrimgeour, resigned. One of its retired partners, Mr James Scrimgeour, put the case in a letter to *The Times*. 'It is, to my mind,' he wrote, 'a reappraisal of our whole private enterprise joint stock system, visualizing the total gradual abolition of separate and individual specialized investments and corporate activities and, in turn, the demise of that part of the market function that provides the machinery for investors to select and discriminate between different types of commercial, industrial and investment activity. We have to face the eventual abolition of that yardstick of relative market status, credit worthiness and management efficiency. The separate and individual activities would be submerged in vast corporations generally controlled at the top by a diminishing number of "businesscrats".' It was tantamount to saying: 'Once a property company always a property company.'

The second, and perhaps more revealing, reaction was that of thinly disguised self-interest among the merchant banks. Had the merger gone through, it would have taken Hill Samuel into quite a different league in terms of size and financial strength to that of its competitors. It was in the face of this threat that the subsequent deal (which was also abortive) whereby Commercial Union and Trafalgar House, the property company, were to carve up M.E.P.C., should be seen. I have already mentioned the large number of merchant bankers on the board of the Commercial Union who would have been capable of cooking up these blocking arrangements. *The Economist* described it as 'a nice example of the folklore that merchant bankers are quite brilliant, that they set the limits of their own profession, and that they have a happy knack of advancing their own interests at the same time as doing the best by their customers'.

A natural consequence of the infusion of outsiders has been greater competition among City businesses. Many of the cosy cartels have broken down under the strain of pressures from outside. The Bank of England has attempted to revolutionize the banking system by outlawing price-fixing on interest rates and most of the other orderly arrangements which made the clearing banks the constipated bureaucracies into which they had developed. The discount houses have been banned from operating their cartel in tendering each week for Treasury Bills. Outside banking, the chill winds of competition have also been blowing. The emergence of a daring outsider (Vehicle and General) caused the motor insurance companies to abandon their collectively agreed premium-fixing arrangement. Those unreadable pages of small print in newspapers advertising the wonders of this or that unit trust indicate, one supposes, the desperate battle to profit from the frugality and prudence of the so-called 'small saver'.

Yet having said all this, one still comes back to wondering *how much* the City really has changed. Has a new order been created? Or are the changes only a matter of degree? It would be hopelessly inaccurate to suggest that the same standards and values exist right across the City or that these are in any way commensurate with those that prevail in many other sectors of the country's economic community.

Take, for example, nepotism. Still a phenomenon in the City, not only widely spread, but also publicly justified. Consider Mr. Jocelyn Hambro, chairman of Hambros Bank and an exponent of 'enlightened nepotism', whatever that may mean. 'Some banking families,' he says, 'continue to produce hybrid vigour – others do not. There is competition within the family; they undergo rigorous selection and training, and not all members make the grade. But let us hope there will always be some that do.' The head of another prominent merchant bank wanted to find employment for a not altogether intelligent son-in-law. He approached a friendly firm of stockbrokers who kindly agreed to employ his relation for a trial period.

At the end of the trial period, the stockbrokers informed the merchant banker that their own future and that of the son-in-law did not coincide. For a brief spell the merchant bank diverted its share deals to another stockbroker. The son-in-law was retained. Such are the forces of capitalism.

The City is still a long way off from a meritocracy. Public school values are disproportionately rewarded and in almost no other field of human endeavour in Britain – save possibly the Church – are women quite so unjustly rewarded as they are in key sectors of the City. Of course, patterns differ within the City. Some of the merchant banks have set a heavy premium on intelligence in their recruitment. The traditional barrier between gentlemen and players in the insurance companies and clearing banks is being dismantled – because of the increasing complexities of the business, career professionals have been gradually admitted to these institutions' main boards of directors. Over the last few years, almost all the large insurance companies, for example, have appointed at least one or two of their senior full-time executives as directors.

The most reactionary sectors, significantly, are those which control most effectively the conditions of entry.* The Stock Exchange is one. Stockbrokers have persistently voted against admitting women as members of the London Stock Exchange** – a fact which, incidentally, says a lot about the feebleness of the Stock Exchange Council, the body which administers the London stock market and whose only clearly identifiable distinction is the longevity of its members. The Baltic Exchange has similarly entrenched views about women. A film company was recently commissioned by the Baltic Exchange to produce a documentary film about its activities. The film director's female assistant was barred from entering the floor of the Baltic and he was forced to find another assistant.

* Lloyd's has recently allowed women to become members, but they are not yet allowed to take part in the day-to-day activities of the insurance centre. They can provide money but cannot take decisions.

** In 1972 the London Stock Exchange decided to admit women members for the first time.

If virtue is not consistently rewarded in the City, there are other things which are. The earnings of top men in the City are way out of line with financial rewards in other sectors of the economic community. In a single month individual stockbrokers can earn anything up to £2000 when turnover, on which their commission is based, is high. Senior partners of some of the large stockbroking firms, such as Cazenove, de Zoete and Bevan or Hoare Govett, in a good year are thought to earn sums well into six figures. Insurance brokers, too, earn astonishingly large sums. Ian Skimming of C. T. Bowring has been earning £53,000 a year; P. W. Milligan of Sedgwick Collins, £44,000. Top merchant bankers also are richly rewarded – Sir Kenneth Keith of Hill Samuel heads the list with £48,000 a year. Sums such as these may be insignificant compared, for example, with what a portfolio manager or a stockbroker could make out of share-dealings on his own behalf. It is common practice among some merchant banks and stockbrokers for employees to have their own share trading companies as vehicles for their own personal speculation.

Below a certain minimum level, employees in the City are appallingly badly paid – a fact about which the trade unions have become increasingly concerned, particularly in the insurance and banking industries. But middle and senior management in many parts of the City make considerably more than their counterparts in industry. This is a distressing fact. It means in effect that a disproportionately large amount of the country's economically sophisticated population are attracted to spend their lives for the most part in the redistribution (or more accurately concentration) of wealth rather than in the creation of wealth. The British business schools which ironically are financed largely by a combination of manufacturing industry and the taxpayer, have a distressingly large quota of graduates who end up in City activities of one sort or another. 'Somebody has got to go back to manufacturing lavatories and things,' one plaintive City entrepreneur told me. 'Managers in important factories in the north of England,' he went on, 'are paid £2500 or £3000 a year. I can't get an assistant investment manager at that rate. The

City attracts people because it provides an easy job. Stockbrokers earn £50,000 a year, while poor old so-and-so in Cleckheaton is worried stiff on £3000.'

Power without Accountability

The City represents a massive concentration of power. This is an indisputable fact. Daily, insurance companies invest several million pounds' worth of new money. Daily, decisions are taken by banks of every description which have a direct effect on huge areas of the country's economic life. Daily, decisions are taken in the stock market which can directly affect the livelihoods of millions of people. Daily, whole businesses are bought and sold as a result of decisions taken in the City. Yet, at the same time, the framework within which these decisions are taken contains few, if any, effective checks against the abuses of power. The City enjoys an immunity which other sectors of the country's economic community do not have.

Only to itself is the City in any real sense accountable. Values are established essentially by the City, for the City, in the City. Accountability, such as it exists, is at two levels. In the first place, there is the Bank of England, the supreme authority in the City. The Bank performs the nightmarish balancing act of being the spokesman of the City in Whitehall and Whitehall's voice in the City. Yet if the Bank is responsible for the City, it is not (as a House of Commons committee has found) effectively accountable to Parliament, as it should theoretically be. Below the Bank is another tier of authority composed of the professional clubs representing the main forms of activity in the City. They set standards and regulations for their members, whether they be merchant banks, insurance companies, stockbrokers, clearing banks, unit trusts or whatever. The clubs in a sense answer to the Bank and are in turn responsible for the orderly conduct of their members. But the sanctions which they can apply to errant members are, as in all forms of club life, decidedly limited. Proof of this has been demonstrated time and again in the field of take-overs and mergers. When one of the members of the British Insurance Association crashed through reckless trading (Vehicle and General) there was precious little the club could do both before and after the unhappy event.

If there was evidence that the City interpreted its responsibilities widely, there would be less cause for anxiety. This is not the case. While industrial companies are beginning to develop a more sophisticated and enlightened concept of their responsibilities in society as a whole, there is little evidence to suggest that the financial community of the country has widened its own horizons of responsibility. It is patently untrue that the economic values sustained in the City invariably coincide with those values which reflect the interests of society as a whole.

In one sense, the City is more accountable than it was: in another sense, less so. It is more accountable in the sense that more is now revealed to the public about its activities by, and through, the Press. The process of self-revelation has been gradual. Financial journalism stands in an uneasy relationship with the City. Geographically speaking, the financial press is part of the City – almost all the journalists who write about the City have their offices in the square mile. The association goes further than that. In the first place, there is the question of ownership. Lord Cowdray's diverse financial empire, centred on S. Pearson and Son, includes the *Financial Times*, the *Investor's Chronicle* and a substantial stake in *The Economist*. It also owns Lazards, the merchant bank. Secondly, many of the large newspaper publishing companies have established City figures on their boards of directors. The company which publishes *The Times* and the *Sunday Times* includes among its directors Sir Kenneth Keith of Hill Samuel and Sir Eric Roll of Warburgs. Evelyn de Rothschild is chairman of *The Economist*. Thirdly, there is advertising. The City pages of daily and weekly newspapers have grown fatter in recent years largely on the strength of financial advertising, which now annually provides more than £21 million worth of revenue for the national Press. Finally, many of the brighter City journalists find their way into jobs in stockbroking firms or merchant banks when their newspapers can no longer reward them adequately.

These are the main facts that have to be borne in mind when considering relations between the City and the Press. To infer from them that the financial press is merely a puppet of the City would be naive, and largely wrong. The Press has played a vitally important part in encouraging the City to disclose more information. The fact that the clearing banks, for example, now publish their true profits is in some measure the result of prolonged nagging by financial journalists. It is doubtful whether the Take-over Panel would have been set up when it was had it not been for the bitter outcries from the Press. There are no doubt many other useful reforms which would not have been made without the Press.

Nevertheless, the facts as I have presented them provide an uncomfortable framework in which the City and the Press must co-exist. At times the framework strains objectively beyond all credible limits. One City editor circularized a number of companies with the promise that if they advertised their results in his newspaper he would guarantee editorial coverage of their financial results when they were published. Stories are not infrequently held out of newspapers on the grounds that they would be offensive (even though true) to prominent City personalities or institutions. Far more disturbing is the practice of share-pushing which in some City pages is thinly disguised. Share-tipping in City columns originally developed to attract a large financially unsophisticated readership – the sort of people on whom unit trust salesmen and exponents of wider share-ownership had set their sights. As the followers of share tipsters grew, the extent to which a newspaper tip could influence the price of a share increased. Share tips could become almost self-fulfilling prophecies, provided only a limited amount of money could affect the price of a share. City operators have not been slow to see the possibilities which this opened up. Skilful 'massaging' of journalist share tipsters became an important factor behind the success of a 'go-go' stock. It is worth noting that in recent years a large coterie of public relations firms, specializing in financial public relations, has grown up in the City.

There are two points further worth considering. Good news in the City is easier to come by than bad news, and with a thriving City public relations industry* to grease the channels of communication there is no shortage of the former flowing into newspaper offices. Secondly, newspaper journalists are in continuous need of instant explanations of market phenomena. And as rumour plays a very significant part in market phenomena, it is not difficult for a newspaper to find itself retailing rumour. Cynics would argue that behind every newspaper share tip is a block of shares to be bought or sold. This is an exaggeration. Newspapers, however, do provide the most effective means of communicating prejudices, facts or rumours around a market, whether it be concerned with securities, commodities or money.

In another important sense, the City is less accountable than it was. In recent years, there has been a gradual concentration of financial power in the hands of a new professional élite: the money managers. These people are entrusted with vast sums to invest. They are the people who manage the portfolios of the insurance companies, the unit trusts, the pension funds, the investment trusts and all the money which is referred to darkly as belonging to 'the institutions'. In a real sense, there has been a shift in the City's whole decision-making process. These men represent an enormous conglomeration of power. Their success or failure is judged exclusively on the financial efficiency with which they put the vast funds under their control to use. Their emergence and methods are the subject of the next chapter.

* There are around a dozen substantial financial public relations firms based in the City, most of which have been started in the last five to ten years.

'It is power concentrated in relatively few hands, working at the apex of a handful of giant bureaucracies, technically supported by a group of professional experts, and accountable, in practice, to virtually no one.'

Professor Richard Titmuss,
The Irresponsible Society

2. THE INSTITUTIONS

Over the last ten years, a comparatively new professional people has risen to prominence in the City: the investment managers. This is not to say that before there were not people actively engaged in managing investments. Investment managers have existed as long as money has been professionally channelled into stock markets. And that's the best part of 100 years in this country. But the point is that the decisions of investment managers until quite recently were carefully circumscribed and controlled by the traditional City establishment – the directors of banks, the trustees of pension funds, the boards of investment trusts and insurance companies and that mystical élite which has attracted so many antagonistic clichés (the public school educated, grouse-shooting amateurs).

The revolution in the field of investment management has been dramatic. A group of people who before were little more than executors of their masters' decisions have assumed responsibilities which even now are scarcely understood outside the City. They are an integrated part of the City's new power structure. They take decisions daily of enormous proportions. They are men, typically in their late twenties or early thirties from a wide variety of backgrounds, with almost complete discretion to manipulate assets equivalent in size to the total assets of many of Britain's largest companies. These assets which they effectively control are theoretically the property of shareholders (in the case of investment trusts), company employees (pension funds), unit-holders (unit trusts), or policyholders (insurance companies). But the separation between the control of these assets and their ownership is virtually total. More important, the effective control of these assets has shifted increasingly from the hands of a group who at least in the last resort are publicly accountable to their owners and into the hands of an irresponsible technocratic élite.

Generally speaking, investment managers fall into two organizational groups. In the first place, there are those who are responsible for the management of funds accumulated by a single corporate entity. These are the managers of what in City jargon are the 'self-managed' funds. The big pension funds, insurance companies, unit trusts and investment trusts have their own full-time professionals. Perhaps even more important are the managers who control massive portfolios as the delegated agents of private and institutional investors. These are the clearing and merchant banks, the stockbrokers and, in growing numbers, the management groups which independently undertake to manage their clients' investments. In short, investment management transcends the traditional compartments within the City. It is a vital common link communicating almost all the City's institutional entities.

No one knows with any certainty the size of this powerful City élite, nor quite how much power they do in fact exercise. Investment managers operate under a cloak of great secrecy. This is partly because of the nature of the game they play. If to be 'right' about a share is to be ahead of the generality of opinion, then clearly it is not in their interests to publicize the details of their decision-making.

There is no single professional body to which investment managers belong. Indeed there are no professional qualifications which make for an investment manager. Some, particularly in the insurance world, have qualified as actuaries: others as accountants. But, for the most part, no qualities are more highly prized in investment management than 'a cynical approach', 'an independent mind', 'the ability to listen to reason', or tautologically 'the ability to pick the right investments'. The essence of investment management is informality. Managers operate in a curiously unreal world of telephones, telex machines and complicated electronic paraphernalia, where little is written down and much is done by word of mouth. 'My word is my bond', the motto of the Stock Exchange, is the great ethic of this disparate community. Investment managers do belong to clubs. Investment trusts, pension funds, unit trusts and insurance companies have their own associations, and within these have grown up formally or informally sub-groups which operate under the genteel term, 'investment protection committees'. Within the framework of these organizations, investment managers can air their grievances about companies in which they have invested. Some 'protection committees' are more hawkish than others: they will assemble the combined muscle of their members and see that this is flexed against the offending investee, if they consider that the grievance is serious enough. But on the whole, investment managers communicate with each other under cover and informally. A lunch at merchant bank X, a chance street meeting with someone from stockbroker Y, or simply the telephone are the more usual points of contact between investment managers.

How much money investment managers handle is again uncertain. The London Stock Exchange lists £120,000 million worth of securities. Round about thirty to forty per cent of this is generally reckoned to be controlled by the institutions, the City's blanket term for the corporate bodies which invest in Britain. Take the insurance companies alone. Their investments world-wide amount to nearly £18,500 million. More significantly, each year they have almost £5000 million of new money to invest. Pension funds follow a long way behind with £10,000 million worth of assets, and in turn are trailed by investment trusts (£6000 million) and unit trusts (£2000 million). This is by no means the entire picture. Professional managers exercise discretion over the management of large company and private client portfolios. Throw in these, together with the funds of charities, universities, trade unions and virtually any substantially moneyed body you would care to think of, and the total potential power at the elbows of the investment managers becomes almost unthinkably massive.

How they Manage at Fleming's

In a discreetly opulent building situated in a small cul-de-sac off Bishopsgate, no more than 100 people play a part in advising and managing £1200 million worth of investments. With typical City false modesty, Robert Fleming and Co describe themselves as 'a rather remarkable merchant bank'. Apart from some of the biggest insurance companies, no other organization in Britain commands so much power in the stock market. No one has yet disputed Robert Fleming's claim 'that we transact more U.S. investment business than any other British institution'. If you substituted 'non-American' for 'British' the claim would probably still be true.

Until recently, Robert Fleming seemed to be quite happy to be known outside the City as the bank connected with authors Ian and Peter Fleming. Their elder brother Richard, who has a military, down to earth presence, is chairman of the bank and has always been very much the lesser known member of the family. 'We hide our lights under a bushel,' said a Fleming's director. Yet with the aid of a public relations firm, the bank is beginning to let a little light be shed on its internal workings. The Flemings became investment managers when the bank's founder, Robert, was sent off to the United States in 1870 to investigate the possibilities of investing money there. He was working for a firm of Dundee jute merchants, who were looking for opportunities to invest some of the large sums they had accumulated in the jute trade. On his return, Robert Fleming established the first Scottish investment trust 'for investment in American railroad bonds carefully selected and widely distributed'. Around 1900, Robert Fleming moved to London to the small square off Bishopsgate where the bank has been ever since. The Scottish flavour is still there. There is no shortage of Scottish accents in the board-room, and guests at lunch are offered a special blend of whisky by their hosts with pride.

Today, investment trusts still represent the lion's share of the money under Fleming's wing (£775 million). These range between the 'in-house' funds over which Fleming's have complete discretion and those which are independent but use Fleming's service in one way or another. The destiny of the 'in-house' funds is controlled entirely by Fleming's. The relationship with the latter is looser. The tendency over the years has been to diversify into other investment media. In the City, Fleming's are probably best known as managers for the major part of Britain's biggest unit trust group, Save and Prosper – they look after £284 million worth of S. and P'.s money. The rest consists of pension and charitable funds (known as gross funds because of their tax-free status) and private client portfolios which are managed for a minimum annual fee of £750.

There is a gloriously informal way in which Fleming's funds are looked after. As one bank official admitted to me, 'The organization is not as clear-cut as it ought to be'. Writing in the *Institutional Investor*, Nicholas Faith described the set-up as looking like 'the affairs of a highly sophisticated tribe'. 'The elders know the extent of their parishes, responsibilities and powers, and their juniors get to learn them, but a stranger has no white lines, no frontier posts and no charts to guide him into the organizational pigeon holes.'

The elders consist of five or six (again it is difficult to be precise as several functions are interchangeable) directors who hold a brief for different parts of the bank's investment empire. There are thirty-nine investment trusts, some of which are advised, others managed, by Fleming's. Members of the bank, usually the directors, sit on the boards of over half of them. The bank, therefore, does not only exercise control over the day-to-day investment decisions of the trusts which it manages. It also has a marked influence on the broader strategic considerations governing the investment of a trust's portfolio, which are in theory the prerogative of the trust's board of directors. Ultimately, the boards of those investment trust companies are responsible for the decisions taken. In practice, virtually all the investment decisions emanate from the investment directors and, further down the line, from the ranks of the bank.

Fleming's do their best to refute the charge that they are an investing 'monolith'. 'We are more like a shingle beach,' a director told me, 'with lots of pebbles widely spread.' Nevertheless, there are occasions where size does bring its problems. What happens, for example, when Fleming's decide to unload their entire holdings in a company? 'There's not much difference between managing a portfolio of £250 million and looking after one of £25 million. One's just ten times the size of the other,' I was told by a bank official. On the other hand, size can mean inflexibility. Fleming's try to confine the average number of holdings in a fund to 400 securities. It becomes difficult for one manager to police more than that number very regularly. But by sticking to that rule, it becomes equally difficult not to accumulate a holding in a company which ultimately becomes virtually unmarketable. Fleming's try to get round this by maintaining a golden rule never to acquire more than ten per cent in a quoted company. An elaborate filing system is kept of all 7000 companies in which Fleming funds are invested and of shareholdings in each company. When holdings move near to the ten per cent mark, warning signals are flashed to the fund managers and directors who take action appropriately.

One occasion when Fleming's sold out of a company lock, stock and barrel caused not a few red faces in the City, but for other reasons. It arose from a determined effort on Fleming's' part to secure themselves a big foothold in the market for corporate advice. In the middle of 1969, Fleming's found themselves for the second time in a year advising Robert Maxwell's Pergamon Press in a take-over situation. The first occasion was during Maxwell's abortive bid for the *News of the World*. On 18 June, Maxwell announced to an astonished Press-gathering a deal handing control of Pergamon to Leasco Data Processing Equipment Corporation, a high-flying computer leasing company headed by a twenty-nine-year-old, Saul Steinberg. Within a month of the announcement Leasco had demonstrated its intentions plainly enough by mopping up in cash £9 million worth of Pergamon shares, most of which were sold by investment trusts managed by Fleming's. Had Fleming's any prescience of events that were to follow? Relations between Maxwell and Steinberg turned to bitter hostility, and in the tangled web of events which developed Leasco withdrew its bid. Wild charges followed on both sides and Fleming's withdrew their support for Pergamon.

A Conflict of Interest

Whatever the rights and wrongs of this particular episode, the Pergamon/Fleming's affair threw up a wider and more significant issue. Is there a conflict of interest where a merchant bank acts in the twin roles of investment manager and company adviser? More specifically, can a merchant bank consistently sell shares in a company and at the same time advise that company on the terms of a take-over bid? In hindsight, Fleming's did a fine deal for its investment trusts, but was it a fair deal for the rest of the Pergamon shareholders?

The City was rife with speculation and gossip about whether Fleming's had acted with propriety, and it was decided that an enquiry should be made by the City's watchdog, the Take-over Panel. The Panel took nine months to deliver its views on the general issues at stake – the sale of the Pergamon shares had already been cleared by the Panel at the time they were sold. The findings of its report, discreetly termed 'The Use of Confidential Price-sensitive Information', were strangely revealing.

The main conclusion of the Panel, at which the City breathed a sigh of great relief, was that it was not practicable to separate legally the investment management side from the corporate advice operations of a merchant bank and that 'an attempt to secure it would gravely endanger the legitimate exercise of commercial and financial services which are of great economic value to the country'. But in reaching its conclusions, the Panel did go a long way to admitting that abuses were not only possible but actual. 'In all cases, therefore, the theoretical or indeed actual possibility existed that information gained in the one capacity, as for instance about an impending take-over transaction or about some alteration in a company's affairs or profitability, could be used with advantage in the other capacity in advising a sale or purchase of securities.' And it went on: 'Human fallibility and cupidity being what they are, it is obviously impossible to guarantee that in every case this duality will not be abused.'

The good names of Robert Fleming in particular, and merchant banking in general, were upheld in the City. But dissatisfaction lingered on after the Panel's findings. Many investment managers feel that the wearing of two hats by a merchant bank is dangerous for other reasons. They believe that 'dud' stocks or new capital issues are foisted on merchant bank portfolios by the corporate advisory side of the bank. Certainly, there is plenty of scope for a merchant bank to parcel out blocks of stock into a tame 'house' fund in order to support the price of that stock. This certainly is common practice with new capital issues. And the task becomes conspicuously easier when the manager in charge of investments is a weak-minded individual. Merchant banks arrogantly argue, however, that the paper of their company clients is of such a high quality that their portfolio clients should be only too glad to have 'a taste of the cherry' before the public at large gets a look in. The question is: how often does the public really want a look in?

One investment management company, in which a merchant bank has a minority stake, 'won't let that bank anywhere near the place'. Chartered accountants have taken the problem rather more seriously. They reckon that their professional reputation is very much at stake where they perform investment management functions in addition to their normal run of business. The awful prospect of publicly revealed leaks of information from the auditors to the investors has prompted at least two firms of accountants in recent years to hive off their investment management businesses into separate legal entities. They hope to have bolted the stable door before the horse escapes.

Performance

Investment managers rose to prominence on the crest of a wave called Performance. As the post-war equity boom got under way in the 1950s investment management became highly competitive. The more alert and ambitious investors believed that making money meant not just investing to keep abreast with inflation but doing better than the general trend – beating the index. To do this required full-time attention to the daily movements in the stock market. It was no good investing for the long term, for, as investment managers are only too keen to quote Lord Keynes, 'In the long term we are all dead.'

The upward thrust of the professional investor, if one can call it that, was given impetus by the growing importance of unit trusts. For here was an investment medium heavily sold and advertised to the public. The message which unit trust men had to get over to the public was that this was a form of investment in some way superior to other investment media. Performance was much of the message. 'An amateur cannot hope to compete with the institutions,' wrote Oliver Stutchbury, formerly managing director of Save and Prosper, 'and since these latter in the case of unit trusts will manage his investments for him, he is wiser not to issue a challenge.'

Unit trusts got off the ground in Britain in the early 1930s, but for a large part of the post-war period the movement was hampered by restrictions, imposed during wartime, on new capital issues. These restrictions were lifted in 1953, but it took four years before the opportunities for expanding the movement were really seized upon. At the beginning of 1957 the starting gun was fired for the rapid boom in unit trusts in Britain. And it was Edward du Cann, the former Conservative Minister (and former Chairman of the Conservative Party), who fired it by starting his Unicorn Securities, a group which set the pattern for future unit trusts in this country. Within fourteen years the unit trust movement has grown from £90 million to £2000 million. Almost all the major clearing and merchant banks now have their own unit trusts.

Performance meant different things to different professional investors. To the insurance companies and pension funds, the stodgier elements of the investment scene, it meant only just beating the index. Everyone was infected with the performance bug to varying degrees. It was the unit trusts who threw up the arch-priests of performance.

One of the great gurus or 'go-go' men of the movement was John Ormond. Ormond is an engineer by training, he has a boyish self-effacing appearance, and at the age of twenty-six he set out on his own to develop what he calls 'certain investment philosophies and ideas which I wanted to put into practice'. His origins in investment management were humble – a converted bedroom in Epsom for an office and a company called Surinvest. His rise was dramatic. He started off looking after the investments of four clients worth £20,000. 'I set out to beat the index by ten per cent. If I could do that I would be able to attract clients,' he told me.

Ormond's magic touch was soon to show itself. It consisted of an all too simple formula: 'I concentrate on a small number of the most promising shares selected from among a large choice of quoted stocks and on getting to know them really well. Success in investment will equal the quality of a selection multiplied by the amount of money put into it. It follows that it is much better to put ten per cent of your money into one excellent selection than two per cent into five quite good selections.' It sounded infallible and for four balmy years it worked. In one glorious year (1968) he became the proud manager of Britain's top performing unit trust (Oceanic Growth). Not surprisingly, his skills soon became known to that very embodiment of the performance cult, Investors Overseas Services, which entrusted nearly £8·5 million to his hands.

By the middle of 1969, Ormond had assembled £12 million

worth of funds under his corporate belt and decided that the time had come to project himself in a still bolder image. He had already launched a number of unit trusts under the Surinvest banner and was busily soliciting to manage private portfolios of £5000 and over (most merchant banks do not touch anything under the six figure mark). So in that classic City manoeuvre, a reverse take-over, Ormond decided to float his company. Pat Matthews, managing director of the First National Finance Corporation and one of the City's zippier financiers, obligingly provided the vehicle for the move in the form of a stagnant 'shell' company, the Anglo-Scottish Tea Investment Trust. A.S.T.I.T. bought Surinvest, changed its name to the latter and became the third unit trust management company to be publicly owned. 'A publicly quoted company,' commented *The Economist*, 'has readily accessible accounts, is critically appraised by the Press and is altogether more visible than a private group.' It was a development 'which many many whiz kids would fight shy of'.

Ormond's activities were always viewed with suspicion by the traditional City establishment. He had once headed a well-publicized campaign to ginger up the management of Cunard, but the more solid institutional investors had left him to do the job on his own (though many of them no doubt shared his views about the ailing shipping group). 'They wouldn't even meet me for half an hour,' he told me. The feeling had always been mutual. Ormond has a healthy disdain for merchant banks, 'who are used to living in expensive offices and employing expensive people to chat up clients'. His offices are in Surrey, and he confines his visits to the City to a token once a week.

Ormond's espousal of the performance cult brought him no further into favour with the City elders. Poised like vultures, they waited for the youthful innovator to put his foot wrong. Their moment of thinly disguised pleasure was near.

As rides go, the one taken by the City investors in E. J. Austin International in 1969/70 was one of the more expensive of recent years. John Ormond was one of the investors – it cost him and his investment clients not far off

£700,000. The story really began in the spring of 1968 when Kenneth Howarth, described as a 'globe-trotting mining buff', and a former associate of two City financiers, Harley Drayton and Oliver Jessel, called in at the West End office of Jim Slater's Slater Walker. Slater was interested at the time in revamping a luckless Cheshire company of builders merchants, E. J. Austin.

Slater has never claimed Howarth as a protégé, but before the summer was out the directors of E. J. Austin found themselves with a new colleague, Howarth, who was already preparing great plans for extending their company beyond the boundaries of north-west England. Slater disposed of his twenty per cent stake in Austin at the end of the year, and six months later, after a palace revolution, Howarth was firmly in the saddle as chairman. By this time Howarth was all set to capitalize on two chance meetings he had had in London in the past fifteen months. The first was with the head of a Cypriot mining company, which claimed to have established chrome and copper deposits in the Troudos mountains. The second was with an Oklahoman mining engineer, called Wayne Chambers, whom Howarth had met a few years back prospecting for manganese in the Kalahari desert. Chambers claimed to have discovered a cheap method of leaching materials from ore. Not only that, but Chambers could, and did, lead Howarth to a forty-acre site near Los Angeles with nothing short of 'fabulous' mineral prospects.

Howarth was suitably impressed. Within a few months of his moving into the chair of the company in 1969, Howarth unveiled his two-pronged plan which was to make E. J. Austin for a few splendid moments a wonder share. The company, he told his shareholders, now controlled the mineral rights over an eleven square mile area in the Troudos mountains of Cyprus. It was all set to make nothing less than £900,000 a year worth of profit on its venture, and it had already spent large sums on investing in roads and equipment to fulfil these plans.

That was only part of the story. The company was also on the verge of buying forty acres of land in California, 'which has extensive above-average mineralization in the form of copper, silver, gold, and platinum bearing ores'. As if this was not enough to impress even the most unexcitable shareholders, Austin had acquired rights to a process which would knock stitches off any existing method of extracting minerals from ore. Finally, the company's name was to be changed to E. J. Austin International.

In the autumn of 1969, the Australian nickel boom got under way, headed by Poseidon, and it is against this background that subsequent events in relation to Austin must be judged. Investors love a good story, and who would doubt that the psychological climate was just right for another big gamble? Poseidon and a host of other Australian mining companies had done their stuff for the performance-hungry investment managers. Why not another Poseidon, but this time rather closer to home? John Ormond was amongst those who were suitably impressed. Dubbed as one of 'seven wise men' by *The Economist*, the 'gunslinger' of Wallington, Surrey, plummed straight for E. J. Austin in that august magazine's annual exercise of inviting investment managers to select their shares of the year.

The shareholders of Austin were to go for a giddy ride. On 19 January Howarth pulled out all the stops. He announced to his shareholders a deal of staggering proportions. 'We always knew literally there was a crock of gold at the end of the rainbow,' he told an astounded audience. This was no ordinary gold mine he was describing in California. Its name was El Sobrante (it means 'the surplus'), and it could yield $5000 of gold a ton compared with $35 by normal standards. 'With a flourish,' reported the *Financial Times*, 'Mr Howarth produced from a black case samples he said had been taken from the mine: gold, silver, platinum, copper (a shareholder shouted: 'What, no oil?'). There were also colour photographs of the mine.' Comparisons were inevitably made with Poseidon.

The nub of the whole package was a proposal to issue seven million shares in Austin to Howarth and Chambers in return for the two maestros' El Sobrante Mining Corporation. This deal would more than double the existing equity of Austin and would give Howarth and Chambers sixty-four per cent of the equity of the enlarged group. The share price took off like a sky-rocket – from 19s. 6d. it leapt to 60s. within three days. Meanwhile, the company had its quotation suspended on the London Stock Exchange to allow time for more evidence of Howarth's amazing claims to be brought forward. Dealings in John Ormond's performance unit trust were also suspended – that was heavily invested in Austin, though Ormond had already disposed of a small part of his holding in the company with a tidy profit.

City interest in El Sobrante hotted up some time before Howarth's public revelations. Early in the New Year, Christopher Spence, a friend of Howarth and a partner in the stockbroking firm of Spence, Veitch which advised Austin, got in touch with that paragon of City respectability, merchant bankers Morgan Grenfell, which shortly afterwards dispatched an emissary to Los Angeles to visit the site of the mining venture. Quite why Morgan's sent one of their men all that way has never been quite clear. True, Austin had recently lost their merchant bank advisers, Keyser Ullmann, and needed a solid City name to lend weight to their claims.

But Morgan's wisely confined their involvement to a brief encounter. 'We have not been, are not now and have no intention of being advisers or backers to the company,' they said with their noses in the air. The official explanation was that they were simply investigating the state of affairs on behalf of clients of theirs who were shareholders.

The E. J. Austin bubble was not long in bursting. Within two months of his 'crock of gold' announcement, Howarth had severed his two-year connections with Austin. A terse statement from the company revealed that Howarth had resigned from the company and added 'It is understood that Mr Howarth wished to pursue his interests in the El Sobrante Mining Corporation.' So the 'fabulous' deal was off.

Scepticism about Howarth's claims was already widespread long before Howarth's departure from the company was announced. In February, *The Times* sent two of its men to

California and Cyprus to find out what was going on. In California, the newspaper's man made some interesting revelations about the company's geologist, on whose findings 'the entire case for E. J. Austin International's multi-million pound Californian venture stands or falls'. In Cyprus, *The Times* writer concluded that 'trying to find where E. J. Austin International is prospecting . . . is almost as difficult as assessing what mining prospects it has. There appears to be no activity whatsoever on the chrome prospects referred to so confidently in the circular last July.'

The demise of E. J. Austin was near. A week after Howarth's resignation a receiver was appointed to wind up the company. On 3 April, the Board of Trade announced that it was appointing a Q.C. and a chartered accountant as inspectors to investigate the affairs of the company.

All this time, John Ormond's problems were compounded by rapidly diminishing confidence in Investors Overseas Services, the giant mutual fund business built up by Bernie Cornfeld. In a sense, I.O.S. had blazed a trail for the performance fanatics, such as Ormond, to launch themselves on to the investing world at large. Ormond's investment philosophy, of course, coincided neatly with that of I.O.S., and it was something of a mixed blessing to Ormond that as the more traditional City elements were growing not a little suspicious of I.O.S. methods (partly thanks to a bout of bad publicity at the end of 1966) the giant mutual fund empire approached Ormond to manage part of its portfolio. Ormond willingly acceded to its request for his services, and at one stage I.O.S. accounted for eighty per cent of the funds managed by Surinvest. So when confidence in I.O.S. evaporated as 1970 drew on, Ormond was one of the hardest hit. He was obliged to dump huge quantities of largely unmarketable stocks in a market which was loath to accept them.

The City establishment was not slow to brand Ormond and the other 'go-go' addicts with their own words. Whether the performance boys will ever again reach their previous heights of eminence remains to be seen. When I saw Ormond shortly after the Austin and I.O.S. débâcles, he was 'going through a rough patch', to use his own words. 'I buy all sorts of funny stocks,' he said. The trouble is that 'funny stocks' have a nasty habit of going down as well as up. The Greeks had a word for it: Nemesis.

The Analysts

In the old days, a stockbroker would have lunch with a company chairman or director. He would arrive back at his office late in the afternoon remembering the odd snatch of useful information about that company. Maybe he would know what dividend the company was to declare in a day or so's time. And before you could say 'bull', he would have bought for, or recommended to, his clients a tidy parcel of the company's shares. It was known as the Old Boy Net. It may have consisted of any number of permutations of different types of City investor. It could have been a stockbroker recommending to a private client. It could have been an investment trust director instructing his investment manager, an insurance company director advising his professional investor and so on. Now the saying goes that if you listen to the managing director of a company, you'll lose twenty per cent of your money in that company: if you listen to the chairman, you'll lose forty per cent.

In 1969 a firm of researchers surveyed nearly 200 professional investors in the City and arrived at the startling conclusion that forty-three per cent of investment managers rely on 'the research department' in considering shares to buy. And stockbrokers relied even more heavily on their research departments than the institutions (fifty compared with thirty-four per cent). Was there any more positive proof that the Old Boy Net had withered away? No, and it was conclusive evidence that the investment analyst is now a force to be reckoned with in the City. No one has ever yet gone as far as insisting that investment is a science. If it were, share price movements could be predicted accurately, and computers would now be occupying the spaces in the City now filled by the desks of investment managers. Mercifully for the expanding numbers of analysts and investors, investment remains an art. But this does not stop the technicians from searching to the point of frenzy to find the reasons why shares go up and down. The greatest enemies of the technicians are the random walk theoreticians. They maintain that shares move about without any order. Mercifully again, the random walkers are more often than not university professors and business school academics. Their influence on the City is therefore minimal.

Investment analysis has been one of the big growth activities in the City over the last fifteen years. By 1955, a small group of analysts, like most active, unrepresented minorities, decided that they needed a corporate identity. So they formed the Society of Investment Analysts. The Society is justifiably proud of its record. It now has over 1200 members and seems to be taken quite seriously by outsiders – it gave evidence to the Jenkins Committee on company law reform and has been collaborating with the chartered accountants in improving company accounts. Three times a year it goes into print with a journal offering such esoteric items as 'Growth Yields Investigated' and 'The First Four Years of the F.T. Actuaries All Share Index and the Large, Growing, Widely Spread Fund'.

Investment analysts come from a number of different walks of professional life – they hesitate about calling themselves a profession since they don't yet have any qualifying exams (though they may soon have). One group of professionals which has taken a keen interest in investment analysis is the actuaries. There are only 1200 of this rare breed in the country, and most of them are to be found among the insurance companies, tucked away inconspicuously. They were once described as people 'who pass as experts on the basis of their prolific ability to produce an infinite variety of incomprehensible figures calculated with micrometric precision from the vaguest of assumptions based on debatable evidence from inconclusive data derived by persons of doubtful reliability, for the sole purpose of confusing an already hopelessly befuddled group of persons who never read the statistics anyway.'

No one quite agrees about how the investment analyst rose to fame. One rather cynical explanation is that one day the stockbrokers woke up to find that they weren't talking to the insurance companies on the right wave-length. The point is that insurance companies started to stand their actuaries on clerical pedestals. Actuaries are the people who work out the terms on which money is collected from the insurance companies' policyholders, and they are also employed (not the same actuaries, of course) to invest that money when it comes in. And as the power of the investment manager in the insurance companies grew, so brokers found themselves in need of experts to converse with them.

That is perhaps a rather narrow explanation. Certainly, stockbrokers had to sell their services to an increasingly sophisticated clientele, and instead of competing on price they plumped for research. This had a ricochet effect. The investment managers were bombarded with pounds of documentation, and they in turn needed experts to sift through it all and analyse what was there. Once within the space of a fortnight I was sent four stockbrokers' reports on a single company (it was Fisons): two were recommending their readers to buy the shares; the other two to sell. Imagine the predicament of the professional investor without the back-room boys to help him make up his mind.

The investment analyst was basically the invention of the Americans. Wall Street realized at an early stage that as the technologist was creeping into almost all forms of business life so it should become a little more technological. The City in many respects was aping the American experience.

The cult of the equity was another major factor in the growth of investment analysis. Investing in fixed interest stocks and gilt-edged securities has always been relatively undemanding. But since the early 1950s the institutions have invested an increasing proportion of their funds in equities. By 31 March 1970, there were ordinary shares (equities) worth £37,793,324,334 invested in some 10,000 public companies in Britain. The equity game was a very different game to the one that investors had been playing before. It had a different set of rules and the risks were far greater. Capital appreciation became the thing, instead of income. A new art was born to assess the risks.

A steady improvement in the information available about companies fed the flames of investment analysis. A succession of Companies Acts, enforcing companies to disclose more information about themselves, brought a lot more raw material for the analyst to feed on. Then there were the repeated demands of the Press and the analysts themselves which played a big part in creating a new climate of disclosure.

Investment analysis has now become a highly specialized profession. It is not good enough in many concerns to be just an analyst. An analyst must be an expert in a particular sector of industry. Investment managers point proudly to their mining expert, or their oil and chemicals man. At Robert Fleming's they even have a Japanese to keep an eye on what's going on in the Far East.

Almost every investor in the City, even the great cynics and even the staunchest protagonists of the old order, pay homage to the investment analyst. But not everyone, by a very wide margin, is agreed on the virtues of a curious sect among them: the chartists. Jim Slater described this minority group as a bunch of 'long-haired men in ragged overcoats with big overdrafts'. They got rather worried about their image and towards the end of 1969 formed themselves into the Association of Chart and Technical Analysts. It's amazing how insecurity brings togetherness in the City.

Chartists, or technical analysts, which is the more respectable term which some chartists prefer to give themselves, are to be distinguished from the bulk of investment analysts. Basically, the difference lies in their approach. Chartists are concerned with charts – that goes without saying – and they are interested simply in the price of a share, whether it goes up, down or remains the same. The majority of analysts is concerned with what are known as 'fundamentals', all the relevant information and data which they think makes a share move. Fundamental analysts are interested in the causes: chartists in the effects.

Chartists have developed for themselves a splendid jargon, which sounds wonderfully professional. They point to charts and talk of 'flags', 'pennants', 'diamonds', 'triangles', 'triple tops' and 'head and shoulders' formations. Some chartists use line charts, others bar charts, and others 'the point and figure approach'. But from all this baffling paraphernalia, little objectivity emerges. Two chartists are quite capable of standing in front of a chart: one will say that the share will go up; the other that it will go down.

The doyen of British chartists, and probably the longest established investment analyst in the country, is Alan Ellinger, an endearing sexagenarian who looks more like a public school classics master than someone versed in the vagaries of the stock market. Ellinger runs a firm called Investment Research, from the porter's lodge at Downing College, Cambridge, where he looks after clients' money and supplies share charts, an elegantly written monthly Investment Letter and other investment services to anyone who wants to buy them. He likes being in Cambridge because he feels there is an advantage in not being caught up in the 'emotional steam of the City'. 'I'm less likely to buy Poseidon in Cambridge than I am in Copthall Avenue,' he told me. He describes himself as 'the first independent investment counsellor to practise publicly and survive', a role he is proud of, as evidenced by an indignant letter he wrote to a more recently established investment counselling firm in the City which was making a similar claim.

Ellinger's existence in Cambridge is explained by a long, carefully prepared monologue which the stranger receives on meeting him. He returned from the war with three strongly held convictions: that he mustn't live in London; that he didn't want people ordering him about; and that the only thing he knew anything about was investment (he worked for a London stockbroker before the war). So in 1945 he founded his own portfolio management service in Cambridge based largely on technical analysis. Ellinger is full of reminiscences: of how he forecast the 1947 fuel crisis, of how he spotted I.C.I. in the late 1950s right at its very low, and of how investment analysts at one time were so out of favour that in order to obtain a copy of Rolls-Royce's annual report he had to become a shareholder in the company. Ellinger has little time for the new breed of City financial operator. 'If they are looking after companies worth more than £10 million they oughtn't to be and soon won't be.' 'We only invest in companies worth over £10 million,' he added contemptuously.

A less conventional figure among the chartists is Bob Beckman, a puckish, loquacious American, who arrived in Britain in 1963 having decided to get away from 'a very sour Wall Street market'. Actually, 'chartist' is a term which, applied to himself, Beckman resents strongly. 'Comparing a chartist with a fully-fledged experienced skilled technical analyst,' he insists, 'is like placing a house-painter in the same category as a Picasso. All they have in common is that Picasso and the house-painter both use a paint brush. Similarly, a chartist and a technical analyst both use charts.' The latter, he claims, uses a combination of charts depicting the activity of business, the economy, the market and the individual share to form only an opinion, 'which he remains ready to alter whenever and as soon as the price action dictates'. Shifting to another metaphor, he says that 'the chartist sets the course of the ship towards the point of objective and proceeds blindly on his voyage. The technical analyst steers his course to keep in fair weather and avoids storms while on route to his destination.' His key to investment is to combine the fundamental with the technical approach, 'for basically we are then combining a study of cause and effect rather than favouring one over the other'.

Beckman commutes a few hundred yards from a penthouse flat to a discreet suite of rooms in an apartment block on the Edgware Road from which he forms and disseminates his strongly held, controversial investment philosophy. On his desk stands a small brass bear, a mascot which betrays these views. For Beckman, by his own confession, has made 'most of my money in bear markets'. In other words, he sells shares one day (which he hasn't got) in the hope that sometime later he can buy them back at a lower price. This is possible on the London Stock Exchange because of the two-week accounting system – transactions are normally settled at the end of a fortnightly accounting system, and even longer periods are allowed. It is known in City jargon as 'shorting'.

Beckman was converted to chartism when he was working on Wall Street. 'I lost $35,000 in the American market, which at the time was close to all I had to invest. The reason? The chart of the Dow Jones Industrial Averages pointed to a severe market but I didn't believe it.'

When Beckman bought up an ailing British publishing business and decided to publish his ideas in the form of a twenty-five guinea a year monthly newsletter, he had already tested them in the market on his own account. When he arrived in London, he found 'all sorts of lovely things like the account system and shorting'. Having failed to convince stockbrokers of the wonders of chartism, he decided to forget about selling charts and trade himself.

It was perhaps the desire for recognition that led him into the open. He now makes no bones of the assertion that 'mine is the only contribution to English chartism'. His business, Investors Bulletin, began publishing his *Monthly Haller Theory Report* in 1970, in which Beckman attempts to apply the chart theories of a Wall Street pundit, Gilbert Haller, to the London market. The whole venture, Beckman admits, is geared to provide him with the information he needs to deal in the stock market. The text of the report is spiced with Cassandra-like prophecies. 'Readers will please take note of the fact that we have reached the screaming point in the course of our latest four-month battle against the forces of conservatism, pacificism, and standpatism. It is not the function of this paper to deride our competitors and the popular financial press, however, when we read statements such as: "The market has fallen so far it cannot fall any further"; "Now is the time to buy shares at low price"; "The market looks good". We can only assume the motives behind such statements are intended primarily to sell newspapers and investment services rather than protect investors. Such wide-eyed optimism is irresponsible and as fictitious as the once accepted notion of a massive cataract at the end of the Atlantic Ocean....

The human species has become so masochistic that the masses will go to any lengths merely in order to believe what they want to believe and avoid the facts at all costs.' Beckman justifies his title, The Great Bear.

The Power of the Institutions

The equity boom has had a number of important effects on the City's power structure. In the first place, it has conferred on the institutions, as they have switched an increasing proportion of their investments into equities, the right to control a huge slice of British business, by virtue of the fact that equities carry voting rights. More specifically, it has conferred on the group of people who manage this money the almost uncontrolled power to intervene in the management of the companies in which they have invested. And there can be little doubt that as fund management has become increasingly competitive, and as performance has become the message from the City's institutional pulpits, the temptation to apply pressure on company managements has been less easy to resist. There are two important interrelated questions: how much power do the institutions wield; and how far do investment managers feel themselves restrained from wielding this power?

The last time anyone made a detailed study of the stake held by the institutions in British business was in 1971. The Department of Economic Affairs in Cambridge published a document which revealed that between them the insurance companies, pension funds, investment trusts and unit trusts owned thirty-two per cent of the quoted securities in the country. The stake controlled by private individuals was only 44·7 per cent, the rest being made up of a group of other institutional bodies, including banks, charities, and universities, with investment management common to a significant extent with the four principal institutional groups.

The survey also revealed that the institutions held larger stakes in bigger companies: private shareholdings in companies valued at over £66 million amounted to only 41 per cent. Since then, the institutional elements generally have almost certainly gone on rising.

There has been another important development. Over the last ten years there has been a tendency for investment decision-making among the institutions to be concentrated in fewer units. There have been mergers on a massive scale among the insurance companies. Investment trusts and unit trusts, too, have gone through periods of consolidation. And with mergers of industrial companies on an unprecedented scale, more power has been concentrated in the hands of pension fund managers. We have yet to see, too, the full implications of another development: the growth of organizations whose business it is to manage institutional portfolios. Merchant banks will continue to attract institutional funds, and there are certain to be further inroads made into fund management by the specialist groups which concentrate exclusively on portfolio management. So there are two isolated trends: first, the growing stake of the institutions in British business; and, second, the concentration of decision-making in the hands of institutional investors.

Traditionally, the institutions have been shy to show their strength. Immediately after the war, it was the scare of nationalization that kept them at bay. The first post-war Labour Government talked about nationalizing the insurance companies and although they never got round to it, 'I reckon they got pretty near to it in 1948,' says the investment manager of one insurance company. Another bogey appears to have been the Trades Union Congress. 'If we had put Arnold Weinstock in as managing director of A.E.I. and he had closed down factories, it would have been us who got the blame from the unions,' he added.

Ironically, it was the institutions which effectively gave Weinstock's G.E.C. control of A.E.I. But happily for the institutions, they never got the credit for the mass redundancies which followed the take-over. G.E.C.'s take-over of A.E.I. was in many ways an important landmark in the development of institutional power. All City eyes were glued on the institutional shareholders as the take-over fight developed. Which way would Prudential Assurance, Pearl Assurance, the Church Commissioners and the rest of them vote? The answer was only known at the eleventh hour. 'The City has grown up,' proclaimed *The Economist*. 'The investment analysts and professional managers are now in charge. The consequence of this new pre-eminence is that their arguments made sense in terms of long-term industrial economics as well as short-term cash.'

No doubt the institutions took heart from the favourable public response to their handling of the G.E.C./A.E.I. affair. But the prevailing mood is still curiously schizophrenic. Angus Murray, a willowy Scottish actuary who until recently had the joint responsibility for managing the Prudential Assurance Company's £2600 million investments, sees the situation in this way. 'Whatever we do, we must be wrong. If we don't take steps occasionally to put our views to directors, we are told we are sitting on our bottoms. If we do, we are accused of throwing our weight about.' In fact, the 'Pru' has turned out to be one of the more active interventionists. Its ex-chairman, Sir John Mellor, announced that it would use its weight to 'revitalize flagging industrial managements'. This is just what the mighty insurance company, in collaboration with other institutions, did with Vickers, the ailing engineering giant. Pressure was put on Vickers to revamp its top management, and the company was gently forced to appoint a chief executive from outside the group.

As one might expect, institutional investors divide themselves between doves and hawks. The dove line is that an investment manager should 'vote with his feet' and simply sell the shares of a company which turns sour on him. Doves argue that they have neither the time nor the knowledge to involve themselves in the management of industrial companies. 'A glib industrialist, talking about the wisher washer on the scrumger cap, could twist me round his little finger,' admitted one investment expert.

Hawks can be pretty interventionist if they feel like it. John Hoffmann, a former director of merchant bankers Keyser Ullmann, is one. He has formed an advisory service for institutional investors to instruct them on how best to persuade the boards of companies to perform better. He is planning to help 'make shareholder democracy work'. 'There are many cases,' he says, 'where selfish interest as an investor, duty as a representative of an above-average shareholding, concern for the future of the workpeople, the "national interest", all combine to require the articulate, professional management of institutional funds to take the initiative and associate with each other to force action on inadequate management.'

Intervention can take a variety of forms. One pension fund manager told me how in the course of the previous twelve months he had kicked out directors of one company, prevented board-room changes from being made in the case of another, and forced another company to sell off some of its assets to protect its loan stock holders. He casually related an instance of where he could have technically put a company into liquidation, but refrained for fear of blood being publicly let.

Institutional investors can often have a decisive influence on the whole future direction of a company. Vast industrial companies have been deflected from their diversification and expansion plans through lack of cooperation and opposition from their institutional shareholders. The Rank Organization was stopped in its tracks by institutional investors as it was contemplating a massive involvement in British brewing – by a take-over of Watney Mann. The plan of Hill Samuel to merge with the Metropolitan Estate and Property Corporation was greeted with howls of protest by the institutions and came to nothing. (Oddly, one of the principal institutions which objected to a merchant bank joining forces with a property company on that occasion was quite happy subsequently to see another merchant bank, Keyser Ullmann, merge with another property company, Central and District – which says something about City opportunism.) Burmah Oil's planned merger with Laporte, that of P. & O. and Bovis, the Imperial Tobacco bid for Courage, to name only a few, all ran into institutional investor difficulties of one form or another.

Support for intervention has powerful advocates outside the

City. Harold Wilson made little secret of his views that the institutions had a part to play in restructuring British industry. Charles Villiers, when he was managing director of the Government-backed Industrial Reorganization Corporation and as such the country's arch-interventionist, put in an eloquent plea for more positive action. 'If large investors opt out in this way,' he said, 'we shall never get the management of industry we so much need to recreate our national wealth. It seems, therefore, that there is scope for investors to concern themselves more deeply with their investments, to prod lazy managers and shift weary willies.' 'Institutional investors,' he added, 'hold too many shares to be able to sell if things start to go wrong and in any case are holding too large a portion of the national assets of a country no longer rich enough to be extravagant.'

Intervention by professional investors in the managements of British companies is comparable to an iceberg. Only a very small part of it is visible. If one can extend the iceberg analogy logically, it does seem that the icy mass has got bigger in recent years because there is greater public knowledge of intervention. More incidents of intervention have come to light. If the top of the iceberg has loomed larger, the iceberg as a whole must have expanded. And this has happened in spite of the fact that investment managers assiduously seek to avoid publicity in their efforts to shift the 'weary willies'.

In the first place, they are loath to admit publicly that they have made a mistake. 'A London borough whose investments we manage wouldn't be too happy if they were seen publicly to be associated with a dud share. What would the ratepayers think?' one investment manager puts the case.

There are other reasons for secrecy. Professional investors usually find themselves prodding around in the affairs of companies because they haven't been able to sell their shareholdings – their stake is too large and the market price would be seriously depressed if they sold. Any public knowledge of intervention would almost certainly send the share price skittling downwards. Secondly, intervention depends for its success to a great extent on the cooperation of the existing management of a company. And when institutions get to the stage of throwing out company managers the whole affair comes out into the open with dire effects on the company and its share price. 'We prefer backdoor moral suasion,' said one pension fund manager. 'It is better than shouting from the rooftops.'

The institutions have received encouragement for their interventionist activities from the associations to which most of them belong. Each of the four major groups of institutional shareholders has its own body. There is the Association of Investment Trust Companies, the British Insurance Association, the Association of Unit Trust Managers and the National Association of Pension Funds. Only the Unit Trust Managers tend to be passive when it comes to intervention.

In the past, it has been the Investment Trust Association which has made most of the running in terms of taking action against bad management. It has nearly 300 members, and until recently operated for seventeen years under the guiding hand of William Gammell, who has done much during that time to champion the rights of shareholders. Under Gammell's aegis, the Association tended to take a ruggedly independent line. It even started to publicize itself and has produced glossy literature extolling the virtues of investment trusts, at the same time taking a mild swipe at their competitors, the unit trusts, in the process. The difference between unit trusts and investment trusts has been described as 'the difference between supermarkets and Savile Row tailors'.

Like a big game-hunter, Gammell, monocled, used to sit poised in his look-out point in a small back passage behind the Stock Exchange, whence the Association operates. His tales of past trophies are legion. He recalls proudly his finest hour when he led a campaign against the Treasury which successfully led to an amendment in the 1965 Finance Act. 'Had the Bill gone through as planned, it would have killed off investment trusts,' he remembers. 'They defined us in such a way in the Bill that we could not have existed.' Then there was the time that he organized a bus-load of shareholders to attend a company's annual general meeting. The company was Crown Cork, which to the howls of dissenting shareholders decided not to pay a dividend to its shareholders in 1964. Another of Gammell's *causes célèbres* was over the decision by a property company to sack its auditors. Gammell intervened (only the shareholders can technically appoint auditors, and the company in question had not consulted its shareholders), and within a short time the auditors were restored.

This type of activity has all happened in the last fifteen years of the Association's operations. Before that, the Association was concerned mainly with the capital structures of companies. Typically, a company wanted to reorganize its capital, and it would approach the Association for its advice. Since 1955, the theatre of activities has widened. Gammell rallies his members on any number of issues where the rights of shareholders are felt to be at stake. He justifiably believes that the A.I.T. is now 'part of the City machine'.

Pension funds throw their weight about in the guise of an Investment Protection Committee (an arm of the National Association of Funds) headed by a bland north-countryman and ex-insurance man, Ken Parry, who in another role looks after the £35 million worth of investments for the Iraq Petroleum Company's pension fund. Historically, the pension funds have lived up to their stolid reputation as investors. But in the past few years, they have become more agile. Seven years ago a group of pension fund managers got together and formed an investment protection committee 'to protect the member funds' interests as stockholders against actions which might be detrimental to those interests'.

Parry has decidedly hawkish views about using shareholdings to stir up bad management. He explains how his committee works in the following terms: 'Matters requiring attention are brought to the Committee mainly in two ways: where a company proposes to take some action affecting stockholders, and wishes to have prior consultation with stockholders' representatives, the company or its advisers may approach the Committee directly, or via the secretariats of the British Insurance Association or the Association of Investment Trusts; alternatively, if a company has made proposals without prior consultation the matter may be raised by a member of the Investment Protection Committee itself. Examples are the treatment of a particular class of shareholders in a take-over situation or otherwise, and the issue of further loan stocks.

'When a matter has been raised its broad implications are considered by the Chairman or Vice-Chairman of the I.P.C. to determine the degree of importance of the subject. The next step is to establish the extent to which member Funds are involved in the particular company or stock concerned, and this is done by asking members to disclose their Funds' holdings. On receipt of this information a sub-committee, made up of a member of the Standing Committee and two or three holders (who will be members of the I.P.C.), is established. The presence of a Standing Committee member ensures consistency in the decisions reached. The sub-committee usually operates by telephone operations and for this reason the fact that an I.P.C. member is not in London does not prevent his involvement in the work of the Committee. A secretary has recently been appointed to carry out the liaison of ideas.

'When considered necessary, the sub-committee makes representations to the company or merchant bankers, or whoever is concerned, often after liaising with the British Insurance Association or the Association of Investment Trusts; and it is often possible to obtain, for example, fairer compensation as between different classes of capital in a reorganization. Even when we have not been successful in a case, there is some evidence that the views expressed have been borne in mind in subsequent similar cases, and the existence of a watch-dog body like the I.P.C. must have an indefinably beneficial influence on the thinking of companies and their advisers. We have to bear in mind that our holdings alone are rarely sufficient to be critical in any particular case, and so it is necessary to use moral suasion by force of argument in major issues.'

The insurance companies' Investment Protection Committee admits through its secretary to 'spending ninety per cent of our time in very unglamorous work'. Insurance companies are heavily invested in loan capital, so much of the attention of the B.I.A.'s Protection Committee is devoted to the terms on which loans are made by companies. 'Intervening in the affairs of a company's management is a matter for the insurance companies themselves,' I was told by the I.P.C.'s secretariat. 'In this capitalist jungle,' their man added, 'there is no obligation to stay in.' 'While we believe in shareholder democracy, why should we impose our views on other shareholders?' 'Our work is of a legal/accounting nature, and concerned in many cases with the nuts and bolts of capital reconstructions.'

The number of occasions when the institutional bodies band together to apply concerted pressure on a company appear to be rare. There are, however, a number of issues involving matters of principle, which the institutions are unanimous in denouncing. One of these is the non-voting share. The views of the B.I.A. are echoed by other institutional bodies: 'The only method of ensuring equitable treatment for all the proprietors of the company is a capital structure which provides all equity shareholders with voting rights directly proportionate to their stake in the business.'

Shareholder Democracy or Autocracy?

'When politicians suggest,' wrote Alex Rubner, 'that corporate democracy has been advanced because tens of millions of people have become indirect investors through these institutional channels, this is little short of claptrap; the institutional managers are autocrats in their fields and subject to little democratic control.'

The most important question to ask in relation to how far the institutions are disposed to wield their power is: how much of the decision-making process is in the hands of the investment manager? He is the man, after all, who is in charge of the day-to-day running of a portfolio. And it is he who is likely to take the initiative on an interventionist issue. To what extent are his powers circumscribed?

My own view is that an increasing amount of authority has been vested in the investment manager in recent years. But there is still a very wide spectrum of power, ranging from virtual autocracy at one end to reasonably democratic processes at the other. The big insurance companies still tend to stick rigidly to the committee system of investment management. 'The investment policy of the Pru,' says Angus Murray, 'is rather like British foreign policy – subject to constant change.' It is formulated by two joint investment managers – of which Murray was one – at the head of a sizable team of economists, accountants, actuaries and tax experts.

The investment decisions of the Pru are effectively taken by the board of the company. Each week a finance committee, consisting mainly of the company's directors, meets to consider investment possibilities put forward by the full-time investment department of the company. The board of the Pru is responsible for all investment decisions taken by the Pru.

The Commercial Union operates a similar system. It has a finance committee (comprising half the members of the board) which meets fortnightly after board meetings to ratify and discuss investment decisions.

Other institutional investors tend to abhor the committee system. They prefer to give one man the job of managing a portfolio, at the same time keeping close control of the decisions he takes. 'Just after the war,' an investment trust manager told me, 'investment managers would have to ring up a director and ask for his permission to deal. Now we cannot afford to wait a month and we take decisions off our own bat.'

One man who has little time for the committee system is George Ross Goobey, the flamboyant investment adviser to the £200 million Imperial Tobacco Pension Fund and a host of other portfolios. Ross Goobey holds strong views on investment matters. 'If I am convinced that a thing is right I will back it 100 per cent.' One of the things he was convinced was right was the attraction of the equity in the late 1940s, and he is generally credited as being the man who foresaw the equity boom before anyone else. One of the first things he did when he joined Imps in 1948 was to ditch most of the pension fund's entire holdings in fixed interest securities and go into equities.

Ross Goobey has virtually a free rein to apply his controversial investment ideas. The Imps pension fund has an investment committee of three men and they talk fairly regularly on the telephone. But they have not met formally for years.

Most institutional investors operate under a minimum of formal restraints. Ultimately, they are responsible in the decisions they take to a board of directors or trustees (very often the investment manager will be on the board himself). The role of the directors or trustees is essentially that of laying down broad policy guide-lines which an investment manager is expected to follow. A manager will be typically advised that *x* per cent of his portfolio should be in gilt-edged securities, *y* in property, *z* in North American shares and perhaps *q* in unquoted securities. But within these broad guide-lines an investment manager typically has more or less complete discretion. And if the investment manager is hardly circumscribed, his directors or trustees have few restrictions imposed upon them either. Ross Goobey told the Government-appointed Radcliffe Committee in 1958: 'It is the practice nowadays not to put limitations in the trust deed but leave it to the good sense of the committee operating the trust deed to make their own limitations from time to time.'

Two examples in recent years demonstrate how unfettered the powers of institutions really are. They both relate to pension funds. In 1969, a pension fund took the unprecedented step of acquiring a publicly quoted property company. The fund was the BP pension fund, and it paid nearly £19 million for Western Ground Rents. The initiative for this deal came almost entirely from the manager of the pension fund.

The other affair has stirred up much dust in the City.

Investing institutions with hundreds of millions of pounds' worth of new money to invest each year have come to find even the stock market a limited outlet for their funds. Over the years they have turned increasingly towards, on the one hand, property and, on the other, businesses without Stock Exchange quotations as repositories for their vast flow of funds. The unquoted company has obvious attractions for the big institutional investor. The growth of a company in its early stages of development can be very dramatic. And though the risks inherent in such an enterprise may be greater than those associated with a company in a more mature state of development the potential rewards can be enormous.

Understandably, investors who put their money at a high risk feel the need to contain their risk within reasonable limits by having some sort of control, or at least detailed knowledge, of the situations in which they are investing. This raises the question of management. The big institutional investors have always felt reluctant to put money into unquoted companies without some form of control or supervision of the businesses they are investing in. But the type of management skills needed to keep tabs on industrial companies are not usually to be found among the institutions.

It was into this uneasy situation that Mr Charles Gordon stepped. Born of Russian parents and married to the one-time prima ballerina, Nadia Nerina, Gordon had had a varied career before he presented his ingenious scheme to some of the country's leading pension funds and insurance companies. His history has been described as 'one of missed opportunities and avidly grasped opportunism'. He went down from Cambridge without taking a degree, flirted briefly with the idea of becoming a chartered accountant and then took on a job as a journalist with the *Investor's Chronicle*. This was small beer compared with the ambitions he entertained. From financial journalism he went to work in property development for Charles Clore and Jack Cotton. And from there he joined

Hambros Bank. At Hambros he got his first taste of the so-called venture capital business – backing young, unquoted companies with money and management ideas.

While at Hambros, Charles Gordon forged an alliance with Boris, known as Bobby, Marmor, a Czech émigré, who had served a British prison sentence for a 'youthful indiscretion', and a property developer, who had already enticed at least one large institutional investor to participate in his business projects. In harness, Marmor and Gordon conceived of the idea of a company backed by institutional investors to manage and invest money in small unquoted businesses where the amount of management required would be quite out of proportion to the funds each institution individually would be providing. Thus, Spey Investments was born.

The birth took place formally in 1965 when the company was registered. Eighteen months later it became active. Its backers have been some of the most impeccable names in the shadowy world of institutional investment. Through their pension funds, the employees of such august organizations as Imperial Chemical Industries, Unilever, Barclays Bank, and the electricity industry supplied a large part of the backing. The Royal Insurance company and the Salmon family of Joe Lyons fame were also backers. All in all, more than £50 million was entrusted to the care of Charles Gordon and his associates.

Nor were the names of those recruited to assist Gordon in his venture any less impressive. Some of the most prestigious names in British industry and finance were enlisted to oversee the project. There were Sir Julian Salmon, a former deputy chairman of J. Lyons; Sir Paul Chambers, former chairman of I.C.I. and chairman of Royal Insurance; Mr. Jasper Knight, former finance director of Unilever; Sir Joseph Lockwood, chairman of E.M.I.; Lord Chalfont, the former Labour minister; and more. All at some stage have been directors of Spey Investments or one or other of its subsidiaries.

For a few glorious years, it seemed that Gordon's ambitions knew no bounds. Large interests in industrial businesses, ranging from plastics to National Car Parks, were acquired at breath-taking speed. Take-over bids were launched for as much as £20 million at a time. Property was added in huge lumps. And then came plans to establish a vast merchant bank to challenge the established citadels of the City at their own game. There were publicly reported plans to take over an important discount house, to bid for a major merchant bank, to enter unit trusts and to launch property bonds.

Meanwhile, signs were beginning to emerge that all was not well in the house of Gordon. Heavy losses were mounting up on the plastics side, directorships in the group of companies were changing hands with uncomfortable frequency, and one of the major backers, the Unilever pension fund, pulled out along with its representative, Jasper Knight. The climax came at the end of June 1971, when Charles Gordon quit the company. 'This is a case of a genuine difference of opinion on policy,' declared Sir Paul Chambers. Less than a month later Spey's 'powerful new banking group', whose formation had been announced only in April, under Lord Chalfont and Sir Joseph Lockwood, was sold off to Pat Matthews' First National Finance Corporation. In the eighteen months to the middle of 1970, Spey as a whole lost more than £1 million; not quite what the institutions had in mind when they put their money where Charles Gordon's mouth was.

Spey continues, but in a much lower key. What is astonishing from this unhappy saga is that the pension funds and other institutional investors had so little control of the uses to which their money was being put. Under its creator and founder, Spey was effectively controlled by Charles Gordon. He himself held most of the shares which carried the voting rights in the company.

'Whatever the facts,' commented *The Times*, 'the institutional shareholders in this case do not emerge with much credit. Most investment carries risk, but one of the basic responsibilities of institutions investing other people's money is to take all the precautions possible when investing that money. In this case those precautions do not appear to have been as full as they could, indeed should, have been.'

'In a capitalist society there will always be a lot of chicanery and a lot of accidents. A lot of mergers have been a mammoth exercise in mutual deception.'

A partner in Baring Brothers

3. THE RICH MARKET FOR CORPORATE FINANCE

Most British companies, small and large, have at various stages of their corporate lives employed the services of a merchant bank. Many retain a very close working relationship with their merchant banking advisers. Some companies employ no fewer than two or three merchant banks at a time. In some cases the relationships are almost incestuously close. In every case, the heart of the relationship can be summed up in one word, finance – or, to use a slightly less glamorous word, money. If it is money to finance exports a company needs, or money to finance an acquisition, or money to pay for a capital investment project, a merchant bank is ready to lend a helping hand – for a fee. Hill Samuel calls itself the 'Companies' Company'. In rather more grandiose terms, Kleinwort Benson claims to have entered 'the era of comprehensive planning for financial productivity. . . . We help each of our clients to make optimum use of all the resources available both from within their business, and from the financial facilities offered throughout the world. That is financial productivity. What the businessman wants from Kleinwort Benson may be easily summed up. He wants credit, finance, capital to meet the short, medium and long-term needs of his business. He wants these in the right proportions, in the right currencies, at the right times. He wants, too, advice, on the technical aspects of organizing and deploying these funds, particularly when they cross frontiers. In short, every facility that he may consider employing.'

If the innocent industrialist finds himself perplexed by the welter of merchant banking jargon – the acceptance credit, the Eurocurrency loan, the sterling certificate of deposit or factoring, to list only a tiny fragment of the merchant banker's esoteric vocabulary – he may be forgiven. He may be excused too if he thinks that behind those discreet portals of Wood Street, Bishopsgate or Cheapside lies a benign fraternity of friendly bank managers who are always there, simply waiting to 'meet the short, medium and long-term needs of his business.'

But he would be wrong. For underneath the mystique which has always surrounded the merchant banks and which the recent revelling in public relations has done little to dispel, merchant banks have assumed the role of kingmakers of the corporate world. In their hands are the powers to make or break huge industrial undertakings, to merge them with equally huge undertakings and to plot systematically the foreseeable future of their corporate clients.

It is a role they have assumed with about as much effortlessness as the British monarchy. If there has been one weakness of many British industrial companies, it has been in the realm of finance. Lacking any real financial expertise a terrifying procession of impressive enough industrial enterprises have paraded their merchant bank advisers as if they were financial crutches.

The merchant banks have a long tradition of being held in awe by the industrial community. Even companies as large as I.C.I., with their not inconsiderable financial know-how of their own, depend on their merchant bankers to tell them how they are to raise the odd £60 million and when the time is ripe.

Historically, and perhaps more importantly, merchant banks have a rich past in the role of financial folk heroes. It was the Rothschilds, after all, who financed the British purchase of the Suez Canal, the Barings who helped the Americans buy Louisiana from the French, and the Hambros who backed Cavour's antics in Italy.

For decades, the cream of the merchant banking fraternity thrived on financing foreign governments and institutions. This was the foreign bond business. But by 1930, for a number of complex reasons, not least U.K. restrictions on foreign lending and the world-wide economic recession, the collective minds of the merchant banks were being exercised on pastures closer home. More specifically, it was to financing British industry that the merchant banks turned. From bond issues for the state of San Paolo, merchant bankers turned to meeting the financial needs, as the euphemism goes, of companies like English Electric or E.M.I. It was a swift transition from political to industrial kingmaker.

Take English Electric, for example, which is now under Sir Arnold Weinstock's control as part of G.E.C. How the former was saved from financial collapse by Lazard Brothers is told in detail by Robert Jones and Oliver Marriott in their *Anatomy of a Merger*: 'In 1929 English Electric made yet another loss, this time of £47,000. The company's financial situation was extremely serious. It was into this situation that the City merchant bankers, Lazard's, stepped with an offer first of £600,000 worth of new capital, later raised to £850,000. Until this time English Electric's merchant bankers had been Higginson and Co. Lazard's proposed a scheme of reorganization which was approved by the shareholders in June 1930.

'The effect of this reorganization was to give the Lazard's group some sixty per cent of the English Electric ordinary shares, more than enough for control of the company. *Yet the shareholders were not told who had gained control of their company and the English Electric official history treats the episode very briefly, as if it were a straightforward merchant-banking operation to re-finance an ailing company.*' (My italics.) And it was Lazard's, in the form of Lord Kindersley and Sir Holberry Mensforth, who invited the first Lord Nelson to become managing director of English Electric.

Nearly three decades later Lazard's took over the merchant

banking house of Edward de Stein and Company. Edward de Stein, described in *The Times* obituary as a 'small sprightly man' and 'a keen bird watcher, but his eye was not unerring', was one of the great industrial empire builders of the 1930s and 1940s. *The Times* said that 'the story of his career is essentially one of companies built up, often from small or difficult circumstances – Gallaher; Columbia Gramophones, later to be merged into E.M.I.; and Mercantile Credit, to take the most notable examples. All this was achieved by methods more usually associated with a banker of the old school: he had little head for figures and little respect for statisticians and economic theorists. What he did possess was a superb ability to pick the man for the job, an indefinable flair, and intuitive judgment.'

De Stein may indeed have belonged to 'the old school'. But it would be quite wrong to think of the 'old school', in the sense of merchant bankers being responsible for the creation and careful planning of large industrial enterprises, as being completely dead. Bankers with 'little head for figures' may be fewer and farther between, but the relationships which merchant banks have with their client customers are, if anything, closer.

At the heart of the merchant banking nexus are the seventeen members of the Accepting Houses Committee. These are the *corps d'élite* of merchant banking. Since the War only five houses have joined the Committee – Antony Gibbs, S. Japhet (now Charterhouse Japhet), S. G. Warburg (which acquired Seligman Brothers, which was already a member), Arbuthnot Latham and Rea Brothers. The Committee was founded in 1914, has no written rules, and its condition of membership is that each member has to have a sizable business in credits and these have to be available for discount at the Bank of England. In effect, this means that the members' acceptance credits can be discounted at the finest rates in the market. To be a member of the Accepting Houses Committee is to have one's ear closest to the Governor of the Bank of England. When the Old Lady of Threadneedle Street turns, the Accepting Houses will be the first to know about it.

The power and influence of the Accepting Houses can be best summarized in a few figures. Between them, the seventeen merchant banks have assets of over £3000 million and their acceptance business, which, of course, is only a part of their total business, amounts to over £400 million a year.

More interesting are the people who run the Accepting Houses. These are the comparatively small group of around 400 men who sit on the boards of the Accepting Houses. They hold an astonishing number of directorships – over 2000 in all – and by my reckoning no less than thirty-six of the top 100 British industrial companies have an Accepting House director on their boards – for example, Shell (Hill Samuel), British Petroleum (Morgan Grenfell), General Electric (Wm. Brandt, Lazard's, Morgan Grenfell and Hill Samuel), Courtaulds (Guinness Mahon), Beecham Group and Bowater (Hill Samuel) and Cadbury Schweppes (Kleinwort Benson).

DIRECTORSHIPS OF DIRECTORS OF THE ACCEPTING HOUSES

Bank	*Ratio of Directorships: Directors*	*No. of Directors*	*Their Directorships*
Brown Shipley	8·4	9	76
Hambros	9·8	30	295
Arbuthnot Latham	12·7	9	114
Barings	3·6	15	54
Wm. Brandt	7·5	17	128
Charterhouse Japhet	6·4	17	109
Antony Gibbs	5	8	40
Guinness Mahon	7·7	12	92
Hill Samuel	5·3	52	278
Kleinwort Benson	5·9	29	170
Lazard Brothers	6·1	23	141
Morgan Grenfell	4	21	83
Samuel Montagu	4·6	25	115

Bank	Ratio of Directorships: Directors	No. of Directors	Their Directorships
Rothschild	6·8	24	163
Schroder Wagg	5·9	34	201
S. G. Warburg	4·9	43	208
Rea Brothers	6·5	13	85
		381	2352

Source: *Directory of Directors*

J. Henry Schroder Wagg has its representatives among an impressive array of industrial bastions. Its chairman, Gordon Richardson, sits on the board of the new Rolls-Royce. Other Schroder directors are to be found in the board-rooms of Boots, Scottish and Newcastle Breweries, Powell Duffryn, Unigate, Bass Charrington, the British Sugar Corporation, Wimpey and Harland & Wolff, to name only part of the labyrinthine network of directorships held by directors of that merchant bank.

These and the formal client/merchant bank relationship are the overt links between merchant banking and industry. Less formal and carefully shrouded from the public gaze lies a powerhouse full of instruments and levers which can be brought to bear on the world of business at large. In the first place, there is the massive potential power which a merchant bank can exercise through the investment decisions it controls. Merchant banks are deeply involved in the management of investment and unit trusts, of insurance company portfolios, of charitable trusts, of rich individuals' portfolios and of company pension funds; the last unhesitatingly entrusted to a merchant bank's care by businesses in search of 'financial productivity'. It is seldom possible to make any quantitative assessment of the influence that merchant banks exercise in this way. With few exceptions, merchant banks prefer not to be associated with industrial companies as holders of the latter's equity capital. The cases where links of this sort are seen publicly to exist tend to be in the nature of small companies which merchant banks have colonized at the early stage of the former's corporate lives.

No, the real power of the merchant banks is to be found among the arcane world of that uncertain collection of City beings – the institutions. If merchant banks are the focal point of the City power nexus, they are also invariably the centre-point for mustering support among the institutions. Only very rarely does this clout or strike power really emerge very far above the surface. One occasion when it did was in 1970, when a powerful group of institutional shareholders raised their collective voices against the mismanagement of Vickers. It came as no surprise to find a merchant bank, Hill Samuel, leading the battle-cry.

The second, and perhaps more obvious, point about the latent power of merchant banks is their influence on the purse-strings of their client companies. The degree of dependence on a merchant bank as a source of finance, of course, differs enormously from company to company; from banking house to banking house. But at the heart of every merchant bank/client relationship lies the simple truth that the bank is the money agent. The merchant bank can provide finance in any one of three ways: it can put up all the money itself; it can join forces with a consortium of other merchant banks or financial agencies to provide the money; or it can arrange for other banks or agencies to provide all. Every request for additional finance from a client business can be met either with a firm veto or with the attachment of formidable strings. There is no very clear distinction in merchant banking between, on the one hand, deciding how much money a client company is to have and at what price, and on the other, determining the uses to which that extra finance is to be put. The client company may have its own fixed ideas, but these are capable of being modified by a merchant bank. If a merchant bank considers a proposed new widget factory to be an unsuitable investment for a client and that the money could be more profitably spent elsewhere, it will not hesitate to influence the client's judgement. More often a merchant bank's advice is restricted to financial matters – dividend policy, the raising of finance, the financing of trade, etc. But it is difficult, almost impossible, to say where this advice or influence ends. A merchant bank advises/influences its client to raise its dividend. This means usually that less money is available for investment within the company. This in turn means that a company cannot afford, for the time being, to put its money into some favoured investment project. Where does the advice/influence end? The fact is that it is absurd to separate the financial from the commercial and industrial decision-making processes of a company.

The Corporate Financiers

No self-respecting sizable merchant bank these days does without a corporate finance department. This is a banking house's Panzer regiment: the troops on whose success and failure, when all is said and done, a merchant bank's reputation rests. Other departments of a merchant bank may earn most of the profits. But it is the corporate finance division whose glorious job it is to fight the battles. And when they are not deep in the fray of take-overs or mergers, the corporate financiers are raising huge sums of money for their corporate clients, bringing new companies to the market (that is, arranging for their shares to be quoted on the stock exchanges) or juggling around with a client company's capital structure. It is these men who have become an established part of the folklore known as the management revolution in Britain. These are the people whom the Press has tried hard to immortalize; these to whom industry has made obeisance.

No one is quite sure when and how the name of the game changed. Corporate finance has only been going under that title for a decade or so. Before that, merchant banks assembled their financial advisory services for companies under their 'new issues' departments. Corporate finance, in the guise of 'new issues', was a fairly timid occupation for the merchant banks compared with what goes on nowadays. Typically, it involved tinkering around with the way that client companies had their capital organized. In technical terms, it might have meant reconstructing the preference shares of a company into unsecured loan stock or upgrading the debentures in a subsidiary company into the debentures of the parent. It also meant raising new capital for companies and assisting companies to go public. But this was somehow mundane, not to say dull, stuff compared with 'comprehensive planning for financial productivity'.

Two events seem to have heralded 'the challenging new era', to continue the words of Kleinwort Benson. They both took place in or around 1958. One was the opening up of the Eurodollar market: the discovery of a vast pool of dollars in non-American hands which could be used to finance international operations. This added an entirely new international dimension to corporate finance. The other was the great Aluminium War.

In 1957, Reynolds Metals, an American company based in Virginia, set its heart on acquiring Britain's only aluminium manufacturer, British Aluminium. The Wall Street banking house, Kuhn Loeb, were advisers to Reynolds and they put their client in touch with their London affiliate, S. G. Warburg. Reynolds were advised not to run the risk of chauvinistic opposition but to team up with another British company, Tube Investments, and make a joint bid for British Aluminium. The Reynolds/Tube Investments camp began buying shares of British Aluminium under the guise of nominee shareholdings. By November, when the consortium had acquired ten per cent of B.A., the cards were laid on the table. Tube Investments made it clear that it wanted a closer association with British Aluminium which in turn replied that it had already reached agreement for a link-up with Alcoa, the major American rival of Reynolds.

The subsequent drama, which ended in victory for the Reynolds/T.I. camp nearly two months after the first shots had been fired, was rich in plots and sub-plots. The theme was essentially the conflict between the City Old Guard and the newcomers: a battery of established merchant banks, led by Hambros and Lazard's, against two parvenus, S. G. Warburg, whose founder Sir Siegmund Warburg had lived in England for barely twenty years, and another unconventional City banker, Lionel Fraser, head of Helbert, Wagg, which was also advising the Reynolds/T.I. axis. The Old Guard accused the newcomers of lack of patriotism. But their appeal to 'the national interest' fell on unsympathetic ears among the Press. Like the first signs of senility, the antics of the Old Guard awakened many people to the realization that all was not well among the City establishment. Commenting on the reactionary consortium of banks afterwards, Anthony Crosland, the Labour M.P., said that 'their outlook appears about as contemporary as the architectural style in which the City is now being rebuilt – both make one shudder'.

Frank Smith, who joined Warburg's just after the war and is now still a director of the merchant bank, looks back on the Aluminium War like a general. 'After the war (Second World) there was very little in the way of opposed take-overs. The Aluminium War created a situation which had not previously arisen in the City: a clear division of all the leading merchant banks. After that, merchant banks had to be more on their toes. The comfortable unenergetic life was coming to an end. Merchant banks began to realize the importance of specialist departments to deal with these special situations.' These were the words of a military hero twelve years after his greatest victory. Sadly, Mr Smith, when I saw him, had just been outmanoeuvred in a take-over battle by a man who had barely left school at the height of the Aluminium saga – Jeffrey Sterling's company had just battled through the defences which Mr. Smith had neatly constructed around Gamages, the ailing Holborn department store. It seemed rough justice for such an eminent campaigner.

Every merchant bank worth its salt in corporate finance has its tale to tell of an early escapade in the take-over field. The one Lazard's likes to tell relates to a deal several years before the Aluminium War broke out. It centres around Lazard's bid to gain control of the Matador Ranch, 800,000 acres of Texas countryside on which grazed over 47,000 head of cattle.

'Matador had been acquired by Scottish interests,' wrote T. A. Wise, 'in the nineteenth century. A public company, it was incorporated and headquartered in Dundee, Scotland, and its shares were traded on the London Stock Exchange. A number of entrepreneurs had suggested converting the land-rich corporation into cash, but the job seemed insuperably complicated by U.S. and British tax laws, British investment rules, and Texas land laws.' Lazard's was not to be put off. The bank and its New York affiliate, Lazard Frères, offered Matador shareholders \$23.70 a share, convinced the British Treasury to allow shareholders to reinvest the money in other U.S. securities, hived off the mineral rights of the company to a separate company and proceeded to carve up the ranch into fifteen separate corporations. For all its efforts the Lazard group earned itself profits of somewhere in the region of \$10 to \$15 million. 'It was something of a fairy tale,' said Derek Willis, one of the bank's managing directors. As part of the fiendish complications of the deal he was on the board of Matador for only seven minutes, in order to meet some quirky requirement of British or American tax law. This was Lazard's first significant foray into the take-over battlefield after the war. All merchant banks revel in the complications of finance.

During the 1950s, most of the spadework on take-overs and mergers was carried out by an army of independent lawyers, accountants and stockbrokers operating quite outside the merchant banking nexus. Solicitors like Freshfields, Slaughter & May and Linklater & Paine, and accounting firms like Peat Marwick and Touche Ross were the creative forces in corporate engineering during the heydays of Charles Clore, Isaac Wolfson and Hugh Fraser.

'In those days,' says John Gillum, now one of Samuel Montagu's corporate finance experts, 'take-overs were down in our books as "sundry fees". When I joined Kleinwort's in 1956 the corporate finance department (or new issues department as it was known) was a very small show consisting of one manager, one senior assistant, one clerical type and a couple of hopeful trainees. Those were the days when directors of merchant banks did not get involved in the small print.' The same pattern was more or less repeated in every leading City merchant bank at the time.

Merchant banks, as one distinguished observer has pointed out, have 'a protean capacity to invent new methods'. If the Aluminium War shook them into awareness that the old style of merchant banking was fast becoming obsolete, it also prompted circumspection. A merchant banker surveying the scene in, say, the year 1960 might have observed two things: first, that the take-over cult was tending to spread; and second, that up till then most merchant banks had made precious little money out of take-overs and mergers. He might have also observed that the work involved in marrying companies off to one another was becoming increasingly more burdensome. This was largely the function of the Stock Exchange insisting on disclosure of more detailed information in take-over deals and new issues. So how did 'the protean capacity to invent new methods' manifest itself? The answer is that virtually all the leading merchant banks systematically raided the bar and the leading firms of City solicitors and accountants to staff up a wonderful new organizational invention to be called the 'corporate finance department'.

It was symptomatic that in the year following their defeat at the combined hands of S. G. Warburg and Cecil King's *Daily Mirror* group, Rothschild's, who had advised Odhams (the company taken over), decided to set up a corporate finance department. The delicate task of running it was entrusted to Philip Shelbourne, a recent entrant to merchant banking and a distinguished practitioner in the field of company law.

It would be superfluous to mention many of the other men who have crossed the divide from law into merchant banking in recent years. A few of the more prominent names are Robert Clark, ex-Slaughter & May and now of Hill Samuel; Sir Henry Fisher, ex-judge and now of Schroder Wagg; H. Monroe, ex-Q.C. and now of S. G. Warburg; and Stanley Berwin, a solicitor and now of Rothschild's.

Nowadays the corporate finance department of a substantial merchant bank typically consists of twenty or thirty executives drawn largely from the ranks of accounting firms and solicitors. The business schools have also provided a rich recruiting ground. Presiding over the team of executives are the directors or partners of the bank – usually somewhere in the region of five to ten of them are specially assigned to corporate finance. 'We look more at the personality type of chap,' says John Gillum. 'He has to be a tough personality, exuding authority, but in a rather subtle subordinate way.' 'There's more in corporate finance than knowing how,' says Frank Smith. 'One has got to present a front of culture.'

The image which a merchant bank likes to project of its corporate finance team is that of a group of alert, clean-shaven, self-confident technocrats bristling only with slide-rules and instant answers to the most complicated financial puzzles. Baring's have even gone as far as installing a computer to help them out in complicated take-over transactions. 'We can manipulate different assumptions about a company's future,' says Peter Baring.

Such talk of cold, bureaucratic efficiency overtaking merchant banking is misleading. Merchant banks still take a highly personal approach to their corporate clients. 'There is almost no large industrial company,' a managing director of Lazard's told me, 'where we have no connection. Anybody can do the arithmetic. No amount of looking at textbooks will replace the grapevine.'

The grapevine, as we have seen, has not a few industrial and financial branches. Lazard's own grapevine is every bit as strong as that of Schroder's. You'll find a Lazard's director in the board-rooms of no lesser industrial and financial powers than E.M.I., G.E.C., P. & O., British Aircraft Corporation, Chloride Group, Babcock and Wilcox, British Match, Dalgety, Gallaher, Royal Insurance and S. Pearson, the rambling corporate empire of Lord Cowdray of which Lazard's are a part. Through the grapevine a merchant bank is capable of finding out things about industry which neither a shareholder nor the avid readers of the business press would come anywhere near to discovering. Join the grapevine of a banking house such as Lazard's to the grapevines of other merchant banks (and, of course, they touch in several places) and you have a vineyard of almost infinite proportions.

The fact is that, however much space is devoted in glossy

brochures to computers, financial productivity and highly skilled teams of technocrats, merchant banking, and corporate finance in particular, is still a very personalized business where hunch takes precedence over scientific analysis. For merchant banks to make any claims beyond this would be simply misleading. The merger mania which gripped British business towards the end of the 1960s has now provided many bitter cautionary tales. Merchant banks played an important role in selling the dubious concept of bigness and the need for concentration to their industrial clients. In so doing, they were not only overselling their own competence; they were succouring the megalomanic ambitions of many British industrialists. Only now are some of the great accidents resulting from this chicanery becoming apparent.

Who Carries the Can?

Responsibility is not a word about which those in such a pragmatic profession as merchant banking pause to think very deeply. To take a very cynical view, one might say that a merchant bank claims responsibility for the performance of an industrial client when it suits a merchant bank to be responsible. And such occasions might arise when the prestige of a merchant bank can be enhanced. Responsibility in merchant banking, the cynic would argue, is about nothing more or less than public relations.

At the end of 1969 Baring's offered to the public shares in Home Counties Newspapers, a small, hitherto family-controlled newspaper publishing company. Among the usual welter of small print contained in the formal offer document, Baring's put their wholesome name to a forecast that profits of Home Counties Newspapers for 1969 would be approximately £225,000. The shares were being offered to the public at 11s. each. The flotation duly went ahead, although a substantial proportion of the shares was left in the hands of the underwriters. Less than three months later, the forecast had gone badly askew. The wretched publishing company declared its profits would be 'substantially less than the estimate included in the offer document'. To be precise, profits were less than half what they were forecast to be. In a strikingly unusual move for a merchant bank, Baring's decided to do the decent thing and buy back the shares at the price they offered them. 'We are not obliged to do this,' they declared. 'But we lent our name to a financial assessment which has not stood the test of time.' It could have cost them around £500,000 – quite a lot of money even for the mighty Baring's. 'While one must criticize both Baring's and H.C.N.,' proclaimed the *Daily Mail*, 'for the forecast that failed so badly, Baring's deserve warm thanks for a generous response and a manly apology. Very few would have done as much.'

The new issue market is a deeply sensitive area of activity for merchant banks. And understandably. For this, and a merchant bank's performance in advising clients on take-overs and mergers, are where the spotlights of the public focus. These two areas, if you like, represent the delicate interface between merchant banking and the outside world. The rest of a banking house's activities can be subtly hidden from the public gaze. If daylight has to be let in upon magic, to paraphrase Walter Bagehot, then unavoidably it must light up the merchant bank *qua* issuer of new capital or adviser on take-overs and mergers. The two functions are intertwined and fall neatly within the realm of the corporate finance department.

But it is in the area of new issues that a merchant bank's reputation is most obviously at stake. 'It doesn't do a bank any good,' one merchant banker told me, 'to have a series of flops.' In order to discover what a merchant bank's responsibility is as an issuing house, it is important to understand the functions and rituals associated with the new issue market.

The *dramatis personae* in the new issue market consist of sixty so-called issuing houses which collectively form the Issuing Houses Association, a club consisting of all seventeen members of the Accepting Houses Committee, but for obvious reasons lacking the exclusiveness of the latter. The I.H.A., formed just after the war, in many ways typifies the representative machinery of the City. It has no formal rules of conduct. 'We do not control how people manage their own businesses,' Peter Samuel (Hill Samuel) told the Radcliffe Committee. 'But we like to think that the fact that we are there means that members of the Association would not do things which would not be directly in accordance with what one would think would be the right practice.' The Association embraces a wide cross-section of City organizations from the older respected merchant bankers to financial trusts, large stockbroking firms and some of the more recently established banking houses. Like any heavily diluted representative body, it seldom carries the authority and *gravitas* of the smaller élitist body.

While issuing houses act as the delicate go-betweens with lenders on one side and corporate borrowers on the other, their importance in providing finance for companies must not be overstated. In 1970 money raised from the new issues market amounted to only £539 million, small beer compared with the total capital needs of companies. Most companies find the majority of their financial requirements from profits, depreciation provisions and future tax reserves. According to Richard Briston of the Bradford Management Centre, 'new issues of share and loan capital accounted for not more than twenty per cent of such finance (the financial requirements of quoted companies) in each year except 1961 and 1962, when they reached a peak of thirty-two per cent.' Nevertheless, though companies may depend predominantly on the amount of earnings they retain, the marginal amount of new capital they raise through the new issues market does in some cases have a disproportionate importance for a company's future operations.

The extent to which an issuing house believes its reputation to be pinned on its success or failure in the new issues market is underlined by the elaborate preparation which takes place before the shares of a company are marketed for the first time. 'Because the issuing house is lending its name to the borrower or vendor and is thus giving the issue the stamp of respectability,' says Richard Briston, 'it must investigate the affairs of the issuing body to ensure that it warrants such backing....

The issuing house must satisfy itself that the company is strongly-based, has good prospects, is well-managed and is worthy of a Stock Exchange quotation.' The investigations, according to Briston, are exhaustive. Full details of the company's financial history are required by the issuing house together with 'details of the management of the company, the current level of capital commitments, the scope for expansion and the specific uses to which the funds raised by the issue are to be put. If favourably impressed, it will send a representative to the company to obtain a first-hand impression of its management, reputation and prospects. His opinion will be reinforced by reports from financial contacts both in the City and in the vicinity in which the company operates. In this way an impression of the past performance, current reputation and future prospects of the company is created. If the result of these preliminary enquiries is favourable, then a more formal and intensive investigation is begun. A firm of accountants will be appointed to examine the accounts of the company for the past ten years, ascertaining that these have been prepared on a consistent basis, and in particular, that stock and work-in-progress have been valued consistently.' All this is done under a thick cloak of secrecy. Before they floated £12·5 million worth of their shares in their own parent company, S. Pearson (which was one of the largest new issues of all time), Lazard's went through an elaborate dress-rehearsal, which contained something of the cloak-and-dagger intrigue of a television series about high finance. Detailed documents passed round the merchant bank months before anything was announced about the new issue purporting to relate to Millbank Ltd., a concocted pseudonym for S. Pearson.

All this is impressive, not to say dramatic, stuff. It is also highly rewarding. A merchant bank normally charges a one per cent commission on issues up to £2 or £3 million. After that it is somewhat less. The broker takes a cut of 0·25 per cent, although he may sometimes do more than the merchant bank. But how competent is the merchant banking system in providing companies with new capital?

There is a priestly solemnity about floating companies. The

novice has exposed himself to all manner of ritual investigations by the arch-priest (the issuing house). The time is near for the formal initiation into the solemn rites of the City. The arch-priest must assemble his acolytes who are to play an important part in the initiation ceremony. These are the underwriters, a variety of financial institutions ranging from investment trusts to insurance companies, who dutifully undertake to buy up a specified part of the shares offered in the novice company which are not bought by the public. And for a fee, of course – ranging from 0·25 to 3 per cent of the cost of the shares underwritten.

A week, or possibly more, before the formal ceremony is due to take place, the novice must be displayed before the acolytes and another important group of attendants – the scribes (financial press). Whether it be a tropical fruit dealer in the west of London or a scrap merchant in Wolverhampton, the novice must be solemnly interrogated by both sects. An awesome meeting place will be arranged – around the lunch-table of the Dorchester Hotel, in the panelled board-room of a merchant bank or in the quiet recess of a stockbroking firm. Both the acolytes and the scribes will want to know how deeply committed is the novice to the City vows. There will be talk of profit forecasts, price/earnings ratios and possible future trends in the markets for yams or non-ferrous metals. The acolytes will retire, communicating to the arch-priest their assent with mystical signs. The scribes will repair to their quarters to give their verdict in the knowledge that the novice's record and intentions will be heavily advertised adjacent to their writings – or not, as the case may be.

The moment of religious truth finally arrives. The public at large make their subscriptions. If the arch-priest has done his job successfully, the speculators will be there in force. They are known as stags. They will have no intention of keeping the novice's shares as an investment. With the ceremonies over, the stags will retire with either profits or fingers burnt, the arch-priest and the acolytes with their commissions, and the novice with his new-found status of public company.

The cost of this elaborate ritual is not inconsiderable. Many would argue that it is excessive. The point is that an issuing house's reputation is firmly staked to the success of a new issue. If the public pay less than the price attached by the issuing house to the shares of a newly floated company, the issuing house will have visibly failed in its task. This explains why issuing houses tend to be excessively cautious in establishing the price at which they issue shares in companies coming to the market for the first time. How far does this caution benefit the client company? Not at all.

'Many issuing houses . . .,' says Briston, 'have established issue prices which, while ensuring the success of the issue and maintaining the reputation of the issuing house, have been far below the price which investors have been prepared to pay, with the result that the issuing company receives much smaller proceeds than would have been obtained had the issue price been more realistic.' The offer for shares in one company, Headquarters and General Supplies, was oversubscribed 177 times when it was floated in 1963. The shares in Penguin Books when they were first marketed were oversubscribed 150 times. The sacred ritual of flotation takes a heavy toll on companies in terms of both commission and caution. It is not always necessary to go to usurers to find expensive money in the City.

One of the beauties of capitalism is that built into the system is a finely tuned mechanism of checks and balances. Any economic activity which for any considerable length of time becomes inherently profitable attracts marauders. As the elderly fraternity of merchant banks woke up to the new-found delights of corporate finance they were not alone. Others soon discovered that the magic of corporate finance was not as exclusive as it seemed. The raiders have come from two camps. In the first place, there has been competition from the clearing banks. Lloyds with its forty-one per cent interest in National & Grindlays were the first of the clearing bankers to obtain a financial stake in an existing merchant bank – N & G bought a two-thirds interest in William Brandt. Midland followed suit and bought its way into Montagu Trust, the parent company of Samuel Montagu. Meanwhile, several clearing banks have been growing their own merchant banking timber. Williams & Glyn's and National Westminster both have active merchant banking set-ups. How much further the clearing banks will go in future is difficult to say. The Bank of England has traditionally been none too happy about this sort of cross-pollination but recently changed the rules so that U.K. clearing banks and banks in the E.E.C. can buy into British merchant banking. The rest of the competition has come from independent marauders – the new generation of City financiers which have risen to challenge seriously the dominance of the established fraternity of merchant bankers.

All this has generated the unhappy predicament: too many merchant banks chasing too few companies for too little business. Or as Sir George Bolton, president of the Bank of London and South America, elegantly puts it: 'The merchant banks may now have reached the point when they are beginning to wonder whether there is enough domestic business to go round to warrant the existence of such a large number of concerns competing for the attention of a smaller and smaller number of large industrial organizations in conditions where it has become impossible to raise capital resources on any scale.'

'The protean capacity to invent new methods' was not slow to show itself. Merchant banks have responded to the potential embarrassment of this competition by surreptitiously redefining the conceptual framework of their client relationships. If you like, they changed the rules of the corporate finance game. They set out to establish relationships with their corporate clients of such deep intensity that it would become practically impossible for a client to move from one merchant bank to another. This could be done in a variety of ways. It could involve seconding personnel from a merchant bank to the corporate planning department of an industrial company; or *vice versa*. Several merchant banks have done this. In doing so they can play a key role in planning the future of their clients. The involvement of merchant bankers in the whole decision-making process of large industrial companies cannot be underestimated. Two recent take-over bids have revealed the merchant banking community in some of the least creditable match-makings the City has seen for some time. The abortive merger between P. & O. and Bovis, the construction company, was essentially the work of Lord Poole, chairman of Lazard Brothers, which for some time had the unique distinction of acting as merchant bankers for both P. & O. and Bovis. Another bid, at about the same time – that of Bowater for Ralli International, the merchanting group run by a former Jim Slater protégé, Malcolm Horsman – was also largely the work of merchant bankers. Bowater's merchant bank, Hill Samuel, had its own man, Robert Clark, on the Bowater board. A meeting between Clark and Jim Slater, whose Slater Walker merchant bank, advising Ralli (and owning fifteen per cent of it), had amassed a twelve per cent holding in Bowater, set this particular merger on the move.

There are few merchant banks who regard corporate finance as a routine service function akin to soliciting or auditing. In the field of take-overs and mergers, most banking houses consider themselves to be 'finders as well as processors', in the words of one banker. They regard themselves in business to steer their clients into the right directions. And this may well involve putting ideas into their heads about juicy take-over situations. Merchant banks have set themselves up increasingly in the business of 'industrial logic', a favourite merchant banking phrase. The astonishing thing is that as merchant banks have begun to see themselves as arbiters of industrial or commercial logic they have failed abysmally to develop the competence with which to practise it.

The fact is that while merchant banks have desperately tied themselves closer with their corporate clients by a variety of devices, they are extraordinarily naïve for the most part in their judgement of people and industrial operations. Every merchant banker likes to tell the tale of an entrepreneur who came asking for finance for a flying saucer project: and how he was sent packing. But what criteria are adopted in assessing the merits of more plausible projects? Typically, a merchant bank will first ask for figures: a financial statement of the company in question. If a solid blue-blooded accounting name like

Cooper Brothers or Peat Marwick is to be found at the bottom of the figures the merchant bank may not even bother to see whether they add up. If there is any reason to doubt the reputation of the company, the merchant bank may tap the grapevine for information – another merchant bank or a stockbroking firm may be approached for its opinion. A visit to the company may be arranged, but this is unlikely to yield more truth than would be thrown up by a carefully prepared public relations exercise. The appalling truth is that the main necessary condition for plausibility in the City hangs around the social ease with which the leaders of a company seeking financial assistance can present themselves. In many cases it has little to do with the intrinsic values of their business. A soft tongue and a healthy balance sheet are the prerequisites of success: and the figures on that balance sheet may bear little resemblance to the facts of commercial life.

It is for this reason that merchant banks, knowingly or unknowingly, do from time to time lend their names to soufflés that subsequently collapse. That powerful duet, Hill Samuel and Guinness Mahon, were among the blue-blooded financial institutions which gave their support to the flotation of Bernard Cornfeld's Investors Overseas Services. Ansbacher's, the merchant bank, in concert with the patrician stockbroking firm of Panmure Gordon, launched Robert Maxwell's Pergamon Press to the investing public. Brown Shipley was at one unhappy stage of its life involved in the infamous Salad Oil scandal. There is no shortage of skeletons in merchant banking cupboards. The list of corporate accidents to which the names of merchant banks could be appended would be impressive.

If the merchant banks want to play a more creative and positive role in the British capitalist system (and there is every indication that this is what they have been wanting to do), there are two crucial implications. First, they have to be prepared to accept a considerably greater degree of responsibility in public for what they do. And second, the screening process, which tells them what companies and people to back and what not to, will need to be redesigned to look less like a very leaky sieve.

'Sentiment and prestige are nothing except where there is some tangible backlash in the form of profit.'

An American banker in London

4. THE AMERICAN CHALLENGE

Diagonally across the street from the Lothbury/Princes Street corner of the Bank of England stands Number 1, Moorgate. It is the normally stark, comfortless type of City building on the outside. But inside, a sea of fitted carpets and (what once must have been) a forest-full of walnut panelling greet the visitor as he enters the building. This is the City office of the Republic National Bank of Dallas, the thirty-eighth and one of the latest American banks to establish itself in London.

The Texan bankers evidently regarded it as something of a triumph obtaining such prestigious quarters. 'Most of us have an image-consciousness that demands getting something attractive as well as business,' says the bank's American manager with a predictable southern drawl. 'Fit for a Texan and in keeping with the dignity and style of banking tradition in the City', is how the bank likes to see its new City branch.

Further along Moorgate, the American presence comes more sharply into focus. At Number 4 can be found the First National Bank of Boston, at 10 the Chemical Bank, at 13 Mellon National Bank and Trust Company, at 34 the First National City Bank of New York, at 35-39 the United California Bank, at 46 the National Bank of Seattle, and so on. It is not for nothing that the City with its arid sense of humour refers to Moorgate as the 'Avenue of the Americas'.

Within a few hundred yards there are more resonantly transatlantic names – like Wells Fargo Bank, Crocker Citizens National Bank, Harris Trust and Savings Bank, and Marine Midland Bank.

Most of these have set up shop in London in the last few years. In 1960, there were only ten American banks represented in London. Six years later there were fifteen, and there are now getting on for forty. Together with around another 120 foreign banks, ranging in origin from Japan and all the major countries of the continent to Russia and Afghanistan, they form the rich fabric of the City's international banking nexus. They represent a powerful virility symbol which the City has come to cherish.

Not surprisingly, of all the foreign bankers the American banks have a disproportionately greater importance in the City. In Britain as a whole, they have attracted more deposits (over £10,000 million) than any other single sector of the banking industry, except the London clearing banks (Barclays, National Westminster, Midland, Lloyds and Williams and Glyn's). Four years ago the American *Fortune* magazine commented: 'Wherever they go, their aggressiveness and ingenuity have quickened competition in banking, stimulated new kinds of capital markets, shaken the sluggish Old World banking communities out of their complacency, and opened the eyes of businessmen abroad to the possibilities of using money more productively.'

Yet strangely enough, the immediate presence of the American banks in London is noticed only by walking through the streets of the City and the West End (where some of them have opened clinically efficient offices), or by leafing through the advertising pages of business magazines such as *The Economist*. In the latter, the reader will find such baffling claims as that of the First Boston Corporation which says it has 'managed or co-managed the underwriting or direct placement of securities totalling over $60·5 million', or that of Manufacturers Hanover which states that 'more medium term Eurocurrency financing has been arranged at 88 Brook Street, Grosvenor Square, than in any other London office during the past eighteen months', or that of Security Pacific, more simply, 'the creative bank'.

These provide the clue to where the activities of the American banks in London have so far been concentrated. They mostly came to take part in a rich new source of international finance – the Eurocurrency markets – in order to satisfy the increasingly large financial appetites of international corporations, foreign governments and state agencies.

American bankers were unable to do this from their home base for a variety of reasons, mostly associated with the various steps which the U.S. Government took throughout the 1960s to put right the country's balance of payments difficulties. One of the most important effects of the recurrent U.S. balance of payments deficits – which began in the late 1950s and grew steadily larger – has been that large quantities of dollars have accumulated in foreign hands. In successive stages the American administration took measures to correct the imbalance, and at the same time reluctantly propelled U.S. banks abroad to take advantage of this fast growing pool of dollars deposited overseas.

Ironically, the move which opened up on a significant scale the market for Eurodollars (as this elusive breed of dollars is known) came from this side of the Atlantic. In 1957, the Bank of England imposed severe restrictions on the way in which sterling could be used to finance international trade outside the sterling area. International traders automatically looked to the dollar as an alternative currency.

The timing was impeccable. Thanks to the American trade deficits, there was an ample supply – and a growing one – of dollars in foreign hands. And thanks to collective action of Western European governments in 1958, the major currencies of Europe became almost freely convertible into dollars. So a German firm, for example, selling machinery to France could easily obtain payment in dollars. Indeed the dollar became the most favoured currency medium through which to conduct international trade.

The banking environment in the United States meanwhile was to become steadily more restrictive. In 1963, the American Government introduced its Interest Equalization Tax which had the effect of eliminating the advantages for foreign borrowers of going to New York for their money. Almost overnight, the New York market was closed to foreign long-term borrowers. From then on, any American who bought foreign bonds in New York had to receive his interest with tax lopped off. This became an intolerable situation when there were richer pickings in international lending to be found elsewhere. These fortunately turned out to be in London.

The fertile financial brains in the City were not slow to spot the opportunities which were open to them. Those of S. G. Warburg are generally recognized to have been among the first. In 1963 this merchant bank was the leader of a group of banks offering bonds worth $15 million on behalf of Autostrade, the Italian national road authority. Thus the Eurobond market came into existence.

The growth of Eurobonds has been one of the principal products of the development of the Eurodollar. Before the birth of the Eurobond, Eurodollars were almost exclusively used for short-term borrowing. Through the development of Eurobonds, the Eurodollar assumed an extra dimension - as a vehicle for long-term borrowing. Nowadays, not only Eurodollars are used to buy Eurobonds. Other Eurocurrencies, including Eurodeutsche Marks and Euroyen (which have the same relation to their native currencies as Eurodollars to dollars), are also being used. Experts are already speculating about whether one day there will be a market in Euroroubles. As the Eurobond market has developed, the dependence of the Eurodollar has declined. One of the market's recent sophistications is a subtle device whereby borrowers can escape the risks of currency devaluations. Bonds are issued in what are called European Monetary Units so that bondholders can receive interest and repayment in any Common

Market currency at the rate of exchange which existed when the bond was issued.

The magical attraction of Eurobonds is the scope they offer for avoiding tax. Corporations issuing them do this by setting up subsidiaries in tax havens such as Luxembourg or the Netherlands Antilles. From there they can issue bonds and pay interest on them without the slightest need to pay tax on it. From the companies' point of view, the money raised from issuing bonds can be shunted readily to any country where it requires finance. And that for a company with huge international ramifications is an important requirement.

Eurobonds have another big attraction. They are issued as unregistered bearer certificates. This means that whoever buys them remains completely anonymous. There is no record of their ownership. The banks and financial institutions who deal in them would dearly like to know who buys Eurobonds so that they could keep closer tabs on the market. Many of the buyers reside in less developed countries. They are constantly in search of safer places for their money than countries where rapid inflation and continuous currency devaluations are regular features of economic life. Southern Americans and Middle Easterners, particularly oil sheiks, are an essential part of the Eurobond clientele. The majority of purchases are channelled through Swiss banks, appointed by wealthy individuals to advise them on financial matters. 'It is difficult to generate much enthusiasm about the people who purchase Eurobonds,' wrote Christopher Tugendhat. 'They are not concerned with broad concepts about uniting the world's economy or spreading the ownership of multi-national companies among the people of the countries where their subsidiaries operate.' From my own experience, I would endorse this view.

The growth of the Eurobond market surprised even its closest followers. It started off as a fairly modest \$300 or \$400 million a year affair and has since mushroomed into the near \$3000 million a year league. Not surprisingly, the American investment banks, which dominated the international bond business while it was centred in New York, have lost their hegemony to some of the European banks. U.S. investment banks, it should be mentioned, are separate banking entities from the big commercial or deposit banks such as Chase Manhattan or the First National City Bank. They have to be by American law. For the commercial banks are not allowed to underwrite or place securities of any sort. They can buy bonds, of course, and lend money direct to borrowers, but they cannot act as principals when it comes to offering securities to the public. Here in Europe the distinction is not so clear-cut and the boundaries between commercial banks (which in Britain include the London clearing banks and the Scottish banks) and investment banks (merchant banks) are becoming increasingly blurred.

'Eurobond underwriting,' wrote Paul Ferris, 'has become a multi-national affair in which about 200 banks and firms of brokers jostle for prestige and profits, their behaviour a mixture of polite smiles and sharp elbows. It is a "placement market", in which no effort is made to sell the bonds to the public in the first instance: the professionals take them up, then feed them out to buyers. A Eurobond syndicate may contain 90 or 100 names, and the lists of underwriters published in fat oblong advertisements called "tombstones" name the financial establishment of Europe, plus successful hangers-on, with many American names as well. The bonds have already been sold to the underwriters and their friends by the time the ad appears.'

'Tombstones' are scattered across the pages of prestige financial journals and newspapers. White, Weld, the leading American investment bank, displays the 'tombstones' on which its name appears on the walls of its London office like hunting trophies. A typical advertisement is headed 'This announcement appears as a matter of record only'. It continues:

> '$45,000,000
> Beecham International (Bermuda) Limited
> 8¼ per cent Guaranteed Bonds due 1986.'

Then follow the names of the two principals, Hill Samuel and

White, Weld. And underneath, in much smaller print, no less than 130 names, ranging across almost the entire international financial spectrum. There are British merchant banks like Baring's and Schroder's, British stockbrokers like Cazenove and Strauss Turnbull, American investment banks, Luxembourg banks, Dutch banks, Japanese banks, German banks ... the list seems exhaustive. The names appear to be in random order. But as Paul Ferris points out: 'Men agonize over it as theatrical agents agonize over the billing for star names.' Publicity is the key point.

It is hardly surprising that with so many banks active in the market competing tacitly, if not overtly, with one another there is no general agreement about who occupies what rank in the Eurobond management league. The Deutsche Bank is reckoned by most to be the largest force in the market. But using other definitions of what the market is, other banks, notably S. G. Warburg and the American Bankers Trust International, have been able to claim the position of supremacy. Scattered beneath these in the pecking order is the richly European assortment of Banca Commerciale Italiana, the Dutch Pierson, Heldring and Pierson, the Banque de Paris et de Pays-Bas, Morgan et Cie, the Dresdner Bank and a number of others depending on who land up with a significant share of the cake each year.

By the middle 1960s there were two conflicting pressures on the American banking industry which were to impose intolerable strains on the system. In the first place, there was the hunger, growing yearly, among American international corporations for finance to expand their operations overseas. In 1960 the assets and investments of American companies overseas were valued at \$68 billion: by 1969 this had more than doubled to \$143·4 billion. Quite naturally, the American Government acted over the period to stem this gigantic tide of dollars leaving the country. This was the other pressure. From 1965 onwards, the Administration introduced a series of measures, beginning with voluntary guidelines on how much American companies could take abroad and ending up in 1968 with a virtual moratorium on all capital transfers to industrialized countries. But if the dollars were not around at home to borrow, they were conveniently nestling in other parts of the world.

These measures amounted to an additional burden on top of the normally restrictive environment in which American banks have had to operate at home. For one thing, there is Regulation Q, a stricture imposed by the United States' central banking institution, the Federal Reserve, which determines the maximum amount of interest the banks can pay for deposits. It required only a small gap to appear between European and U.S. interest levels for money to flow rapidly across the Atlantic. When the U.K. Bank Rate was raised to seven per cent in 1965, this is precisely what happened. Another restraint imposed on the American banking system is the regulation limiting one bank to one state. The biggest American banks, the Bank of America, First National City and Chase Manhattan, have achieved their size mainly because they operate in two of the biggest states, California and New York: the Bank of America in California, and the other two in the latter. In some states, banks are confined to only one building.

When the American banks invaded Europe on a grand scale, they were not just chasing their native currency. They were also following in the footsteps of their clients – both tourists and companies. And they chose London as their base because according to Robert Blomquist, a vice-president of Chase Manhattan, 'the (British) government is stable and there is a similar culture and language to the U.S.'. He might have added that the City has always been remarkably free and easy in comparison with other European financial centres so far as international currency markets are concerned. And all the time. the Bank of England was extending a welcoming hand to foreign bankers.

The relationship between American corporations and their domestic bankers has always been close. Which explains why some of the big banks have long been established in the City. Bankers Trust International arrived in 1860, Chase Manhattan in 1887, Morgan Guaranty Trust in 1892 and First National City Bank in 1902. They were all serving the interests of some of the first American corporations to make the move overseas.

There is probably nothing intrinsically more profitable in overseas banking. It is simply that the American banks were faced with the grim prospect that unless they expanded their operations into those areas of the world where their clients chose to operate they would lose the business. Many companies prefer to deal with only one bank, and if that bank can serve its interests on a world-wide basis why use any other bank: 'If you are looking for buyers in Singapore,' proclaims a Chase Manhattan advertisement, 'start with our man-on-the-spot. A large American chemical firm did. Our man not only provided an extensive list of local buyers for their Singapore subsidiary – he also found office space for this new operation.'

Not all the American banks have followed the same route into Europe. And many of them have taken more than one route. By and large it is true to say that until the early 1960s most American banks relied on correspondent relations to handle the foreign needs of their domestic clients. It was a gentlemanly sort of relationship. A British bank would look after the American bank's clients in London, and *vice versa* in the U.S. It was irritating, to say the least, for the British bankers when this comfortable way of exchanging favours was sharply called to a halt as the Americans decided to move into Europe with full-scale branches – more irritating when one considers that the British had little to offer in the United States to British or American clients to make up for the loss of business. American banks even have the gall now to proclaim themselves as correspondent bankers in London. 'Chaseman Bob Rummel', reveals the Chase Manhattan's advertising, 'is our correspondent banking manager in London. He takes good care of the banks who bank with Chase – overseas banks in London and London banks overseas. He's a man always in demand, since so many banks prefer Chase as their correspondent bank.'

But branches were not the only way of tapping the rich market which American banks saw ahead of them in Europe. Another road into Europe was by acquiring a financial foothold in an existing European bank. First National City Bank got itself stakes in a British overseas bank and a London merchant bank, a member of the Accepting Houses Committee, for the price of one. It bought itself a forty per cent share of National and Grindlays which in turn controls William Brandt's, the merchant bank. Chase Manhattan owns a slice of the Standard and Chartered Banking Group, and there are at least nine other American banks with footholds in established British banks.

Most City bankers agree that the most significant development in which the American banks have played a crucial part has been the growth of multi-national banking consortia. Unusually, it was a British bank, the Midland, which pioneered this peculiar form of banking. In 1964, it joined forces with two Commonwealth banks, Canada's Toronto Dominion Bank and the Commercial Bank of Australia, and set up Midland and International Banks – known fondly as 'Mabel'. The British Standard Bank was a third partner. The establishment of MAIBL was a timely recognition on the part of a British bank that in order to survive in world banking a bank needed extensive international coverage. It was a belated response to what the American banks had long before realized was an inevitable trend in international banking. And after all, international thinking among industrial corporations was not the exclusive monopoly of American companies. There were plenty of European firms who had similar thoughts.

MAIBL's *raison d'être* has been to provide companies with medium-term finance – funds that are repayable over five to eight years (after eight years, long-term forms of finance such as Eurobonds take over). It was a response to need in the market for funds. Historically, companies have been financed with either short-term loans – in Britain almost always in the form of bank overdrafts – or with long-term funds such as debentures and loan stock repayable over a period beyond eight years. The trouble with the old-fashioned overdraft is that it can always be called in by the bank when it chooses to. When a bank sees a company approaching trouble it may decide to ask it to reduce its overdraft just at a time when the company may need the money most. The bank may be forced to because of a credit squeeze. With a term loan, a company knows where it is: the money need only be repaid at the end of so many years. At the other end of the spectrum, long-term finance also has its disadvantages.

Many of the investments which companies make nowadays have a life of less than eight years. Factories and new processes become obsolete much more quickly these days as the pace of technological change has quickened. Therefore, a company does not want to be saddled with a whole lot of debt whose life is far longer than the assets which that debt has been raised to pay for.

MAIBL started out with the limited objective of providing finance in sterling to clients in those areas of the world where its shareholders were most active. It was a stone's throw to arranging medium-term loans in the Eurocurrency markets. By the end of 1968, the Eurodollar market had grown around thirty-three fold to $33 billion. Since then it has virtually doubled so that it is now larger than the gross national products of several substantial West European economies. There was no shortage of banks willing to pick up stones.

The different permutations of banks which have established teams to take advantage of the demand for medium-term loans in Eurocurrencies are bewildering. At one end of the compass there is a consortium of Scandinavian banks which have set up shop in the City. Continental banks are heavily represented, from Crédit Suisse, to Commerzbank, to Banco di Napoli. Then, of course, there are the Americans, outnumbering by far the banks from any other single country. Almost invariably, the consortia have a British partner, either a clearing bank or a merchant bank. In some consortia, multinationalism has been allowed to run riot. Rothschild's have teamed up with French, Dutch, Belgian, Swiss and American partners in Rothschild Intercontinental Bank. Williams and Glyn's, the clearing bank, have partners from no less than six countries in their consortium, United International Bank.

Medium-term lending lies sandwiched in an unclearly defined area between the traditional activities of the clearing and merchant banks. It is not surprising then that it has attracted banks from both camps. But it is in the area of merchant banking that the most potentially significant future for the multi-national banks is seen. This is the view taken by some of the big American commercial banks. They have skilfully managed to skip over the obstacles which prevent them in the United States from taking part in underwriting and other merchant banking type activities, and have established powerful merchant banking subsidiaries or affiliates in London. Manufacturers Hanover Trust paved the way in 1969 when it set up a London multi-national merchant bank with financial support and participation from Rothschild's and an Italian financial institution. Bankers Trust got in on the act by taking over a British merchant banking operation called Rodo Investment Trust, which had fallen on hard times at the hands of a veteran financier, John Gommes.

The American multi-national merchant banks have not been slow to flex their muscles. Under Minos Zambonakis, an ebullient Greek who, as he puts it, 'started to philosophize about what would happen' at the end of his ten-year spell at the head of M.H.T.'s European operations, the merchant banking arm of this commercial bank has already raised Euromoney for a baffling array of distinguished borrowers ranging from the Governments of Iran and Brazil to such corporate giants as Philips and International Telephone and Telegraph. Zambonakis claims to have raised $1·5 billion in the course of a week.

The logic which the American commercial banks claim has propelled them into merchant banking is their enormous financial strength. American bankers have a habit of telling an outsider that the assets of their bank are $13 billion or some bewildering figure like that. It is as if this is the first thing they ever learn about their bank. Figures like this crop up, too. constantly in advertisements. This financial strength, they claim, gives them an overwhelming advantage over the traditional merchant banks in the international Eurocurrency markets. The tendency, they claim, is for the arrangers of finance (which is basically what the merchant banks are) and the providers of it to move together under one institutional roof. 'If you squeezed some merchant banks,' an American banker told me, 'you wouldn't find $5 million in the whole bloody shop.'

But on the whole there is a curious dualism about the attitudes of American bankers towards their presence in Europe. On the one hand, they have an embarrassingly conscious desire to be 'good corporate citizens' (a phrase they constantly use) in a foreign country. American bankers in London tactfully point out how good relations are between themselves and the British clearing banks. Yet beneath this veneer of *politesse* is a restlessness. It is as if the ghost of the bank president is in the room telling his lieutenant that 'sentiment and prestige are nothing except where there is some tangible backlash in the form of profit'. It is a restlessness which was amply demonstrated to me by a vice-president of one of the big New York banks. He strode across the room of his London office, and picked up a copy of his bank's annual report (written incidentally in three languages) and proudly showed me a photograph in the report of his bank's top brass. There were the chairman and two of his top men climbing out of a helicopter beside the caption: 'Management on the move'. 'Just imagine,' said the American in London, 'one of the clearing banks putting something like that in their stockholders' report.'

The impact of the American banks in the City has been out of proportion to their size. Their sharp competitive edge has cut through layers of deeply entrenched ideas about lending which European bankers have clung to for decades. 'American banks,' says a Britisher now managing the London branch of an American bank, 'have made British banks rethink their attitudes towards the market.'

The differences in philosophy are noticeable at various levels. Enter the central banking hall of a large American bank on Moorgate and you find a large expanse of open-plan office, girl receptionists to direct you and heavy advertising of the bank's services. In a British clearing bank a few doors away, the walls are lined with marble, there is a great mahogany and glass divide between the customer and the bank officials, and the use of display is ascetic.

Part of the differences is bound up with different notions of debt. In Europe, attitudes towards debt have been traditionally based on a sort of puritanism which has dictated that borrowing and immorality are somehow inextricably intertwined. In Britain, in particular, this Micawberism has been as much a feature of the corporate sector as it has among private individuals.

In the United States, there is little in the way of logical distinction between money and any other commodity. Both can be 'sold' with all the ingenuity at the disposal of a powerful marketing organization. To a great extent the American banks were forced into this posture by the regulations restricting banking activities to a single state. In Britain, money has historically been lent when it is needed. This simple truth has profoundly affected the whole relationship between the banks and their corporate customers. American banks, on the other hand, have not been content simply to respond to customers' needs. In a real sense, they have gone out to create needs. 'They start with a conviction,' according to *Fortune* magazine, 'that a loan is a productive instrument'. Many of these attitudes have already begun to change among the British banks, and it is not overstating the case that the American banks have played a very significant part in the whole process of change.

Some of the techniques and methods pioneered by American banks have rubbed off on British banking. It is difficult to be unaware that the British banks are now spending large sums on advertising. Credit cards have been imported by the British banks from the U.S. and are making strides towards converting the country into a cashless society. But as the Americans have not yet confronted the British banks head-on in the latter's richest preserve – High Street banking – the 'rub-off' has been covert. 'The American bank role,' says Richard Vokey, the First National City Bank's former U.K. vice-president, 'has had a significant effect on the City but not a great impact on the U.K. economy.'

One major development which the American banks have

done a lot to promote in the City has been to shift the emphasis in company borrowing from the overdraft to what are known as 'term' loans. This in turn has brought about something of a revolution in lending methods. Traditionally, all a British bank needed to know about when it lent money was what assets a company had to secure the loan. That in a sense was all right as far as overdrafts were concerned because the money lent out could always theoretically be recalled at a moment's notice. But in putting money out to pasture for a year or more without the possibility of recalling it, the banks were taking considerably greater risks. The bank's concern shifted from whether the assets securing the loan were good enough to whether the company was able to generate enough cash to pay the interest on the loan and eventually to pay off the loan. It was a fundamental change in the notion of credit worthiness. The banks were rudely reminded of the penalties of the old system by the failures of Rolls-Royce and Upper Clyde Shipbuilders.

Term lending has long been the established banking practice in the U.S., and American banks have developed a battery of sophisticated techniques to determine what the future earning power of their corporate customers is likely to be. The bigger banks employ teams of experts specializing in individual industries and knowing the ins and outs of a chemical plant, an oil refinery or a department store. They typically have degrees from one or other of the business schools and can talk the same language as the bank's industrialist clients. Long experience with clients at this level has provided American banks with a fund of knowledge about the workings of industry. More often than not, they can tell at once whether someone is trying to pull the wool over their banking eyes. At the First National City Bank's London office, they invite a businessman for lunch and while he is being entertained they run his balance sheet through the computer. When the businessman comes to leave, he can be told some startling truths about the way his business is going from the computer print-out.

Another important contribution the American banks have

made has been in spreading the philosophy that money shouldn't be allowed to lie idle for any length of time. Large international corporations nowadays can have hundreds, if not thousands, of millions of dollars floating around at any moment. The loss of earning power which can result from this money not being made to earn interest can be enormous. The money experts and treasurers in these large corporations have fast developed a reputation for grim-faced commercialism. 'The days are gone when a company would leave £25,000 on current account (not earning interest),' says an American banker. 'Today they might leave 5½p there.' American banks have become masters at not letting money stagnate. In the U.S. they even use specially chartered jets to move it from one state to another. When the big international oil companies were presenting their bids for oil leases in Alaska, aircraft were standing by at the nearest airport to ship the money to the relevant banks. A day's loss of interest on $10 million for example could be as much as $3000, a good deal more than the cost of most air tickets. One of the big American banks sells a service called International Money Mobilization, by which funds can be shunted across Europe in the space of less than twenty-four hours.

For the major American banks, overseas activities have added a new dimension to their whole management structure. Their managers can typically get shuffled round the world from Panama to the Lebanon to Rome without working in the U.S. for years. A bank like First National City with half its business abroad can boast that it has 242 branches in 85 countries on 5 continents. The smaller banks, to whom foreign banking has been a novelty, obviously have not had the same internally grown timber with which to staff their London offices. They have recruited heavily from the clearing, merchant and British overseas banks. This has irritated the British banking community. The price of foreign exchange dealers has been pushed up, as a result, to what many banks would consider extravagant levels – and this on top of City rents being forced up to ethereal heights by the foreign banking invasion. The Americans appear to have little difficulty in tempting British bankers away from what one of the former described as the 'suffocating bureaucracy' of the clearing banks. The big clearing bank mergers too helped a lot – if the atmosphere in a smaller bank was suffocating enough it can only have been worse when that bank doubled or trebled in size.

Talking to some of the Englishmen who have crossed the great divide into American banking, one certainly gets the impression of being in the company of liberated individuals. One of them who made the move after thirty years in British banking in order to set up a branch office for an American bank in the City is impressed most of all by the flexibility of American banking. 'If a British bank gets an unattractive proposition they tell the customer that it is just "not our policy". The answer of an American bank would be "Can we try and do it some other way? Instead of going from A to B, let's try going from A to C and then trying to arrive at B." '

Most of the American banks see themselves as not just in banking but in the finance business as a whole. So far their main impact in the City has been within the rich confines of the Eurodollar market. But there are already signs of restlessness. 'American bankers,' wrote the head of a large American branch in the City, 'like particularly all American corporations operating abroad, look to the patterns already experienced, or at least perceived, in the U.S. and therefore have at least theoretically available for use in the U.K. market those critical skills presently developed for penetrating U.S. markets and in certain cases foreign markets.' Another prominent American banker sticks his neck out even further. 'Pressures exist for them (the American banks) to establish themselves as a major U.K. banking force by 1980. These banks, many of great size in their own markets, are not overawed by the large clearing banks and are fully confident of their own marketing skills to capture a portion of conventional banking business.'

All the American banks have been seriously hampered by the credit squeeze enforced with varying degrees of intensity by the Government and Bank of England in recent years. One new American bank which had just arrived in the City was horrified to be told by a Bank of England official that it could only lend £500,000. 'What sort of a welcome is that?' he added disgruntledly. The squeeze, however, has had the effect of concentrating American minds wonderfully on the Eurodollar market. Lending sterling to British borrowers has tended to take the back seat.

Notwithstanding, the Americans have already begun to extend a menacing finger or two into the British market. One large American bank has wandered into the computer software industry. Another is leasing factory equipment to British companies. Perhaps the cheekiest thing that an American bank has done so far in Britain has been to edge into the clearing banks' most closely guarded preserve – High Street banking. Americans call it retail banking (as opposed to wholesale banking which is the dignified end of the business and does not involve collecting deposits from the public at large). First National City Bank, of the American banks, has gone furthest along this line in Britain by building up a chain of small saving banks. To the stunned horror of native bankers, it has christened them 'money shops' and is opening them up with all the vulgarity which could be associated with selling money (scantily clad 'Citigirls' driving round shopping centres in beach buggies). On a smaller scale, the International Bank of Washington is doing much the same sort of thing in the Midlands with the elusive Jewish tycoon, Sir Isaac Wolfson, as a partner. 'We do all sorts of things,' explained their manager, 'to encourage people to go into our banks.' Briefcases and wallets are handed out to new depositors, autokits are offered to customers borrowing money to buy a car, and children get colouring books and crayons. The persuasive talents of the American banker have no bounds. 'You can't expect Americans not to be like Americans in Europe,' says the manager dolefully.

There are clearly few bounds to what American banks feel themselves competent to do in European banking. On the other hand, they recognize the restraints. It would be madness for them to collide head-on with the clearing banks, for example, at the retail end of the business credit squeeze or no credit squeeze. The clearing banks built up their branches when the cost of a High Street property was considerably less than it is today.

The hearts of American bankers in Europe will continue to be set on the international currency markets. The only nagging worry is what will be the future of the Eurodollar. It took a fearful knock – and so did the American banks – with the 1971 dollar crisis. And if the American Government's measures to set right the balance of payments succeed, what then? Or what would happen if the central banks of the industrialized western world took steps to regulate the market; a source of nightmarish speculation among the banking fraternity? The answer probably is that if anything happened to the Eurodollar, somebody would have to invent something else to replace it. And there are already one or two heir apparents among the major currencies of the world. Whatever happens, the chances are that the Americans would be cast in the role of either inventors or developers, or both.

'We do not want the public to discuss our affairs. We would much rather they did not. The more information we give them the more they will discuss our affairs, and that is what we do not want.'

Mr A. W. Tuke, former chairman of Barclays Bank, in evidence to the Radcliffe Committee, 1959

5. THE CLEARING BANKS

The analogy between large ocean-going liners and organizations is often made. In relation to the clearing banks it has a peculiar appropriateness. Clearing, or 'joint stock', banks, as they are variously known, are mammoth, slow-moving institutions. To get them to change direction requires the temporal equivalent of several miles.

Of all the City institutions, the clearing banks probably emerge as the most institutional – their development being evolutionary rather than revolutionary. They also represent the most pervasive and visible interface between the general public and the City itself. As Anthony Sampson has put it, 'They have become, like town halls or public libraries, part of the face of town life.' It is difficult to imagine a High Street without a Midland or a Barclays, a shopping centre without a National Westminster or a Lloyds. What is very remarkable is how these corporate giants without much more than a twitch or a sigh have survived more than a decade of radical change in virtually every other form of British institutional life. Amazingly, little has rubbed off on the clearing banks. Yet banking, one could argue, is not about change. It is to do with caution, conservatism, stone façades, marble halls, safety, solidity, stability and anything else one might associate with crystallized immutability.

The association is understandable when one considers that clearing banks occupy a curious role in the economy at the very meeting point between the public and private sectors. Their overlord is the Bank of England, which directs, guides and nudges the clearers and which in turn is issued instructions on monetary policy by the Government in the form of the Treasury. The clearing banks, as it were, are one of the main taps by which the flow of money into the economy can be turned off or on according to the monetary policies of the Government.

As David Robarts, former chairman of the Westminster Bank, explained to the Radcliffe Committee, 'What we have to do is, first of all to run our businesses so that they are conducted with safety to our customers, and secondly, as far as we can, to follow the monetary and fiscal policy of the day, whatever the colour of the Government, as described to us by, as a rule, the Governor of the Bank of England, and on occasions by the Chancellor.'

That was the classic exposition of the functions of a clearing bank in the late 1950s. Since then the words, shareholders and profits, have penetrated the clearing bankers' vocabulary. And if, in general terms, one had to describe the biggest single change that has taken place among the clearing banks over the last ten years, it would be this awareness that a third dimension does, or ought to, exist in commercial banking. Today, the banks are continually posing themselves the question of whether their services are too cheap. National Westminster caused an uproar when it tentatively suggested charging its customers £6 an hour for its branch managers' time – an indication that the public have been devoutly led to believe that banks really are there just to perform the public service of safeguarding customers' money.

The gradual recognition that the role of banking was to do rather more than safeguard and transmit the public's money and to cooperate and help carry out the Government's monetary policy led to the sacrifice of some sacred cows. One of these was the dogged belief that the business of clearing banks was one business and one business only: that of borrowing money short and lending it short. Traditionally, the sound banker's prescription for ruin has been to borrow short and lend long. The view has been that only by keeping its lending and assets in the most short-term forms of money can a bank manage its business properly. Its deposits, so the thinking goes, are repayable at seven days' notice (in fact a bank will repay them at even less notice), and therefore there should be equally short-term assets available to meet demands of this sort.

In practice, of course, things have never really been quite like that. Theoretically, overdrafts, the banks' traditional lending medium, can be recalled at short notice. But only on comparatively rare occasions have banks exercised their rights to do so. Clearing banks talk about their 'hard core' overdrafts, meaning lending arrangements which get renewed on the same basis every so often. They really mean permanent or semi-permanent loans.

But over the years in large sectors of the clearing banks' traditional business were emerging areas where short-term finance, even on a revolving basis, was becoming increasingly less appropriate. Financing the needs of small companies was one. In the early 1930s, a Government Committee under Lord MacMillan, the distinguished lawyer, published a report on the monetary system showing that there was a serious gap in the market for longer term finance for small businesses. Then there was the longer term finance needed to finance exports. Capital goods, like ships, machinery and pipelines, accounted for an increasing share of international trade – William Clarke estimates that their share of Britain's exports increased from two to twenty-five per cent between 1913 and the mid 1960s. And all these products by their very nature required far longer gestation between the times of ordering and delivery – anything up to five or even ten years: far longer than the traditional 'seed corn to harvest' view taken by the clearing banks.

Much of these rigid attitudes towards lending stemmed

from the belief that Britain escaped the worst horrors of the 1930s depression simply because its financial institutions were in neat watertight compartments. Bankers point to the fact that in the United States the banks were dangerously hybrid institutions, not just taking money from the public on deposit, but also investing it. The view was that as long as the clearing banks confined their activities to the narrow area of short-term borrowing and lending there could not be the sort of chain reaction that brought down Wall Street like a pack of cards in the early 1930s. In this way, the disease could be isolated and cured. 'The City survived the dirty thirties,' one banker told me, 'far better than New York largely because banking here was highly compartmentalized.'

As the clearing banks surveyed the scene around them in the late 1950s, one thing stuck firmly in their collective gullet. A large number of other financial institutions had grown up which were beginning to encroach on the clearing banks' own business. Both companies and private individuals became increasingly aware that a whole range of other bodies existed which could offer them a higher rate of interest on their money and a wider range of services. In particular, companies were discovering the financial delights of putting their money with merchant banks, the discount market and the overseas banks. Private customers were looking to Trustee Savings Banks, Building Societies and last, but not least, hire purchase companies.

The overall effect of this was that the clearing banks were steadily losing their share of the banking business. In the ten years up to 1956, clearing bank deposits declined from sixty to thirty-four per cent of the country's gross national product. And by the early 1960s, merchant banks were adding to their deposits at the rate of thirty per cent a year, hire purchase companies by twenty-five per cent, building societies by ten per cent, Trustee Savings Banks by nine per cent: while the clearing banks were increasing their deposit business at a paltry five per cent a year.

'We saw these figures and didn't like them,' says Derek Wilde, now a vice-chairman of Barclays. The absurdity of the situation consisted in the fact that to an unnecessary extent the banks were unable to do much to reverse the trend – unnecessary because much of the freedom which could have allowed them to do something about it was restricted not from outside but by the banks themselves. Ever since the turn of the century, all the clearing banks had agreed not to compete against each other on interest rates. The 'cartel', as the banks have reluctantly described it, basically took the form of agreements to fix minimum lending rates and maximum deposit rates by reference to Bank Rate. In short, the banks had closely circumscribed themselves in what they could do to meet the challenge of competition.

One of the more depressing things about innovation among the clearing banks is how each bank follows another with an almost Pavlovian inevitability. At the beginning of 1958, Anthony Tuke, former chairman of Barclays and known throughout banking as the 'Iron Tuke', made the astonishingly patronizing remark: 'It is extraordinary what you can get on hire purchase these days.' Hire purchase companies had long been regarded with a sense of disdain and irritation by the clearing banks. Hire purchase had had a somewhat chequered history beginning in the latter half of the nineteenth century as a way of financing sewing machine sales – Singer was one of the pioneers. It was extended into other forms of consumer goods, and by the turn of the century had become the established method of financing the collieries' purchase of railway trucks for transporting coal. In those days, the railways did not provide their own trucks. This explains why some of the larger hire purchase companies had odd-sounding names like North Central Wagon and British Wagon. Traditionally, the clearing banks regarded hire purchase as being very much on the outer fringes of banking and there was a healthy puritanism which fostered these attitudes. It is significant that even now, in spite of the size of the hire purchase industry, the so-called finance houses, the practitioners in hire purchase, have never really been accepted into the City's power structure. The ill-concealed snub when the Post Office Giro joined forces with Mercantile Credit, one of the leading finance houses, to provide loans to Giro account holders, is a more recent example of the uncomfortable relationship which exists. It may not be going too far to describe the relationship as similar to that between Harrods and Woolworths. The leaders of the finance houses have never had the close attention of the Governor of the Bank of England enjoyed by the clearing banks.

In the middle of 1958, the Government relaxed the credit squeeze to the point where the banking sector as a whole had never enjoyed such freedom since before the war. The clearing banks took this as their cue to move. In one astonishing week at the end of July, no less than four of what were then the Big Seven banks acquired stakes in hire purchase companies. Barclays led the way by buying twenty-five per cent of United Dominions Trust. 'Within one week,' commented *The Economist*, 'a principle of association of the great English deposit banks with companies financing hire purchase has been established.' 'I was away on holiday in Wales at the time,' a leading clearing banker told me, 'and came back to find the whole bloody lot in hire purchase. They went into it like the herd of Gadarene swine.'

It is not quite true to say that this was the first time the clearing banks had got their feet wet in an activity outside their traditional line of business. In response to the MacMillan Committee's report a group of them had set up a joint company, the Industrial and Commercial Finance Corporation, to help close the famous 'gap' by providing longer term finance to small businesses. And the banks would argue that they had long had departments dealing with foreign business and personal estate duty, investment and tax problems. After the hire purchase invasion, however, the clearing banks were never quite the same again. And just to ram home still further the point that they were not happy to see the finance houses run away with new business, two of the big clearing banks in the same year launched personal loan schemes to attract customers who might otherwise have resorted to hire purchase to finance buying motor cars, washing machines, televisions and other consumer goods.

As it turned out, the incursion into hire purchase was something of a false dawn for the clearing banks. In retrospect these moves proved to be more the workings of the clearing banks' defence mechanisms than part of a new aggressiveness. 'My bank,' David Robarts told the Radcliffe Committee, 'regards its hire purchase subsidiary as an entirely separate business.' 'It is recognized as a trade investment in our balance sheets,' added Mr Tuke. The important point is that the acquisition of strategic footholds in hire purchase really did not significantly alter the thinking by the clearing banks towards their business. Banking remained their business, and hire purchase remained a useful bonus to be kept in the background.

There were a number of factors which tended to ossify the thinking of the clearing banks. In the first place, there was the comparatively high Bank Rate which turned out to be a permanent feature of the 1960s. Now it is not difficult to see that as long as the banks agreed not to pay interest on the money deposited with them on current accounts they would be benefiting from a huge bonus on the money they received interest free and the money they lent out in the form of overdrafts. The higher the Bank Rate, the bigger the bonus. For most of the 1960s, the clearing banks were able to make handsome profits simply by sitting and watching Bank Rate. It was an effortless sort of existence which firms in other industries might well have envied.

Secondly, whatever profits they were making, the clearing banks never had to publish. By a curious convention embedded in the 1948 Companies Act, banks, along with shipping companies, are under no legal obligation to declare their true profits. In the case of the banks, the tortuous reasoning behind this is that banks from time to time suffer serious setbacks. And if they are seen to be in trouble the public would hasten to remove its money. A 'run on the bank' had been a bogey long cherished by the clearing banks. The only profit figures the banks did disclose were shown after taking into account taxation and secret transfers to the banks' reserves.

Failure to disclose true profits had a peculiar effect on the banks. It meant that instead of profits being the yardstick by which the outside world judged the banks, growth, measured in terms of deposits, was the canon. And in order to increase deposits, banks embarked on a massive expansion of their branch networks. Between 1945 and 1967, the clearing banks expanded their number of branches from 9600 to 14,000. There was not much else they could do as they were proscribed from competing on interest rates.

It is significant, though, that after Barclays overtook the Midland in terms of deposits in the late 1950s, the latter fast established a reputation for itself as an innovator. It was the first bank to introduce personal loans, the first to bring in night safes, the first to compete for sterling deposits through an associated company (Midland and International Bank) and the first and only clearing bank to buy its way into an established merchant bank (Samuel Montagu).

The third, and the banks would argue the most important, factor restraining their development was their obedience to the authorities (the Bank of England and the Treasury). In the first place, the clearing banks were required to maintain at least twenty-eight per cent of their assets in liquid form, eight per cent of these in the form of cash. This not only meant that a large proportion of their funds had to be set aside and could not be lent in the ordinary way. It also represented a sizable loss of earnings – the money could have been put to better use. At the same time, the banks were subject to repeated official requests for restraint and selectivity in their lending. This again severely limited the earning power and growth of the clearing banks.

By the early 1960s there was already considerable disquiet in the City about the lethargy which seemed to have gripped the clearing banks. Foreign banks were beginning to establish themselves in force in the City, other financial institutions had been making full use of the opportunities available to them and a complex structure of so-called parallel markets had sprung up to feed the financial appetites of local authorities, international companies and finance houses - markets in which the clearing banks by no means were playing a dominant role.

Unease among the authorities about the situation percolated to the surface at the unlikely event of a banquet to celebrate the 400th anniversary of Martins Bank, in April 1963. In what must rank as a moment of high drama in an industry not unduly given to histrionics, the Governor of the Bank of England rose to speak at the banquet, and after a few pleasantries weighed in with the monstrous question 'whether the considerable rigidity in interest rates which has grown up in the banking world in the last twenty years or so is an encouragement to the growth of bank deposits'. If spades tend to go under another name in banking, there was no question that this was hitting right at the roots of the clearing banks. In short, the Governor was making the not so gentle hint that the cartel ought to be scrapped. Not surprisingly, the banks squealed furiously. And, unusually, they had the Treasury on their side. The banks argued that, if they bid competitively for deposits through price competition, the cost of credit would go up. The Treasury believed them.

But when the headmaster makes a very strong hint, which he had done, it is 'not done' simply to ignore it. The clearing banks came up with the classic compromise. Their solution was to set up specialist subsidiary or associate companies which would offer competitive rates for new deposits. This was not to be full-blooded competition since only deposits of £50,000 or more at a time were to be acceptable to these new institutions. It was hardly a benefit a private individual could enjoy.

The Midland was the first into this new-fangled business with MAIBL (Midland and International Bank Limited). Other banks, like Barclays and Lloyds, simply revamped for the purpose existing subsidiaries operating in international banking. Others, like Midland, found another partner or partners to go in with – National Provincial joined forces with Rothschild, an alliance which has since been dissolved.

The Governor's remarks about the cartel were certainly not the last the clearing banks were to hear about the restrictive arrangements. The Press were quick to jump on the bandwagon. 'The opportunity to bid for deposits came and went in 1963,' commented *The Economist*, 'and with it, literally the chance of a lifetime, all because the banks were not quick enough to jump at the opportunity Lord Cromer offered them before the Treasury could step in with its veto. . . . The banks must not miss the chance when it comes again. And it will come again – one day – provided the banks themselves keep the idea alive and help towards creating the opportunity.'

The chance did indeed come again. In 1967, the Prices and Incomes Board in terms less ambiguous than those of the Governor published its celebrated broadside on the clearing banks. The P.I.B. report, largely the work of the Board's outspoken chairman, Mr Aubrey Jones, spoke of the banks in terms of weary, unadventurous institutions. It regarded the abolition of the cartel as 'a necessary step towards the creation of a system in which the banks could play a greater role than they do at present by developing a more diversified pattern of lending', found that the banks could greatly increase their efficiency by 'a radical reorientation of attitudes', and found little, if anything, to justify the banks' practice of not disclosing their true profits. In short, it was a solid indictment of the clearing banks. And not surprisingly it evoked hysterical reactions from the heads of the banks. The bankers were outraged that Aubrey Jones had interpreted his brief so widely – the Government had asked the P.I.B. to look at bank charges. The chairman of Barclays, John Thomson, wrote plaintively, 'I do wish that people who want to throw stones at us, whether they are composing letters to the Editor, or writing editorial comment, or reporting to the Government, would look harder at the facts. Perhaps the shrewdest criticism of all would be that bankers are too often reluctant to argue back.'

There was something else in the P.I.B. report which the banks were to find rather greater sympathy with. It was a small section neatly secreted towards the end of the Aubrey Jones *tour de force*. 'Further amalgamations,' it said, 'among the banks, carried through to the appropriate point, could permit some rationalization of existing networks. The Bank of England and the Treasury have made it plain to us that they would not obstruct some further amalgamations if the banks were willing to contemplate such a development; and we think that a further reduction in the number of independent banking units would not necessarily affect very significantly the degree of competition.'

This, in the banks' eyes, was revolutionary doctrine for a Government agency and the authorities to be preaching. The banks' attitude towards amalgamations had been largely conditioned by a series of events which had taken place fifty years previously. In 1917, a period of consolidation in clearing banking reached a climax when some of the largest banks began to merge. The Government was deeply concerned about this development and set up a committee under Lord Colwyn to look into the matter. The Committee reported in the following year and concluded that some sort of Government control was needed. It proposed that legislation should be introduced requiring the banks to get approval from the Government before they implemented merger plans or other arrangements such as the creation of interlocking directorates. Legislation never was introduced even though the Government at the time accepted the Colwyn Committee proposals. However, the banks came to an informal understanding with the Bank of England that the latter would be consulted before any merger proposals were carried through. And the Governor of the Bank would in turn consult the Treasury.

As it turned out, this arrangement was quite effective. Though amalgamations involving the big London clearing banks did take place afterwards, they did not reduce the number of the large independent banks. Coutts and District, for example, were taken over by National Provincial: Williams Deacon's and Glyn Mills became subsidiaries of the Royal Bank of Scotland. But none of these mergers significantly altered the competitive *status quo*.

Events following the publication of the P.I.B. report in May 1967 are intriguing for the insight they give into the strange ways that changes take place in the City. At this stage, it must be remembered, the London clearing bank line-up consisted of the Big Five (Barclays, the Midland, Lloyds,

Westminster and National Provincial, which together accounted for eighty-eight per cent of the combined deposits of the London clearing banks); and the Little Six (Martins, District, Williams Deacon's, Glyn Mills, Coutts and National, the English rump of an Anglo-Irish bank and the result of a carve-up in 1966 between the National Commercial Bank of Scotland and the Bank of Ireland).

Attention after Aubrey Jones' revelation inevitably focussed on Martins, a Liverpool-based bank trading under the sign of the Grasshopper and at that time the only completely independent member of the Little Six. By 1967, the board of Martins, headed by an illustrious Northern businessman, Sir Cuthbert Clegg, had come round to thinking that there was no long-term future for a small bank in an industry of giants. Branches were becoming increasingly more expensive to open, and the advent of the computer to banking had upped the stakes by a very considerable amount. Not only that, but Martins had most of its branches concentrated in the north at a time when the banks' big industrial customers were increasingly requiring coverage on a national scale.

The courtship for the hand of Martins began in earnest in the four months after the P.I.B. report was published (in previous years, Martins had brushed aside several advances from other banks). It was around that time that the new thinking of the Martins board was communicated to the other banks. This was no great problem as relations between the heads of the banks are extremely close, conditioned, of course, by their gentlemanly approach towards competition. Formally, they meet regularly at meetings of the Committee of London Clearing Bankers. Collectively, they operate a system for clearing each other's cheques which has its operating base in an austere building in Lombard Street. Informally, there is continuous contact between the chairmen of the banks – they are mostly good friends.

At the outset there emerged two suitors, Barclays and Lloyds. They went to the Bank of England and each in turn sounded out the Bank's view on mergers. While they discovered that things were not quite as straightforward as the

P.I.B. had presented them, they found that the authorities would be quite happy about a take-over of Martins provided that it was a British bank that did the taking over. By the end of the year the auction of Martins began in earnest. An intriguing procedure was drawn up, which had the support of the Bank of England, whereby details of Martins' balance sheet were to be supplied to six banks which had shown an interest in acquiring Martins. Under the arrangement, the six banks were given fourteen days to consider their position and submit proposals to Cooper Brothers, the chartered accountants, who were acting for Martins. The three banks which submitted the highest offers were to be told what the offers were and to be given longer to reconsider their position.

The whole affair reached a giddy climax in the last fortnight of January 1968. On 11 January, Cooper Brothers revealed the detailed state of Martins' balance sheet to the six contenders. On 25 January, the last day for submitting first offers, there were only two suitors left. The two banks which were most conspicuous by their absence were the Westminster and National Provincial. The following day, they announced their own plans to merge to an awe-struck financial audience. In the afternoon of 29 January, Barclays and Lloyds heard from Cooper Brothers that their offers for Martins were the only ones left.

At this stage, panic seemed to have taken the place of the usual dignified calm among the banks. The clearing banks have traditionally been unusually sensitive about their position in the league. If the Natpro/Westminster merger went through, and if Barclays remained as it was, then the newly merged bank would force the latter off its perch as the largest bank in the country. Much the same sort of thinking must have gone on in the collective mind of Lloyds, which would end up if the same conditions were fulfilled at the bottom of a league of four. The performance of a bank at that time, it must be remembered, could only really be measured in terms of the size of its deposits.

Two days after they had heard that their banks were the only two in the running for Martins, John Thomson and

Harald Peake, the chairmen of Barclays and Lloyds, met to discuss the situation, and it was only at this stage that the plan for a much wider grouping – a merger between Barclays and Lloyds – was first discussed. What emerged later on, therefore, was a hastily conceived proposal – a defensive reaction which would have dramatically altered the pattern of British banking for years to come.

Barclays, Lloyds and Martins publicly revealed their hand on 8 February. The idea was that the two larger banks should merge and then take over Martins. On the same day, the Government stepped in. Having consulted the Treasury and the Bank of England, the Board of Trade announced that it had decided to refer the Barclays/Lloyds/Martins merger to the Monopolies Commission. To crown it all, two of the biggest Scottish banks, the Three Banks Group (comprising Williams Deacon's, Glyn Mills, and the Royal Bank of Scotland) and the National Commercial Bank of Scotland, announced their merger plans in the same week.

The Monopolies Commission, under its chairman, Sir Ashton Roskill, a lawyer, was asked by the Board of Trade to have its report and verdict ready in six months. By July, the worst for the banks was known. Six members of the Commission voted against the merger and four were in favour. The merger issue, as *The Times* commented at the time, was 'back in the melting pot'. The embarrassment was really the Government's. For there were not enough members of the Commission against the merger to empower Anthony Crosland, President of the Board of Trade, to step in and forbid it under the most recent Act regulating monopolies. There were other powers at the Government's elbow, but for the time being Whitehall decided to do nothing. With such an indecisive verdict, it was probably the best thing they could have done. Meanwhile, the heads of the three banks, like rejected lovers, processed to the Government in the hope that they could achieve something by horse-trading with ministers. By the end of July, Anthony Crosland had climbed off the fence. He told the banks and the House of Commons that the Government supported the majority verdict of the

Commission. Within a matter of a few hours, Barclays announced it was bidding £105 million for Martins and that the board of Martins was recommending the bid to its shareholders. Lloyds had been left out in the cold.

The Monopolies Commission report was an unflattering document. The banks' case for the merger was boiled down to six main points. Essentially these were as follows:

1 A larger banking group would be in better shape to cater for the present and future needs of industrial groupings, which were themselves getting larger;
2 branches could be rationalized to reduce overlapping;
3 savings could be achieved by pooling the three banks' computer systems;
4 the overseas banking interests of the three could be coordinated and extended 'to meet the varied requirements of United Kingdom traders throughout the world';
5 a sufficiently large domestic and international bank would be created to meet the foreign banking challenge; and
6 the country's balance of payments would benefit.

A whole variety of interested parties canvassed for its opinions. Large companies were fairly indifferent about the merger, medium-sized ones were against it, and a hotchpotch of organizations from the Multiple Shops Federation and the Hire Purchase Trade Association to the National Chamber of Trade and the Consumer Council expressed varying degrees of hostility. The Treasury and the Bank of England were worried that the merger might in the end force the two smaller banks, the Midland and Natpro/Westminster, to get together and restrict consumer choice and competition even further.

What disturbed the majority of the Commission members was that the number of sources of finance for small and medium-sized businesses would be greatly reduced. They also felt that private individuals and small retailers would suffer as branches would be closed down *en masse* without any compensating advantages in the form of more and better services at lower cost. 'Furthermore,' they concluded, 'we consider that competition among banks is in the public interest and that such competition as there is among clearing banks is likely to be keener with four large clearing banks of roughly comparable size, than with three banks with one as large as the other two combined. In addition, with four banks innovations of benefit to customers have a greater chance of being tried than with three banks.'

In general, the Commission was no more impressed with the clearing banks than Aubrey Jones and the P.I.B. had been a year before. It shared the P.I.B.'s disapproval of those two banking habits of which the Board had spoken so scathingly – the cartel and failure to disclose true profits. Of the former, the Commission concluded, 'we believe . . . that these agreements have such a soporific effect on the banks that, so long as they exist, no foreseeable change in the structure of the clearing bank system could greatly increase the degree of competition in it.' The banks, it also claimed, 'have escaped the stimulus to efficiency and competitiveness that informed comparison of performances and profitability might have been expected to produce.' Soporific became a word the banks quickly came to resent.

So the battle-lines between the banks were drawn up. But for the time being there were not many signs of battle. Both National Westminster and the new Barclays/Martins combine got down to seeing and sorting out what they were landed with – but at a fairly leisurely pace. Natwest earmarked around 400 branches for closure; Barclays nearly 250. And there was a lot of tidying up to be done elsewhere. Curiously enough, the mergers may have had as much effect on the banks which were not involved.

Lloyds have since thinly concealed their delight that they did not become part of a great super-bank. Towards the end of 1968, they appointed their first ever professional banker chairman. Eric Faulkner, the son of a senior civil servant, went to Lloyds with thirty-two years of banking experience behind him and with a solid determination to shake up the bank.

But whatever the banks did to streamline themselves, they were still working under a set of rules that were more appropriate to the first quarter of the twentieth century than the last.

Many clearing bankers publicly regarded the unflattering remarks of the P.I.B. and the Monopolies Commission as impertinent offerings from uninformed outsiders. But clearly the chorus of criticism had grown so loud that it would have been difficult to disregard it for ever. The seemingly endless occasions when leading members of the clearing banks stood up publicly to justify the cartel and their secrecy over their balance sheets was a sure sign that deep down they were not all that happy with the arrangements. And their justification as time went by became more and more conditional.

The rules were changed – and in the hair-raising (by banking standards) period of two years. The first sacred cow to be sacrificed was the secrecy over profits and reserves. In September 1969, after no little cajoling from the Government, the clearing banks finally decided to disclose their true profits and reserves. On Friday, 20 February, the figures for the first time were actually published. *The Banker*, the staid but not uncritical banking magazine, heralded the decision as a 'new era for British banking'. 'Banking,' it said, 'has at last declared itself an industry. Or that is the import that should be read into the clearing banks' unveiling of their true profits and reserves last month. For the first time in their history, the banks are to be subjected to the same degree of market scrutiny normally reserved for industrial companies. Now they must perform, and be seen to perform, as such.' The magazine went on to say that more competition could be expected within the banks themselves and that a more stringent appraisal of costs within the banks would result. But it added the warning that 'the disclosure of itself can do little to aid competition in the banking system while the authorities continue to maintain a regulating framework which encourages the banks to preserve their restrictive habits'.

When the figures were finally presented, there were some

embarrassments. The figures seemed to confirm what much of the criticism over the past few years had been about: that the banks were not very efficient or competitive. In the first place, the banks had to report that the profits they made in the previous year had actually declined. Secondly, it transpired that the average amount of profits attributable to each of the banks' 12,000 branches was a paltry £10,000 or less. This carried with it the inescapable conclusion that a substantial proportion of their branches were operating at hefty losses – something which any profit-minded management would be loath to admit. The Midland turned out to be the dunce in terms of efficiency (based on profits as a percentage of deposits), which must have confirmed their feelings of isolationism after the big mergers.

The advent of a Conservative Government in June 1970 paved the way for the next big sacrificial offering. The Tories, of course, were obsessed at the outset of their term of office with the idea that competition could provide the much needed spur to efficiency which had somehow evaded the previous Administration in its multifarious attempts to shake up British business. Competition there was to be, and what better industry to put it to the test than banking?

It did not require clairvoyance on the part of the banks to see what the Government's game was. The banks sensed that imminent change was in the air. But interestingly they had begun to shift their ground. John Thomson told his shareholders that it would be no good scrapping the cartel unless the banks were first released from 'the strait-jacket in which we are confined' – meaning the cash and liquidity ratios and the quantitative and qualitative restrictions on lending. John Prideaux made similar noises to the shareholders of National Westminster.

In May 1971, after weeks of mounting speculation, the Bank of England finally produced its revolutionary pamphlet under the discreet title, *Competition and Credit Control. The Times* described it as 'the most important paper that any banker is likely to read in his working lifetime', an 'economic milestone'. The pamphlet was in the nature of a consultative document and, of course, had the full blessing of the Treasury. The plan was that the Bank should discuss the implications of it with the banks and other interested parties before going ahead with implementing its proposals. Change is seldom overtly imposed on the City.

The Bank's message was straightforward. It was asking the banks to scrap their cartel in return for a systematic dismantling of the existing controls about which the banks had complained so volubly. The new system was to be based on a 'reserve : assets ratio' of 12½ per cent, which in effect meant that all the banks would have to hold this fixed proportion of their sterling deposits in certain specified reserve assets. In addition, the Bank of England would have the right to insist that the banks from time to time make special deposits with the Bank. There was to be no ceiling on lending so that the banks could increase their lending as fast as they increased their deposits. Moreover, more or less the same rules were to apply to all kinds of banks – not just the clearing banks but also the accepting houses, foreign banks in London and British overseas banks. And the hire purchase companies were to be included too – a massive report on consumer credit by a Government committee under Lord Crowther earlier in the year had recommended that comprehensive legislation should be introduced to deal with all forms of lending and credit.

The familiar City ritual of consultation between the main banking institutions and the Bank of England took place in the summer months. Gentle horse-trading went on, but the Bank was in no frame of mind to shift its ground. By September the soundings had been taken, the consultation was over and the Bank was ready to set its revolution into motion. The final draft of its proposals was greeted with a great deal of enthusiasm by the Press. *The Times* described them as marking 'the end of an era' – there have been many 'eras' in British banking recently. The paper's banking correspondent, in rather more dispassionate terms, said that 'the new controls are important because they set the seal on a process of change which is already underway. Clearing banks may be slow-moving institutions, but once they are travelling in the correct direction they will tend to carry on doing so.' 'What the Bank of England has done,' he added, 'is to change the traffic lights from red to green at a time when the banks' progress along the road towards greater competition and efficiency was being halted unnecessarily. If the banks fail to accelerate from now on it will be their own fault.'

The Economist saw the changes in a much more dramatic light. It put forward the suggestion that the banks might use their new freedom to become the financiers and controllers of large hunks of industry – a practice that British banks have studiously avoided but which is common in Germany and Japan. 'Might banks,' the journal asked, 'now come to play so large a part in the British capital market that we may move gradually over to what might be called the German-Japanese system of largely bank-controlled industry, and away from the Anglo-American system of stock market-oriented industry?' *The Economist* was worried by what might happen. 'It is really worth remarking,' it concluded, 'that this radical change of Britain's whole internal financial system – which could very well have a bigger eventual effect on British industry, British working habits, British competitive power, than any other single economic reform since the war – has not been the subject of a single clause of legislation. Parliament has barely discussed it. It has all been fixed up as a gentleman's agreement in private conclaves of the City. It would, however, be sensible if Parliament kept watch over how it works.' It is perhaps significant, in contrast, that the Bank announced its proposals on 10 September and the new competitive era was not to begin until 1 October. The banks seemed to be embarking on their much heralded conflict with a sense of charming, if pathetic, chivalry.

The inescapable conclusion seemed to be that, while the Bank had removed the chains, the banks were in no frame of mind to get up and run. 'One should be cautious about overstating the impact on inter-bank competition,' said *The Banker*. 'It is hard to imagine for example that the final demise of the cartel will in fact result in the banks offering very different rates from each other for deposits. The habits of the last decade will die hard. But it is important for the City as well as its customers that they should be well and truly buried.'

The clearing banks have frozen themselves into a fixed philosophy and attitude of mind. The signs of any thawing process having got under way among the Big Four are only vestigial. The banks would have their critics believe that they have made a lot of progress. They point to the innovations they have pioneered, to the diversification they have achieved, and to the management techniques they have adopted. On the face of it, these seem to amount to a creditable record.

Barclays have launched their Barclaycard. Lloyds, National Westminster, Williams and Glyn's and the Midland have teamed up to introduce a rival credit card. Some of the innovations, though, have been little more than window-dressing and gimmickry - such as coloured cheque books with pictures of English castles. Too often, heavy advertising - the Big Four spent nearly £1,250,000 between them on press and television advertising in 1970 - seems to be a substitute for innovation, setting out to establish differences between one another which do not really exist.

Diversification is another much vaunted achievement. The banks have bought their way into hire purchase, unit trust management, insurance, merchant banking, leasing and factoring (a service, copied from America, for settling a company's bills and credits) and have increased their presence in international banking. There has been much talk of a 'one-stop bank', a sort of financial supermarket in which the customer could buy any service ranging from booking an airline ticket to obtaining a house mortgage. 'We have been taking a critical look at our diversification,' said John Thomson, 'trying to ensure that it is consistent rather than capricious and planned rather than defensive. First and foremost, we feel that we are in the business of finance, broadly defined. Banking, like all businesses, is a continually evolving activity. Of course we have to ensure that our traditional services are of the highest possible quality, but to concentrate on them exclusively could be a recipe for declining profits and influence even in a developing and more affluent environment.' Splendid though these sentiments may sound, they seem to have little relation to the way the big banks actually run their businesses. Banking to the Big Four is still banking and not an industry which has a common thread running through called money or finance. The host of ancillary activities is mostly treated by the banks as essentially arm's length investments. They are confined to subsidiary companies each with their own specialists detached from the mainstream of the banks' operations. This was one of the practices for which the P.I.B. had little time. The Board felt that activities like hire purchase and overseas banking should be 'part of an entire spectrum of new activities, each part of the spectrum being related to another and the whole therefore being pursued more effectively together'.

Barclays, in particular, seems to have belatedly recognized this principle. During 1970, they bought out the remaining shares in Barclays DCO they did not own. Barclays DCO (the initials are used to avoid the embarrassingly imperial sound of 'Dominion, Colonial and Overseas') runs a chain of 1500 branches, mostly in developing countries. The bankers of DCO were always a resolutely independent-minded lot who resented any interference from the parent bank itself. And the attitude of the parent bank, as a Barclays man explained it, was a question of 'as long as they don't trouble us, we won't bother them'. That is all changing now that Barclays have brought DCO completely under their ownership. The plan has been to integrate DCO with the international banking operations of the parent bank as a whole.

Much the same has happened at Lloyds, where Eric Faulkner is hell-bent on building up what he calls 'a world bank to see off First National City Bank'. One of the first things Faulkner did when he arrived at Lloyds was to merge the bank's international banking operation (Lloyds Bank Europe) with the Bank of London and South America, whose president and post-war architect, Sir George Bolton, is widely credited as being one of the first British bankers to discover the delights of the Eurodollar. Faulkner's new international banking baby is called Lloyds Bolsa International – shrewd observers are already speculating whether LBI will soon stand for Lloyds *Bank* International.

There is little doubt that the banks by keeping their ancillary activities in separate compartments have been feeble-minded in their diversification.

Discovering the benefits of the management sciences has been a slow and agonizing process for the banks. Clearing bankers still regard themselves as bankers rather than managers. It is a distinction which their narrow logic impels them to make. Nevertheless, they have felt themselves bound to experiment with and apply the methods which have been accepted for decades as standard practice in other industries. I spotted a book by Peter Drucker, the American management guru, in the dark recess of a bookshelf in the office of the chief general manager of one of the Big Four. It was a symbolic recognition that the banks now have a sneaking feeling that the management sciences have some relevance to their business.

By comparison with other industries, the Big Four's application of management techniques has been little more than a flirtation. 'Management by objectives' has been tried out in one of them, and all the Big Four have one or other of a 'marketing department', an 'Organization and Methods' section, a planning department and a 'management services' unit. But non-banking specialists have traditionally never achieved much status in the clearing banks. Barclays informed me they were going on a recruiting drive for chartered accountants – they already had one and were contemplating bringing in two more. The Midland employs around 100 so-called specialists (ranging from lawyers, accountants, economists and planners to investment analysts and public relations men). The trouble is that in each of the Big Four specialist skills are grafted on to the whole like an orange attached to a football. The specialists have at most a glorified backroom role. They speak when they are consulted.

Probably the saddest confrontation between the banks and the management sciences has been over that greatest managerial aid of them all – the computer. Between them, the clearing banks have invested well over £100 million in computers, which seemed to provide the answer to a problem that had long nagged the banks – rising staff and administrative costs. Tragically, the answer has proved an expensive one. Half-way through 1971, *The Banker* revealed that 'the computerization plans of some of the British clearing banks are seriously behind schedule'. Barclays and the Midland, it pointed out, were at least a year behind schedule in their computerization plans and the delay was costing them over £16 million in lost savings. *The Banker* indicated that both banks had strong doubts about the computer equipment they had ordered and concluded that the sorry episode to date showed the 'failure of bank management to deal successfully with major investment decisions outside pure banking'.

All this raises the more general question of whether the clearing banks can cope with the management of change. It is all very well to talk about 'one-stop banks' and financial supermarkets, but do the banks have the right managerial resources to manage such entities if and when they are developed?

It is probably right to look for the root cause of the clearing banks' predicament in the board-rooms. Nowhere is the division in the City between amatures and professionals, gentlemen and players, more apparent than in the clearing banks (the only possible exception being in insurance companies). The gentlemen occupy the board-room while the players, or general managers, run the bank. 'Policy-making in the great British banks,' commented *The Economist*, 'goes largely by default. General managers know too much about banking, the directors too little.'

Between them the Big Four have 115 directors, the majority of whom are industrialists each with seats on the boards of several large companies. There is a total of more than 900 clearly identifiable directorships associated with these men. Many of them represent companies which are customers of the bank. A survey by *The Economist* in 1966 showed that a quarter of the London clearing banks' boards was filled by Old Etonians and that only half had been to a university. It noted that many of the industrialist directors came from declining industries such as shipbuilding, shipping, textiles, steel and mining. Growth industries, such as chemicals and electronics, were sparsely represented. The appearance of general managers in clearing bank board-rooms is a comparatively recent development. Lloyds, National Westminster and the Midland have two general managers on their boards; Barclays one.

It is not difficult to see how this type of board structure is likely to have a deadening effect on the organization as a whole. Ostensibly, directors are chosen for their wide range of contacts and experience in industry and finance. This may be useful for maintaining and expanding a bank's business. But this is hardly what a board of directors is for. There is little evidence to suggest that clearing bank boards have made any really significant contribution to new thinking or policies. Rather the opposite. They seem to contain the worst characteristics of a self-perpetuating oligarchy: resistant to change, unbalanced in their outlook and sterilizing new thinking right down the organizational chain.

The day-to-day running of the Big Four is in the hands of between six and twelve general managers who meet daily to discuss and decide on issues as they crop up. There is a tribalism in these men reflected in their titles which range from chief general manager and assistant chief general manager to assistant general manager and general manager. Banking traditionally has revolved round the short term, and it is not surprising that the issues raised at these meetings are mostly of a short-term nature. There is little time for strategic, long-term policy-making, for this is not in the nature of the decisions that have to be regularly made.

General managers attain their positions in the banks because they are good bankers: and that invariably means conservative bankers. Their careers follow a monotonous pattern: leaving school (usually grammar school) at seventeen, branch manager just before forty, and general manager in the late forties. The loyalty to the bank is astonishing – there is almost no movement of managers between the large clearing banks. A frightening insight into the consistency of this pattern can be seen in the careers of the three recently retired chief general managers of National Westminster, the Midland and Barclays. They were all born within three years of each other, had a more or less identical educational background, and all joined their respective banks at sixteen or seventeen.

The 'cradle to grave' career pattern among the big clearing banks has probably done more than anything else to fossilize thinking in the banks. Most of the present top managerial brass in the banks were recruited towards the end of the 1920s at a time when banking was considered a respectable alternative to entering industry. The banks recruited heavily during this time and for the next two and a half decades cut back considerably on their new intake. The result has been not only an age – almost a generation – gap within the bank hierarchies. The presence of a gerontocracy has created serious recruitment problems for the banks. These problems have been reflected at all levels. At the lowest, wages have declined over the years relative to pay in other industries, and as a result the prestige inherent in banking has been largely dissipated. In 1967, N.U.B.E. (the National Union of Bank Employees) took unprecedented strike action and forced all the banks to recognize the union.

Only comparatively recently have the banks attempted to attract graduates into their ranks in significant numbers. The scarcity of graduates in clearing banks and the 'cradle to grave' pattern have contributed substantially to the inflexibility of the system: to the stultifying belief among the banks' senior executives in the excellence of their organizations. It is significant that Glyn Mills, the only bank for years to pursue an active policy of graduate recruitment, has been the training ground of many of the City's brighter banking professionals (admittedly their graduate intake was mostly of solid public school stock). These include Eric Faulkner of Lloyds, Charles Villiers, head of Guinness Mahon and formerly managing director of the Labour Government's Industrial Reorganization Corporation, and Jeremy Morse, the youngest director of the Bank of England.

Another product of Glyn Mills' graduate school of banking is Richard Lloyd. Lloyd is a clearing banker/iconoclast who at the tender age of forty-two set out to overturn many of the established notions about how to run a bank. There is even something heretical about his title. He is *chief executive* of Williams and Glyn's Bank, the youngest and by a long way smallest of the London clearing banks. The *Sunday Times* proclaimed the birth of Williams and Glyn's – or rather the merger of three banks into one – in September 1970. 'Next Friday a new London clearing bank goes into business. Already it is planning a whole series of new departures and experiments that, if successful, could change the long-term character of British banking much more than all the great super-mergers that created the pattern of four giant banks. Yet only a few months ago, this future newcomer looked condemned to stagnate as a dwarf in the giants' world.'

Lloyd, a self-confessed admirer of the American banks, started with the premise that banking is not fundamentally different from any other business – at least not in management terms. The big failing of the large banks, in his view, was that they simply invested money in new businesses without attempting to manage them. 'It is intellectually more attractive,' he says, 'to diversify one's activities under one's own management. I've felt that the way to diversify is to manage one's endeavours in a synergetic way. Instead of buying businesses we buy people.'

For a clearing bank, Williams and Glyn's went to unprecedented extremes to find people to make its experiment work. They brought in a personnel expert from a machine tool company, a computer man from an electrical company, a marketing man from a publishing group, a Foreign Office official, a don from Manchester University, and three merchant bankers. In the process they dismembered the old hierarchies based on chief general managers and general managers. In their place were appointed executive directors responsible for the seven operating divisions of the bank – each responsibility neatly defined with white boxes and dotted lines on an organization chart. Committees were to be outlawed: the whole organization was to be accountable, one man to another.

Lloyd himself is a career banker whose family once ran a bank in Shropshire called Lloyd's, which is now part of *the* Lloyds Bank but originally had no connection with it. He runs the new bank from a room overlooking the main banking hall in head office just off Lombard Street. To approach his office, the visitor walks up one floor, and crosses an open-plan space occupied by secretaries and modern office furniture. There are no private lifts reserved for the chairman only, no ante-rooms with the ubiquitous *Financial Times* and the latest copy of the bank's review, no sponge-bag-trousered retainers. 'It's not very pompous,' says Lloyd proudly.

Williams and Glyn's is a curious hybrid of merchant bank, clearing bank and financial supermarket: the mixture of a City-orientated semi-merchant bank (Glyn Mills), a Lancashire-based branch bank (Williams Deacon's) and the English rump of an Irish bank (National); and with Lloyd's distinctive ideas imposed on top. 'Management ought to tell sometimes,' says Lloyd confidently.

Rather like the big investing institutions, the clearing banks have so far seldom been seen to exercise their power in the industrial arena. Part of the reason for this is that they have steered clear of actually investing money in companies, in the form of either equity or loan stock. And in so far as they lend money to industry on a fixed term basis, they have tended to fight shy of most of the rigorous control systems and analytical techniques used by the American banks in their lending.

But two events in 1971 may have paved the way to rather closer involvement. The first was the collapse of Rolls-Royce, as a result of which Lloyds and the Midland were faced with £16 million worth of bad debts. The second, which significantly followed shortly afterwards, was Lloyds' tough tactics with the David Brown Corporation. The bank refused to lend the tractor and Aston Martin company any more money, unless the Corporation's chairman, Sir David Brown, ceased to have any executive powers. The company accepted the ultimatum. How far this process continues – or indeed whether this incident is part of a trend – remains to be seen.

Some City observers – not least the Inter-Bank Research Organization which was commissioned by Lord Rothschild's Whitehall 'Think Tank' to examine the future structure of the City – see the clearing banks developing along the German and Japanese models, and becoming substantial shareholders in industry in their own rights. Among the banks themselves, however, there has been scant enthusiasm about this aspect of the IBRO proposals.

BRITAIN'S CLEARING BANKS

Bank	*Rank in world league**	*Deposits*	*Chairmen*
Barclays	4	£5778m.	John Thomson
National Westminster	5	£4899m.	John Prideaux
Midland	22	£3322m.	Sir Archibald Forbes
Lloyds	32	£2877m.	Eric Faulkner
National & Commercial Banking Group	97	£1042m.	James Blair-Cunynghame
Bank of Scotland	168	£451m.	Lord Polwarth.

*Source: *The Banker*

THE CHIEF GENERAL MANAGERS AND THEIR BACKGROUNDS

Chief General Manager	*Born*	*Age when joined bank*	*Education*	*Age when became a general manager*
Geoffrey Cundy (Barclays)	1913	17	Mitcham County School	50
Alex Dibbs (National Westminster)	1918	16	Dover College and Whitgift Middle School, Croydon	47
Charles Trott (Midland)	1911	17	Tottenham County School	48
B. H. 'Peter' Piper (Lloyds)	1918	17	Maidstone Grammar School	47

	Education	*Other remarks*
Sir John Thomson	Winchester and Magdalen College, Oxford	Member of the Jockey Club; Lord Lieutenant of Oxfordshire.
John Prideaux	Eton	Mother an Arbuthnot; joined family merchant bank of Arbuthnot Latham at the age of 19.
Sir Archibald Forbes	Paisley and Glasgow University	Chartered accountant; has spent most of career between Government jobs and private sector; used to run the old Iron & Steel Board; industrial directorships include Dunlop, Shell Transport and Trading and Spillers.
Eric Faulkner	Bradfield and Corpus Christi, Cambridge	Joined Glyn Mills at age of 22; directorships include Vickers and Hudson's Bay Company.

'Quand je me trouve en face de la vielle dame de Threadneedle Street, je regrette que je suis tout-à-fait impotent.'

Winston Churchill

6. THE BANK OF ENGLAND

The Bank of England is a most peculiar institution. Symbolically it is situated right in the centre of the City – a massive quadrilateral with some of the City's main streets leading either towards it or around it. If you stand on the pavement outside the front of the building, you see the Bank at its best – a solid windowless façade punctuated by Corinthian columns. This was built by Sir John Soane and others in the (first three decades of the) eighteenth century. Stand a little further back across the street and the monstrous superstructure – the work of Sir Herbert Baker in between the wars – heaves itself above the elegance of Soane.

The windowless outer walls have their own peculiar significance. For generations, the Bank has guarded its activities from the gaze of the outside world with an almost obsessive secrecy. Ever since it was founded in 1694 to help finance William III's war against Louis XIV, the Bank has resisted intrusions made upon it by outsiders.

To be fair, things have begun to change. Some shafts of light have begun to penetrate through the cracks in the shell of this institutional oyster. In 1971, the Bank for the first time published a set of financial accounts – the profits of its banking department were revealed as £6·3 million. And for over a decade it has been adding to its annual reports and gradually expanding its Quarterly Bulletins, which have become fatter with more statistics and drier with more learned dissertations such as articles entitled 'The importance of money'. But the process of change has been more responsive than self-induced.

What has irritated its sternest critics is that the Bank has traditionally behaved like the most private of private banks. Yet in fact it is a publicly owned organization, and has been so for the last sixteen years. The visitor to the bank is greeted by a tall, pink-coated, top-hatted attendant. At the other end of the hierarchy there is a similar aura of courtly pageantry. There is the Governor, of course, the Court of Directors who, by statute, administer the Bank's affairs, and other such elegant titles as the Chief Cashier, the man whose signature appears on bank notes.

'In the course of two and three-quarter centuries the Bank of England has developed in a typically British way,' concludes an introductory brochure produced by the Bank, 'without any kind of revolution and with experience taking the place of an elaborate written constitution. Nor are old customs forgotten – there is still in the Court Room a wind-vane, which in the days of sailing ships warned the Directors of likely delays in arrivals in the Port of London, and so helped them in estimating the day-to-day demands for money. Though only a relic now, it serves as a reminder that foresight and business skill are not purely modern arts and that, though methods may change, the past is not likely to be disregarded.'

The fact of the matter is that the Bank of England is very different from such other bastions of the public sector as the National Coal Board, the railways or British European Airways. In the immortal words of Sir Leslie O'Brien,* the Governor, 'Let me say that of course we are not a nationalized industry; we are a nationalized institution.'

The process of shedding light on darkness really began around fifteen years ago – and in the most embarrassing cir-

* Sir Leslie O'Brien was succeeded by Gordon Richardson in July 1973.

cumstances. It happened in a week which the City as a whole would long to have forgotten, if it has not already done so. On Monday, Tuesday and Wednesday, 16, 17 and 18 September, 1957, the gilt-edged market, to use the official phraseology, was in 'an extremely sensitive state'. Gilt-edged stocks, Government loans in marketable form, so-called because of their supposed rock-sure investment qualities, were being sold throughout the market. On the Thursday of that week, the Bank of England announced that Bank Rate was being increased by a massive two per cent to seven per cent, a level appropriate to the devastating economic crisis with which the Conservative Government was being faced.

The relationship between Bank Rate, which traditionally has had its most marked effects on the interest charged for loans and overdrafts by the banks, and the gilt-edged market is a fairly mechanical one. The yield on gilt-edged naturally goes up and down according to the price of stocks. If the price of a gilt-edged stock goes up, the yield goes down. Take, for example, Treasury Loan 5½ per cent 2008–2012. (That means that the Government has to repay this loan between the years 2008 and 2012 and in the meantime pay interest at the rate of 5½ per cent a year.) The point is that the interest is fixed, so that if the price of this stock goes from say seventy to seventy-five (per cent of the price at which it will be finally redeemed)* the yield automatically drops. Now if Bank Rate goes up by a substantial amount, interest rates rise and gilt-edged stocks automatically become a relatively less attractive form of investment. So people sell, the price of gilt-edged falls, the yield rises, and hopefully and eventually the gilt-edged market is back in business. There is another important point about a sudden rise in Bank Rate. Insofar as it reflects a crisis in the British economy, investors are less happy to have their money with an ailing lender, however gilt-edged it may appear to be. It is worth remembering that 3½ per cent War Loan has never been repaid.

* Gilt-edged stocks which have a long life ahead of them before they are redeemed are less liquid or money-like than shorter dated stocks. It is this and their yield which largely determines their price.

Before virtually any substantial movement in Bank Rate, there is invariably some movement in the gilt-edged market which reflects accurately the imminent change. It just so happened that in the early part of that unfortunate week in September 1957 there seemed to be an unusually large number of operators in the market who had got it right. The story is told at length by Paul Ferris, part of whose excellent account I quote:

'Rumours began to fill the City and get into the papers that some of the selling had been the result of a leak. Newspaper references crept towards the libel mark. Hints, smears, and dark allegations were made in Parliament, and finally, after much denial that anything was wrong, the Government was forced to hold a public enquiry to clear the names of public figures. It lasted twelve days in December and probed deep, concerning itself with holidays and train timetables, examining cables in code and private correspondence, cross-questioning a slice of London, from top bankers and journalists to unsuspecting investors and clerks, dissecting a cocktail party, peeling back the roof of one of the proudest merchant banks – and finding in the end that no one had talked, no one had cheated, no one had behaved with anything but total propriety. But for the outsider it was a window and a shaft of daylight into the City.'

The Bank Rate Tribunal under Sir Hubert Parker, the distinguished lawyer, provided some splendid ammunition for the City's critics. Its report did much to confirm what most of the critics had long suspected: that the City was dominated by a conspiratorial collection of not very gifted pluralists, knitted together to form a complicated pattern of personal relationships. From the evidence submitted to the Tribunal, this particular fragment was particularly memorable: 'Sorry to bother you with such problems when you should be concentrating on the grouse.' This came from a letter written by Hugh Barton, the managing director of Jardine Matheson, the well-known Far East merchants, to John Keswick, a proprietor and director of the company. Barton, based in Hong Kong, was asking whether 'Tony and you would let me have your recommendations, so that I can take whatever action may be necessary when I return, as naturally I do not want to miss the bus with the firm's Gilts.' On 18 September Jardine Matheson sold £1 million worth of gilt-edged securities.

'Tony' referred to William Johnston Keswick, who apart from his association with the family firm of Jardine Matheson was, and still is, a director of the Bank of England. Nor was he the only Bank of England director in the *dramatis personae* of the Bank Rate affair. Lord Kindersley, chairman of Lazard's (sellers of £1·5 million of gilt-edged on 17 and 18 September), governor of Royal Exchange Assurance (sellers of £500,000 worth of gilt-edged on 18 September) and chairman of the British Match Corporation (sellers of £375,000 of gilt-edged during the week), was another.

From the Bank of England's point of view, the embarrassment could hardly have been greater. Smoke and fire inevitably go together in the minds of the City's critics. The Tribunal's main finding that 'there is no justification for allegations that information about the raising of Bank Rate was improperly disclosed to any person' only barely extinguished both the fire and the smoke. The fire-fighting operation, in the case of the Bank of England, was not helped by the questioning attitude of Sir Hubert and his colleagues about the whole role of non-executive directors of the Bank. 'It will be observed,' the Tribunal concluded, 'that our inquiries into the dealings of companies with which Lord Kindersley and Mr. W. J. Keswick were connected has focussed attention on circumstances in which a Director of the Bank of England, who has other business interests, may find himself in a difficult and embarrassing position. This is particularly so in the case of a Director of the Bank, who, like Mr. W. J. Keswick, is the one person to whom his business colleagues look for advice, and where he cannot escape his duty to give such advice.' The Tribunal added that it did not feel it could pronounce on such issues of general policy.

Eighteen months later, however, the Radcliffe Committee did, having been asked to do so by the Chancellor of the Exchequer. The Radcliffe Report, published in August 1959, exploded the myth that the outside directors of the Bank played any real part in the policy decisions of the Bank. 'In our view,' it concluded, 'the misgivings that have been expressed about the position of part-time directors and their possible embarrassments are due to the belief, not unnatural in the light of the special circumstances which attended the Bank Rate move in September 1957, that policy decisions about central banking operations must be the product of prior discussion and agreement by the Court in general. This . . . is not the case.'

By law, there have to be twelve part-time directors out of a total of eighteen members of the Court. Until the late 1950s, they were drawn heavily from the City – merchant banks and clearing banks.

At the time of the Radcliffe Report there were three merchant bankers, one clearing banker and one overseas banker. The present breakdown of the part-timers on the Court is: six industrialists, five bankers and one trade unionist. The industrialists include Sir Val Duncan of Rio Tinto-Zinc, Sir Maurice Laing of John Laing, the builders, Lord Nelson of General Electric, Lord Pilkington of Pilkington Brothers (the only director of the Bank to ride to Court meetings on a bicycle), Adrian Cadbury of Cadbury Schweppes, and Lord Robens, ex-chairman of the Coal Board and now boss of Vickers. The bankers are Leopold Rothschild, W. J. Keswick, Gordon Richardson of Schroder Wagg, Sir Eric Roll of Warburg's and Sir John Stevens of Morgan Grenfell. The trade unionist is Sir Sidney Greene, the general secretary of the National Union of Railwaymen.

The part-timers only get £500 a year, but their perks are not inconsiderable. According to *The Economist*, they get 'a free lunch on Thursday, the use of a car on Bank business, and the privilege of being able to bank with the Bank and flourish that most respected of all cheque books, old fashioned pale-grey at that'.

The Radcliffe Committee, with its wide-ranging brief to examine the whole of the British monetary system, went much further in its scrutiny of the Bank. In particular, the

Committee was sternly critical of the amount of information the Bank disclosed about itself and the various workings of the financial system generally. In a famous phrase it referred to the Bank's annual report, 'the meagreness of which has become a byword'. In addition, the Bank publishes a sort of weekly balance sheet (showing among other things the levels of note circulation and bankers' balances) called the Bank Return, which the Committee said 'no longer performs its intended function of proving to the public that the Bank of England is behaving itself according to accepted principle'. The Radcliffe Report sparked off the Quarterly Bulletins and the expanded annual reports.

The Radcliffe Report shed a lot of light on the workings of the Bank of England (about which more later). But it was a decade later that the real moment of reckoning came.

The Parliamentary Select Committee on Nationalized Industries is an energetic body, which has burrowed deeply and fascinatingly into those monolithic institutions – the nationalized industries. Under its vigorous chairman, Mr. Ian Mikardo, the Labour Member of Parliament for Poplar, it has seldom been uncontroversial in its investigations within the public sector. For years, however, the Bank of England, the first institution the first post-war Labour Government nationalized, failed to come under the Select Committee's aquiline scrutiny.

Round about 1968, the Select Committee, a body incidentally like all Commons committees of its kind composed of members of both major parties, began making suggestive noises that the Bank should come within its gaze. Undoubtedly, the pressure came from within the ranks of the Labour Party. The Bank and the Labour Party have been uncomfortable bedfellows even at the best of times. The Bank has long been viewed by men of the Left as a deeply conservative body, showing a callous regard for such social problems as unemployment and the need for expanding the social services. Tension between Bank and Party is naturally always at its greatest during a Labour Administration.

Nowhere has this been more amply demonstrated than in

Harold Wilson's memoirs. His account of his dealings with Lord Cromer, the Governor of the Bank at the time, during the 1964 sterling crisis is illuminating.

'The Governor of the Bank,' wrote Wilson, 'was in a peculiarly difficult position. He had to maintain the confidence of sterling. Whatever Lord Cromer's personal or political views – and in later years after his retirement he made little secret of what these political views were – it was his duty, at any rate, to represent to the Chancellor and the Prime Minister the things that were being said abroad or in the City; to indicate to the Government the issues on which, in the City's view, it was necessary to win confidence if a disastrous haemorrhage were to be averted.

'This was why we had to listen night after night to his demands that there should be immediate cuts in Government expenditure and particularly in those parts which related to the social services, even where money was already committed. Indeed, once later at a private lunch at No. 10, I challenged him specifically on this point. I told him that Government expenditure was committed far ahead; schools which were being built, roads which were part-way to completion, had been programmed by our Conservative predecessors in 1962–63.

'Was it his view, I asked him, that we should cut them off half-finished – roads left as an eyesore on the countryside, schools left without a roof, in order to satisfy foreign financial fetishism? This question was difficult for him, but he answered "Yes". That was, in fact, what he felt he had to ask.'

Mr Mikardo and his colleagues had a difficult job persuading the Government to give their Committee wide enough terms of reference for their investigation of the Bank of England. The Government, at first, pressured by backwoodsmen in the Treasury, appeared to be trying to limit the scope of the Committee's inquiry, which brought about angry cries in the Commons of a 'watch dog without teeth'. As it turned out, the brief given to the Committee, which omitted the sensitive area of relations between the Bank and the Treasury over the formulation and execution of economic policy, was interpreted widely by Mikardo and his colleagues. Some would say too widely.

During the course of the inquiry a galaxy of figures was paraded before the Committee representing such diverse sectors of the economic and financial establishment as the Treasury, the clearing banks, the Stock Exchange, the accepting houses, the discount market, the financial press and, of course, the Bank itself. The Governor, Sir Leslie O'Brien, gave evidence to the Committee on no less than nine different occasions. The Committee's searches included visits to the central banking parlours of the United States, West Germany and the Netherlands.

When the Select Committee published its report in May 1970, the picture it painted of the Bank was of an arcane assortment of machinery which not so much defied, as operated outside, the normal laws of commercial gravity. To be fair, the Bank had done a fair amount to come to grips with the second half of the twentieth century. A couple of years back, it had called in McKinsey and Co, the American management consultants (to the intense irritation of British management consultants who thought they could do the job just as well), and a hefty amount of money had been spent on computers. Phrases like 'budgetary planning and control' had entered the Bank's vocabulary, and when I spoke to one of the Bank's officials, a financial controller was about to be appointed – they had already given somebody (Roy Heasman) the job of looking after a new 'management services' department.

But in almost every other respect, the Bank behaved like no other commercial organization in the public sector. It did not charge the Government, its customer, the true cost of providing services, it did not apply the same sort of criteria to evaluating its investment programmes as other nationalized bodies, and, above all, it did not publish a set of annual accounts. There seemed to be an almost Dickensian charm about the relationship between the Bank and its owner, the Government - once every six months the Bank had been paying to the Treasury the unlikely sum of £873,180 and 'such less or greater sum as may from time to time be agreed upon between the Treasury and the Bank, in lieu of dividend'.

What disturbed the Select Committee greatly was the fact that no one – not even the Treasury (let alone Parliament) – seemed to have any control over how the Bank managed its affairs. In short, the Bank was not properly accountable, either to the Treasury or to Parliament. 'The Bank could go on operating inefficiently for years,' the Committee claimed, 'without anyone outside knowing about it. For all anybody knows with certainty to the contrary, it may have gone on operating inefficiently for years.'

The Committee did not manage to find much evidence to support this case. Mr Mikardo was alarmed that the Bank was 'building replicas of the Taj Mahal in a number of provincial English cities', referring to new branches of the Bank in Manchester, Birmingham, Leeds and Newcastle. This was stoutly countered in the evidence to the Committee by Roy Jenkins, Chancellor of the Exchequer at the time. 'If,' said the Chancellor, 'the Bank – I have no evidence of this at all – were to start managing the foreign exchange market in an extremely foolish way or even an absolutely brilliant way the effects of that would far outweigh the building of Taj Mahals in every city in the country.'

It was the way that the Bank had used its statutory immunity to shield itself from the outside world that worried the Select Committee. There was nothing embodied in the Bank's charter, or in the 1946 Act which nationalized the Bank, to suggest that it should disclose its financial accounts: nothing saying that it should have its capital spending plans vetted by the Treasury or any other Government department. 'But the fact is,' the Committee said, 'that any institution which is protected by secrecy and shielded from scrutiny is in danger of becoming unselfcritical and complacent.'

One thing which particularly appalled the Committee was the fact that the salaries of the full-time directors had never been disclosed. 'The Court,' said the Committee, 'is the only body of men in Great Britain, in either the public or the private sector, which determines the remuneration of its members and then reports it to nobody. Your Committee consider this practice inappropriate in a public corporation.' In the course of his lengthy dialogue with the Select Committee, the Governor in fact revealed his salary. He told the Committee he was paid £25,000, of which £2000 was statutorily provided under the terms of the 1946 Act. Jasper Hollom, his deputy, received £18,000, and the other four executive directors upwards of £14,000, the starting salary of a full-time director. Since then, Sir Leslie and Mr Hollom have been voted a pay rise. The Bank's first annual accounts revealed that Sir Leslie was getting £27,182 (precision is a nicety among bankers) and Mr Hollom between £20,000 and £22,500. Interestingly, the top mandarin at the Treasury, Sir Douglas Allen, only gets £15,000 a year.

An official of the Bank confided to me afterwards that the justification for not publishing all the things the Select Committee wanted publishing and for not adopting practices that had become accepted in other parts of the public sector really boiled down in the end to tradition. Time and time again, the Bank's answers to the Committee's questioning came back to this. It was like knocking one's head against a brick wall. 'The Bank,' said the report, 'seems ready to fall back on the broad view that an institution that is nearly 300 years old does not need to use other people's instruments of measurement and control because its longevity indicates that there cannot be much wrong with it.'

The Bank's resistance finally broke down. It had to. In March 1971 the Government published a White Paper indicating its support in broad principle for the main recommendations of the Committee. In future the Government expected the Bank to make charges to cover the full costs of its main services to the Government and to pay over the profits to the Treasury after suitable provision had been made for working capital and reserves. The Treasury was also to be kept informed about the Bank's programme of capital expenditure which was to be subjected to 'approved techniques' of evaluation. Mr Mikardo and his colleagues could have justly claimed a major triumph – another scalp, if you like – for the Select Committee.

What baffles most people about the Bank is that it is a curious amalgam of different pieces of financial and economic machinery. In short, it is all of a number of things. It is an arm of Government, an adviser to the Government, and a banker to the Government. At the same time, it has a peculiar and very delicate relationship with the City. 'Guardian of the financial system', 'representative of the City', 'banker to the clearing banks' . . . these are only some of the epithets bestowed on the Bank in relation to the City. And as if that is not enough, the Bank also has a special relationship with other central banks abroad. It is a member of the Bank for International Settlements, essentially a central bankers' bank whose monthly meetings in Basle Sir Leslie O'Brien or Mr Hollom invariably attend. It is essentially concerned with short-term operations between European central banks – it takes deposits in the form of gold and currencies, and issues mainly short-term credits. Besides the B.I.S., the Bank of England has relationships with a galaxy of other international monetary bodies (not least the International Monetary Fund, the International Bank for Reconstruction and Development (otherwise known as the World Bank), and the Organization for Economic Cooperation and Development), not to mention the hundreds of other central banks with which it deals individually.

As an agent of the Government, the Bank does four clearly defined jobs. In the first place, it issues bank notes – nearly 1800 million of them a year. Secondly, it handles exchange control – keeping a check on the amount of sterling that leaves the country, and comes into it for that matter. Thirdly, it looks after the Exchange Equalization Account, the depository for most of the country's gold and foreign exchange reserves. The Bank has commitments to keep the value of the pound within prescribed limits of the values of other currencies – when the dollar was floated in 1971 and the pound in 1972, the prescribed limits, of course, tended to fluctuate considerably more. And it does this by buying or selling sterling in the foreign exchange markets. The Governor told the Select Committee that the Bank's turnover in the foreign exchange markets could be anything up to $250 million a day. In the 1964 crisis, the drain on sterling became so acute that the Bank just could not afford to keep propping up sterling in the foreign exchange markets. From a day's worth of telephone calls to his central banking friends overseas, Lord Cromer managed to raise $3000 million – a feat which must rank as one of the most productive acts of money-raising in banking history.

Probably the most important job the Bank has to do is controlling the monetary system of the country. Central to this is the national debt – all £32,000 million of it, available in a variety of shapes and sizes ranging from short to long, marketable to unmarketable, national savings, tax reserve certificates, Treasury Bills and, above all, gilt-edged. Britain has the doubtful honour of having a national debt which is larger as a proportion of its gross national product than that of any other country. And it has an awkward habit of growing inexorably larger every year in spite of what Conservative Governments say they can do to stop it.

It is the gilt-edged market where nowadays the Bank can leave its most pronounced mark on the monetary system. By buying or not buying, selling or not selling, Government securities it can profoundly influence the amount of money actually floating around in the system. The Bank's operator in the gilt-edged market is the old-established stockbroking firm of Mullens and Co. of 15 Moorgate. They have held the august title of 'Broker to the Commissioners for the Reduction of the National Debt' for about as long as most City memories can be stretched. The present individual incumbent at Mullens is Thomas Gore Brown, an old Etonian in Government broking traditions who took over from the more familiar Sir Peter Daniell in 1973.

The traditional device used by the Bank for regulating the monetary system has been Bank Rate. But in recent years Bank Rate has had a declining significance and was formally abolished by the Government in 1972. In the years leading up to its demise, the banks no longer kept their lending and borrowing rates so closely aligned to it and an increasingly large amount of borrowing by corporations and public sector organizations was done in markets quite outside the influence of Bank Rate – in particular, the Eurocurrency markets. Bank Rate was still a sort of thermometer of the British economy – that is, when it went up people automatically suspected or knew the worst about the country's economic health. But as a determinant of interest rates, its use was much more limited than it had been. In any case, in the eyes of the country's economic policy-makers, interest rates, themselves, are not as important as they were in regulating the monetary system. Thanks largely to the energetic efforts of the Chicago academic economist, Professor Milton Friedman, the actual amount of money floating around in the system has become more important than the price people have to pay for it.

Historically, the Bank's independence of Government is something which has been long cherished in Threadneedle Street. The Bank's very sobriquet, the Old Lady, comes from a cartoon by James Gillray depicting William Pitt the Younger attempting to seize the Bank's gold from an elderly lady seated on a locked chest. The cartoon is displayed prominently in the Bank and the Old Lady nickname is something of which the Bank is sufficiently proud to have used as the name of its house magazine. Mr Gladstone, when he was Chancellor of the Exchequer, complained bitterly that the Bank was oversensitive about its independence – a sensitivity, he claimed, which was justified in an earlier age when the Government was 'justly in ill odour as a fraudulent bankrupt'. Other politicians' exasperation with the Bank has been more extreme. In 1916 Lloyd George threatened to move the Government's bank account from the Bank to the Midland Bank.

How much independence the Bank actually enjoys is a moot point. Certainly in the days of the extraordinary Montagu Norman it was highly individualistic and independent. He was the 'strange, elusive, yet dominating personality', to use Andrew Boyle's words, who 'between the wars, bestrode the financial world like a colossus'. It was this curiously psychologically disturbed character who largely shaped the Bank into its present form.

However, the degree of independence the Bank enjoyed in Norman's day was vastly greater than it is now. On one occasion, Norman actually altered Bank Rate without warning in advance Winston Churchill, at the time Chancellor of the Exchequer. The Bank's independence has been gradually eroded. As the Radcliffe Committee found, the decision about Bank Rate 'lies today with the Chancellor of the Exchequer, not with the Bank'. And the Committee went on to recommend that 'it would be better that this should be made explicit by the announcement being made in the name of the Chancellor and in his authority'. The formal announcement of Bank Rate is something the Bank never gave up. Before the Tory Government abolished Bank Rate, a member of the firm of Mullens would formally announce it on the floor of the Stock Exchange.

When the Labour Government nationalized the Bank in 1946, Sir Stafford Cripps is alleged to have said 'The Bank is my creature.' This proved something far short of the truth. Certainly, the Bank of England Act contained powers whereby 'The Treasury may from time to time give such directions to the Bank as, after consultation with the Governor of the Bank, they think necessary in the public interest'. On the other hand, the Act specified that 'the affairs of the Bank shall be managed by the court of directors'. This phrase, 'the affairs of the Bank', has been the subject of more or less continuous controversy ever since. What indeed are 'the affairs of the Bank'? The Act never specified them. The Select Committee concluded that the vagueness 'may have encouraged the Bank to believe that it had more independence than it actually had'.

Other central banks are probably more sensitive than the Bank is about their independence. Dr Blessing of the West German Bundesbank was described by Mr Mikardo in the Select Committee report as saying that 'a bank has to be independent because one cannot really trust the politicians – they are all a rotten lot and any of them might seek to get out of a hole by printing money'.

The extent of the Bank of England's independence probably depends more than anything else on the personality of the

Governor. Until 1966, twentieth-century Governors had a certain dynastic formidableness about them. Lord Norman was followed by Lords Catto, Cobbold and Cromer, all rich awe-inspiring men in their own right, and all ducal figures in the City. In 1966, after the turbulence of Lord Cromer's relations with the Labour Government, recent precedent was broken when Sir Leslie O'Brien was appointed by Harold Wilson from within the ranks of the Bank. 'I went into the Bank forty-three years ago,' Sir Leslie told the Select Committee, 'and earned £150 a year which was £30 or £40 more than one would be likely to get in a similar job in the City which was one reason for going there.'

Sir Leslie has proved himself no mouse. On one celebrated occasion he gave the Government a fair piece of his mind. It was the Lord Mayor's banquet in October 1970, a traditional debating forum for the Governor and the Chancellor of the Exchequer. The new Conservative Government at that stage had firmly rejected the idea of introducing an incomes policy. At the banquet, Sir Leslie, with appropriate gubernatorial decorum, propelled himself into the realms of controversy by saying: 'Over the longer term, I believe that Government will have to set about devising a fair and workable incomes policy . . . ' Not a few observers were somewhat surprised when Sir Leslie three months later was reappointed for a further five-year term of office.

Officially, the Governor, the Deputy Governor and members of the Court are appointed by the Queen. But in fact, the Prime Minister and the Chancellor of the Exchequer lend more than a helping hand in appointments. Unlike in the nationalized industries, the Governor has security of job tenure: he cannot be thrown out by a disapproving monarch, or Prime Minister for that matter, until his five-year term of office has come to an end.

In a straight fight with the Bank, the Treasury could always win simply by virtue of its powers of direction under the 1946 Act. But with two-thirds of the Court non-executive, the embarrassment could be overwhelming. The part-timers could form themselves into a group and walk out if the Government tried to pull any fast ones on the Bank. This could embarrass the Government to the point where they would have to think again. It has never happened. Nor has the Treasury used its full powers under the Act.

From the City's point of view, the Bank fulfils three different roles, which at times can seem like a very precarious tight-rope walking act. In the first place, it has to see that the Government's monetary policy is actually carried out. This can mean any number of things from regulating the levels of bank lending to what are known as 'open market operations' in the gilt-edged market. In this capacity, the Bank is usually referred to as 'the authorities' – which can be a blanket term referring to any decision or action emanating between Great George Street (headquarters of the Treasury) and Threadneedle Street.

Legally, the Bank can direct the banking system to comply with its instructions. Just as the 1946 Act gave the Treasury powers to issue directions to the Bank, it also authorized the Bank to 'issue directions to any banker for the purpose of securing that effect is given to any such request or recommendation' – with Treasury permission, that is. In practice, things have never got to that pitch.

What in fact the Bank relies on to ensure that its desires are fulfilled is the curious device known as 'moral suasion': suasion is a slightly stronger form of persuading than persuasion. In prosaic terms, it really amounts to varying degrees of arm-twisting. It applies to a large number of City institutions. Until 1971, it was most conspicuous as the way in which bank lending was kept under control in successive credit squeezes. The banks – and that included the clearers, the accepting houses, and the overseas and foreign banks – were subject to both quantitative and qualitative controls. They were 'morally suaded' to keep the volume of their lending within certain prescribed limits and they were also 'morally suaded' to lend a certain amount of their funds to particular industries (shipbuilding in particular), for particular purposes (exporting) and for investing in particular regions.

It would be wrong to assume that the powers under the 1946 Act constitute the only weapon in the Bank's armoury, in the same way that the atom bomb is by no means the only device available in modern warfare - though, of course, both are thought to have fairly effective uses as deterrents. There is a wide range of other instruments at the disposal of the Bank to facilitate its 'moral suasion'. 'In fact,' said the Select Committee, 'there are sanctions enough available in the ordinary course of the Bank's business, although some are only a degree less unthinkable than invocation of the Act of 1946. No responsible financial institution would carelessly incur the Bank's displeasure by its behaviour.' As far as the clearing banks are concerned, the ultimate sanction, as the Select Committee explained, would be to withdraw their right to hold a balance with the Bank. The Bank could also refuse to authorize a bank to deal in foreign exchange. An accepting house could be hard hit if the Bank refused to discount its bills at the 'finest' rates. The nearest the Bank has got in recent years towards penalizing the clearing banks was in 1969. In order to bring the clearing banks inside their prescribed lending limits the Bank decided to impose what became known as a 'fine', though the Bank, of course, never called it that. What it amounted to was that the Bank halved the rate of interest it normally paid on the special deposits lodged by the clearing banks at the Bank. The clearing banks screamed with rage, dismissed the penalty as 'irrelevant in the circumstances', claimed it would cost them £8 million a year in lost interest and went round to see the Chancellor of the Exchequer to protest.

This was an eccentric thing for any substantial segment of the City to do. For the second major City role played by the Bank is as the City's representative. It is with the agility befitting a music hall artist that the Governor is able to switch from wearing one hat to wearing another. Some would say that this constant double act is at times too arduous for the Governor.

To the Select Committee, the Governor described how the Bank was not only 'the arm of Government in the City' but also 'the bankers' best friend'. Sir Leslie sees himself as 'a discriminating advocate'. 'I am not then the representative of the City but I do represent City interests where I think it is right and proper to do so.' Sir Leslie added that the Bank was not 'unduly infected by City views'.

One of the most curious, perhaps absurd, chances to see the Governor wearing two hats came and went in 1971. It arose from a few paragraphs tucked away in Anthony Barber's Budget speech in March.

'It is recognized in every country that effective control of the monetary system is an indispensable part of economic management. By effective I mean that the authorities must be able to bring about any necessary tightening of the system when this is called for. But the techniques used should also be flexible and should allow scope for competition and innovation in the banking system.

'The existing arrangements which we took over when we came into office are clearly defective on the score both of flexibility and of scope for competition . . .

'A great deal of preparatory work and study has been done during recent months towards a more flexible régime on these lines. These ideas will now be fully explored between the authorities and the banks and finance houses.'

The collective proposals of Great George and Threadneedle Streets for reforming the banking system were unveiled in May (see Chapter 5). How much of the so-called Green Paper, *Competition and Credit Control*, was the work of the Treasury and how much the work of the Bank is difficult to know. What is certain is that the Bank, having been substantially responsible for the revolutionary proposals, then had to go through the seemingly undignified process of listening to the City's criticism of them, report this back to Whitehall and then, presumably, play a hand in modifying the proposals as was seen fit. After the document was published in May it took four months of consultation with the main City power groups before the 'new arrangements for the control of credit', as they were somewhat obliquely referred to officially, were made known. During the consultative period the Bank for most of the time wore its 'arm of Government' hat – or glove more appropriately. There is not much evidence that the City won any major concessions from the Bank once the proposals had been published. The margin for negotiation was small, in most cases only on matters of detail, which caused ill-feelings among some of the major financial institutions, who thought they could extract major concessions from the authorities. To these, the Bank was perhaps too discriminating an advocate.

The third, and arguably the most important role the Bank plays in relation to the City is as 'guardian of the good order of the financial system', as the Select Committee somewhat tersely put it. 'The health of the banking system is absolutely vital for the health of everyone,' Sir Leslie told the Committee. The Bank's health-giving spirit is pervasive throughout the City. It is prepared to come to the support of not just ailing banking brethren but also other weak-kneed institutions ranging from stockbrokers to the commodity market. Almost invariably, the Bank never discloses when and where it is involved in rescue operations. To use the familiar phrase, it 'does good by stealth'. The argument for stealth rests on the assumption that overt rescue operations would damage confidence in the financial system as a whole. This was one of the principal arguments paraded before the Select Committee against publishing financial accounts.

Over the last ten years, the Bank has been involved in at least twelve rescue operations – consisting mostly of temporary loans to lame financial ducks. On one occasion, there was no stealth. Just after devaluation in 1967 a number of commodity traders got into serious trouble largely because the Nigerians failed to devalue by the same amount as Britain did. This caused mammoth losses on trading in cocoa. The Bank came to the rescue of the commodity market with around £5 million worth of temporary loans. It says something for the achievement of Mr Bernard Cornfeld that two and a half years later the Bank was again mentioned as taking the initiative, in an international attempt to rescue his mutual fund group,

Investors Overseas Services. Nothing in fact ever came of this rescue operation.

The Bank regards its function of guarding the good order of the financial system rather more widely than simply rescuing the tottering. Traditionally, it has had decided views on the right structure for the country's financial institutions – who should own whom. For years until 1958, it frowned on the idea of clearing banks owning finance houses. Until 1973, it was unhappy about clearing banks taking over merchant banks – though the Midland were allowed to go part of the way towards this. And, of course, the Bank was firmly against further concentration among the clearing banks. Almost invariably, Bank approval is sought before a member of any of the major City power groups undertakes a radical departure from its normal business.

The Bank's most visible concern for the good health of the financial system has been in the field of take-overs and mergers, the subject of Chapter 7.

Nor is the Bank's 'doing good by stealth' confined to the financial sector. Historically, industry has been at the receiving end of some fairly substantial strokes of largesse. Andrew Boyle describes how Montagu Norman in the late 1920s and early 1930s became a 'central banker in industry'. 'He did so in the first place most unwillingly and mainly by accident, like a man slipping, fully dressed, into the deep end of a very cold swimming bath. The coincidence that Armstrong Whitworth and Company of Tyneside and Manchester were old and respected clients of the Bank's Newcastle upon Tyne branch could not be overlooked.' It was Norman who negotiated the finance for the merger of the near bankrupt Armstrong Whitworth with Vickers in 1927.

Forty-three years later, the Bank found itself in a not altogether dissimilar situation. This time it was Rolls-Royce which was receiving the Bank's attention. Towards the end of 1970, it had become clear that Rolls-Royce was heading for insolvency. By October it was known that Sir Leslie was canvassing in the City for extra funds for the ailing aero-engine giant. Yet oddly enough, when the Government

TC–II

announced at the beginning of November that another £18 million had been found from private sources to back Rolls-Royce there was no mention of the Bank. There followed an unsightly wrangle in the House of Commons. The Government assured the House of Commons that the 'funds are entirely private' and that 'no public funds are involved'. Under pressure, the Government eventually came clean. The Bank was there all right. *The Times* commented sourly afterwards: 'If through the absence of a public body specifically created for this purpose the lot is to fall on the Bank of England, the Bank will have to adapt itself to the task. It will have to be much more open (and enable Ministers to be more informative), if not about the details of every case, at least about the global sums committed. The confidence factor is a less persuasive reason for secrecy in the case of industrial concerns than in the case of financial institutions. And it will have to equip itself with staff competent to make sound judgements about the condition and prospects of ailing manufacturing enterprises.'

For years the Bank was slow to catch up with developments going on in the City around it. It took some time for it to grasp fully the significance of new developments like the growth of hire purchase companies – which might explain why it held out for so long against the clearing banks being allowed to buy their way into this field. Even today, it is the oldest established members of the City hierarchy who have their ears closest to the Governor – the accepting houses, the Stock Exchange and the clearing banks. There is plenty of scope for improving relationships between the Bank and the finance houses, the building societies, the foreign banks and other newer segments of the City. It is difficult to escape the conclusion that the Bank has traditionally seen itself as part of the banking industry in the very narrowest sense of the term – the president, if you like, of a rather exclusive club to which the uncouth proletariat of the hire purchase and building society worlds have been admitted at a later stage under sufferance, to be seen and scarcely heard.

It is not very surprising that the Bank has become extremely sensitive to criticism about itself. One Bank official I spoke to expressed the hope that I'd 'do a better job' than the previous critical author he had met researching into the Bank. Soon after the Select Committee report was published, the wrath of Sir George Bolton, a former executive director of the Bank, was unleashed. 'The attitude of the Select Committee,' he wrote in *The Banker*, 'towards this professional institution, soaked in the past and future of Britain, was in violent contrast to the importance of the occasion and of the subject. The occasion developed in a search for candle-ends accompanied by a succession of sneers (very noticeable in Chapter II on the Note Issue) where it is suggested that the public ought to like soiled notes and a statement that the branches represent "a waste of resources".' 'The positive mania for information,' he added indignantly, 'reveals the desire to interfere and to direct operations in markets that take a lifetime to understand.'

'A beautiful piece of machinery'

Among the back few pages of *The Times* and *Financial Times* each day the diligent reader will find such apparently arcane references as these: 'A severe credit shortage in Lombard Street', 'The authorities gave assistance described as "exceptionally large indeed" ', or, less dramatically, 'There was no official intervention but, in somewhat uneven conditions, books were generally balanced less readily than on many other days recently'.

This is the esoteric language of the discount market, perhaps the most astonishing British institution to have survived into the second half of the twentieth century – certainly the most self-consciously anachronistic. One of its leading lights once described it as 'a beautiful piece of machinery', a point menacingly taken up by Ian Mikardo during the Select Committee enquiry. To which the former replied: 'Perhaps the word "beautiful" is not quite right, but it certainly is a very effective and efficient piece of machinery. Beauty is in the eye of the beholder.'

Like the Bank of England, the discount market is all of a number of things. Quite simply, it consists of twelve discount houses which for all practical purposes behave and act like banks. In other words, they operate on the thoroughly realistic basis of lending money more expensively than they borrow it. The general principle which distinguishes discount houses from other types of banking creatures is that the discount market's time-span of interest is exclusively the short term.

Of all the City institutions with which the Bank of England has relationships, the discount market receives the most special attention. Essentially, it is the mechanism by which the surplus of cash floating around the country's monetary system can be mopped up. It therefore occupies a critical position – a cog if you like – right at the intersection between the public and private sectors. Surpluses or shortages of cash in the system can arise from any number of different causes. The Government, or, more accurately, the public sector, is continually having to make payments to the private sector – and *vice versa*. Government disbursements might include milk subsidies to farmers or National Health Service payments to the pharmaceutical industry: its receipts would include tax payments.

At any one point of time, there is likely to be a temporary imbalance between the two sides of the equation. And then, of course, within the private sector, there are invariably a whole separate series of imbalances. One bank will have a shortage of cash to meet its customers' withdrawals: another bank, a surplus. Companies and finance houses will be in the same sort of predicament. The discount market is the benevolent Water Board which channels these idle pools of money to efficient uses: or, more accurately, profitable uses.

One of the extraordinary things about the discount market is that its size seems quite out of proportion to both the amount of money it handles and to its prominent role in the whole of the monetary system. It employs only 400 people, yet borrows and lends anything up to £900 million in a single day.

The discount market's most visible presence in the City is

the more or less continuous flow of top-hatted figures walking purposefully and solemnly along Lombard Street or Cornhill between ten o'clock and midday every morning, Monday to Friday. Each morning, the discount brokers, or bill brokers (as they are more usually known), dutifully set off to visit the City's leading banks. The advent of the telephone has meant that nowadays fewer banks are made personal visits. Nonetheless, the emissaries of the average discount house still manage to visit fifty or more banks every day. Whatever the reasons for this personal treatment – I was offered a variety of explanations from 'If you're going to deal in big figures you want to look at a man's face' to 'We want to know who's fond of Spurs and likes gardening' – the object of the exercise is plain enough. It is to find out how much cash each bank is ready to lend to, or call back from, the discount market, or whether the banks want to adjust the rates on the money they have already lent to the market.

The banks are the staple source of the discount market's money. The money is borrowed without any written contracts – purely by word of mouth. With the money, the market has a variety of means, or instruments, by which it can earn more than what it is paying for the money it receives. In effect, the market re-lends the money to the Government, to local government and to a variety of commercial enterprises by buying a varied assortment of short-term monetary instruments. There have traditionally been four outlets for the funds borrowed by the discount market. In the first place, there is the Treasury Bill, a Government IOU maturing ninety-one days after it has been issued. These can be bought in denominations ranging from £5000 to £10,000. For decades until 1971, the various members of the discount market used to get together every week and agree the price they would pay for Treasury Bills. Each Friday, the Bank of England makes a new issue of Treasury Bills, but under the new competitive banking rules introduced by the Bank the syndicated tender, as the cartel was euphemistically known, has been outlawed. Each discount house individually now has to decide what price it will offer.

Treasury Bills are not as profitable for the discount market as they used to be. They have their uses nonetheless. Under the new rules of competition, each discount house has to hold at least fifty per cent of its assets in the form of public sector debt. And, to quote the elegant phraseology of one bill broker, 'As a chicken has to have grit to enable it to digest its food, so the discount market has to have Treasury Bills to enable it to hold its other less liquid assets.'

The more potentially profitable traditional instruments fall into three categories. The first are short-dated Government stocks with up to five years to run before maturity. These are what the market calls its 'make or break assets'. In the past there have been dramatic instances of where discount houses have come dangerously close to the latter predicament because of badly managed speculation in the short-term gilt-edged market. National Discount, one of the largest houses in the market, nearly came to grief for this reason, but was bailed out in the nick of time by Gerrard & Reid, a smaller but more aggressive house. The two are now merged to form Gerrard and National.

Besides Government bonds, there is a wide variety of other similar forms of finance issued by a heterogeneous collection of authorities ranging from U.K. County Councils, Water Boards and River Authorities to large industrial corporations and Commonwealth Governments. All these are traded in by discount houses to varying extents.

Finally, there is the oldest and the most traditionally staple instrument: the commercial bill of exchange. This was the conventional method of financing foreign trade. An exporter cannot wait to be paid until the corresponding importer receives his goods. What he gets is a bill of exchange or an IOU from the importer which he then takes along to a bank (an accepting house) to accept the bill. This guarantees that the bill for his goods will be paid even if the importer defaults. The bill then becomes tradable – the discount broker will buy it at less than its face value, so he gets a fixed rate of interest over the life of the bill (which is usually ninety days). Commercial bills have had a varied past. The Radcliffe Committee more or less wrote off the commercial bill business as 'vestigial', simply because the bank overdraft had largely taken its place. Since then, with successive credit squeezes it has been reincarnated. But since the credit squeeze was relaxed in 1971 it has looked like diminishing again in importance.

Let us return to the day in the life of a bill broker. By midday the various emissaries will have returned from their rounds and by this time each discount house will know what its overall disposition is: whether more money has been called from the banks than deposited. At this stage of the curious drama, a character known as the Special Buyer enters the stage. He is Hugh Seccombe, from the discount house of Seccombe, Marshall and Campion, which is the Bank of England's own bill broker. Seccombe is told of the overall position in the market, and the Bank of England, when he in turn informs it, must then decide how to deal with the situation. The Bank can do a number of things. Whatever it does, each member of the market must end the day with its books balanced.

If there is a shortage of money in the market, the kindest and gentlest thing it can do is to buy bills either directly from the discount houses or alternatively from the banks which will in turn lend the money to the houses in need. This is known in the cryptic language of the discount market as either 'direct' or 'indirect help', depending on which tactic is employed.

The worst thing that can happen is the curious rigmarole by which a director of a discount house in deficit has to present himself at the Bank of England (by 2.30 p.m., for some inexplicable reason) and actually borrow the money from the Bank. If the Bank wants interest rates to rise, it can charge the discount market penal rates (anything above Bank Rate) for this privilege. It is in this way that the Bank of England acts as 'lender of last resort' in the monetary system. The saga is described breathlessly in a brochure published by one of the discount houses with a photograph of middle-aged 'money dealers telephoning to borrow enough money to "escape" from borrowing at penal rates from the Bank of England'. 'It is a matter of judgement,' says the brochure, 'whether to borrow from the Bank of England, and, if so, how much to borrow. Such borrowing has to be by 2.30 p.m. This time limit can cause great excitement in the dealing room as banks are urged to lend to us in the minutes and seconds before 2.30 p.m. There is no limit to the amount which can be borrowed from the Bank of England against eligible security, though the Bank can vary the period and the rate of the loan.' The fact that the Bank will always lend to the discount market makes the latter a safe place for the banks to put their money to rest.

During the afternoon, bills, bonds and other assets are bundled up into lots, put into tin boxes and taken round to the banks where they act as overnight security against the money borrowed.

The discount market is probably the most reactionary citadel of conservatism in the City. Formally, it consists of a closed shop, known as the London Discount Market Association, membership of which is the forbidding qualification of having an account with the Bank of England – a privilege not lightly given away. In recent years, the membership has contracted slightly from twelve to eleven.* It is generally accepted that there will be a further contraction in numbers. The immutability is reflected in the resounding nineteenth-century names of some of the members – like King and Shaxon, Jessel Toynbee, Smith St Aubyn or Allen Harvey & Ross. It is significant that no less han six of the twelve make regular contributions to the Conservative Party. Union Discount, the largest discount house, asked its shareholders to vote money to the Tories during the Labour Government. 'It seems likely,' it told them, 'that the high money rates which have been to the disadvantage of our Market, will continue so long as there is no major return of confidence in Britain's economic position. Many feel that such confidence will not be regained while the present Government remains in power, despite the severity of the domestic measures they have taken or those they may yet take.' The shareholders kindly consented, since when Union has paid more than £150 to the Conservatives through diverse

* A twelfth member was added in 1972.

channels. It is also significant that the discount market once enjoyed the services of Enoch Powell. He resigned from the board of Union because the discount house, to his annoyance, took part in a Prices and Incomes Board survey of top executives' salaries.

The Bank of England has undoubtedly played an important part in maintaining the conservatism (with a small c) of the discount market. From its Discount Office, the Bank keeps an eagle eye on the activities of the market. Traditionally, it has closely circumscribed the type of things that discount houses get up to. In a masterly piece of understatement, one bill broker told me: 'If we started to put our money into deep-sea diving ventures or boot factories in the Argentine, the Bank would show its displeasure.' Heads of discount houses, generally speaking, are not allowed by the Bank to hold important outside directorships. There are a few exceptions. David Jessel, of Jessel Toynbee and a distant cousin of Oliver Jessel, is on the boards of Eagle Star, the insurance company, and Great Portland Estates, a property company. Duncan Mackinnon of Smith St Aubyn is also a director of Eagle Star. Jeremy Smith also of Smith St Aubyn is a director of Transparent Paper, an industrial company. These are very much the exception rather than the rule. Likewise, the Bank is very demanding about the ownership of the discount market. Rothschild's, via the Rothschild Investment Trust, got as far as owning twenty per cent of two discount houses, Clive Discount* and Gillett Brothers (it has pulled out the latter), but twenty per cent was as far as it was allowed to go. Gerrard and Reid once found itself controlled by an issuing house, Minster Trust. The Bank refused to allow it entry to the discount market until its ownership was in other hands. Behind the Bank's supervision of the market is an ultimate deterrent – the ability to close down a discount house's account with the Bank. Mavericks do not get very far in this corner of the City.

Yet in a curious sort of way, the inexorable process of

* In 1972 the Bank went further and allowed Clive to be taken over by Sime, Darby, an Eastern merchanting company.

change has begun to creep into this traditionally insulated niche of financial life. Computers have begun to take the place of low-paid clerks, though one wonders whether at an exorbitant price. At lunch in one of the discount houses, conversation got round to the girl from IBM who had visited that particular discount house. As the conversation developed, it became increasingly unclear whether it was computers or womanhood that was the object of cynical jibes: probably both – the combination seemed too good to be true.

Certainly, the discount market has become more outward looking. Articles have begun to appear in the business columns of newspapers with such outrageous headings as 'The City's money men ride out to spread the gospel of hot cash'. The money men on this occasion came from Cater Ryder, who during the week before had entertained 'fifty more or less dour Yorkshire company chairmen and finance directors' in Sheffield on the miracles of the discount market. It was described in the newspaper as 'a pioneering presentation by the City discount house, Cater Ryder, touting for new business'.

The very thought appalled the discount house I saw the next day – whose two sets of lavatories, incidentally, were marked 'Gentlemen' and 'Principals' (the two were not mutually exclusive, I was told). But most houses in the discount market now resort to some sort of advertising or public relations exercise. One of Union's advertisements shows two bowler-hatted men walking along a busy City street after dark. 'What is your money doing tonight?' asks one of the other. There seemed to be the same faint undertone of sexual frustration which runs through much of City life – when I asked the head of another discount house what he would put in his company's advertisement, he replied: 'Fuck, fuck, fuck, fuck: that should make them sit up.' Gerrard and National have a more staid approach in their advertising. They show a photograph of the Tower of London seen across the Thames with the caption, 'When you want liquidity with a background of security'. Most of the sales pressure is put to bear on County Council treasurers or the financial heads of such esoteric institutions as the River Authorities: all people with lots of money around and the need to put it to profitable use.

Most people in the discount market recognize that it has changed a lot over the last ten years or so. 'After the war, the discount market had become rather effete,' says one bill broker. 'It was full of lazy men who felt rather aggrieved if they had to leave their offices after three o'clock in the afternoon.' 'In the last ten years,' he adds, 'the place has become much more professionalized. There is a new enterprise in the discount market.' It is certainly true that there are more younger men in the market with positions of responsibility than there ever were ten years ago – men like Pat Cooper of Clive, grandson of one of the accounting Cooper Brothers; John Barkshire of Cater Ryder, and Alastair Buchanan of Allen, Harvey & Ross. These men typically exploited the generation gap in the City, a phenomenon discussed elsewhere. They joined their respective firms in the certain knowledge that within a few years the old diehards, some twenty or thirty years their seniors, would move on to quieter pastures.

The emergence of this younger stream of bill brokers coincided with another development. Since the middle of the 1950s, the discount market had no longer been on its own in the market for short-term money. A complex network of so-called 'parallel' markets had sprung up, offering more attractive rates to borrowers and lenders alike. Borrowing and lending in these markets is unsecured (as opposed to the secured lending and borrowing in the discount market) and grew at such a pace that before long it outstripped the discount market itself. On the lending side, the *dramatis personae* consist of the merchant banks, the foreign banks, the overseas banks and the hire purchase companies. At the borrowing end are the local authorities with their insatiable appetite for money (their total borrowing is about £3000 million) and hire purchase companies. The clearing banks traditionally have side-stepped these short-term money markets, remaining faithful to the old discount market.

What really brought the parallel markets to life on a substantial scale was a Government decision in 1955 which virtually deprived local authorities access to the Public Works Loan Board, a State agency providing funds for the public sector. From then on they had to go out to look for money in the open market.

The other big fillip to the parallel markets came in 1958 when controls were relaxed on the convertibility of the pound into other currencies. The flood of foreign currencies (mainly Eurodollars) which found its way into the City afterwards could be converted into sterling and lent to the money-hungry local authorities and hire purchase companies. And, of course, with credit restrictions at home hampering the traditional money market, the less restricted parvenus were able to have a field day.

It is an established law in the City that when buyers and sellers exist in a market on a significant scale there is invariably a middleman – a broker who takes his commission by putting one in touch with the other. The parallel markets were no exception. Towards the late 1950s and early 1960s, a host of middlemen sprung up to perform just this function. There were local authority brokers providing local authorities with money from the banks and hire purchase companies. There also grew up another group of brokers dealing in another market: the inter-bank market. This began around 1964 as a mechanism whereby the non-clearing banks could borrow and lend money among each other without going anywhere near the discount market.

The sight of all these activities developing around them naturally caused the discount houses considerable distress. And their distress initially was in no way alleviated by the Bank of England. The discount houses realized they could check this growing threat to their business if they bought their way into existing firms of local authority and interbank brokers. But the Bank had a fixed idea that broking and acting as a principal in the same market (or jobbing, in City terminology) would be an unsavoury combination. Discount houses have traditionally made their money by acting as principals in the money markets: that is buying bills or bonds one day and selling them (hopefully) at a higher price later. Brokers – the term bill broker is actually a misnomer – only buy or sell on behalf of others. How can a broker, the Bank asked, get the most favourable deal for his client if he (the broker) has a full-scale commitment in the market on his own account?

The Bank's resistance to the idea of discount houses buying into money brokers finally dissolved in 1966, thanks largely to exceptionally friendly relations between the head of the Bank's Discount Office and the comparatively newly established firm of Clive Discount.

When Clive took over the firm of interbank brokers, Guy Butler, it became the first discount house to get involved in money broking. The rules had been bent. The Bank gave way. And Clive's exploits were followed by a stampede from other discount houses anxious to get in on the action.

At first, the discount houses used their new-found freedom mainly in the sterling markets. But in 1968 they were given the opportunity to develop their business on a large scale in the dollar markets. It came about as they were granted permission to deal in dollar certificates of deposit. The C.D. is an American invention which is issued in exchange for a deposit with a bank. It has the beauty of being negotiable, so that anyone who holds it can sell it to a third party before it actually matures.

Nowadays, discount houses divide themselves between those who still regard their business as narrowly confined to the traditional discount market and those who think of themselves as being in the money markets in the widest sense. The former category will probably remain fairly small and City-centred, while the latter are likely to grow bigger and (they hope) fatter. One or two of the larger discount houses already have offices sprinkled over the Continent and the occasional outpost in North America. 'We hope to be doing the same thing in every financial centre,' says one bill-broking optimist. 'Eventually we should be lending money from I.C.I. in this country to Frankfurt county council or whatever it's called.'

This is somewhat of a far cry from the verdict of the Radcliffe Committee or indeed of Sir Leslie O'Brien. In a famous judgement on the discount market, the Radcliffe Report concluded: 'It would not be beyond human ingenuity to replace the work of the discount houses.' And Sir Leslie O'Brien, when asked by Mr Mikardo 'If a thunderbolt fell tonight and all the discount houses were wiped out, what disasters would occur?', replied: 'I will not say that if they disappeared overnight it would be beyond the wit of man – or even of the Bank of England – to devise some mechanism which could take their place.'

The fact of the matter is that the discount houses' biggest customer also happens to be their biggest competitor. Under the new rules of competition, the discount houses can now compete for business with the clearing banks, which have traditionally provided the lion's share of the funds to operate the discount market. 'If we go out and compete with the clearing banks, we'll get bitten,' a bill broker told me. 'The only difference is that in future, retribution won't follow quite so quickly or quite so surely.' The closeness of the relationship is reinforced by the fact that it is common practice for clearing bankers to be directors of discount houses. With or without their top hats, the bill brokers too have a formidable balancing act to perform.

'I am firmly of the opinion . . . that in a few years' time self-regulation in the take-over bid field will be taken for granted even by those who today are its sternest critics.'

Lord Shawcross, chairman of the Panel on Take-overs and Mergers

'It has always to be borne in mind that what seem to be problems today may be dwarfed by the complexities of new types of market operation which are being elaborated for use tomorrow.'

Ian Fraser, first Director-General of the Panel on Take-overs and Mergers

7. THE CITY CODE

The years 1967 and 1968 saw an unprecedented build-up in company mergers and take-overs. No fewer than 2500 companies, valued at over £5000 million, changed hands, and attempts were made to take over another £900 million worth of the corporate sector. An horrific ten per cent of all Britain's industrial, commercial and financial assets outside public ownership became take-over targets. Seventy per cent of the 100 biggest companies in the country were involved in one way or another and a quarter of all British firms worth more than £10 million were taken over.

These are the stark facts behind probably the least creditable two years in recent British economic history. The reasons why merger mania gripped the country's business community at that particular time are now not so important as the trail of wreckage it has left behind. Suffice it to say that the increase in merger activity during this period was born of a number of factors, of which the stock market boom and the Government's hysterical belief that somehow size would provide the solution to Britain's industrial problems were the most important.

The City, of course, not only tolerated all this but also actively promoted it. It was very good business. Stockbrokers and merchant bankers collected their hefty commissions and fees (Hill Samuel, for instance, was paid several hundred thousand pounds for advising G.E.C. in the A.E.I. take-over), along with their acolytes: the accountants, solicitors and advertising and public relations men (there is nothing like a full-blooded take-over battle to fill the financial advertising columns of the Press). The speculators too found their rewards. Once the take-over trend had been established, stock market values became almost self-sustaining. As share prices rocketed, so it became easier for acquisitive companies to trade their shares for what they considered to be undervalued companies. And the more the take-overs came to light, the more the speculators expected there to be.

The reality of these frantic years has only since come gradually into the open. Two years after the merger boom had petered out, a study by Gerald Newbould, an academic at the Manchester Business School, exposed the whole narrowly self-interested nature of the episode and came up with the tentative conclusion that among a sample of comparable firms those that were not involved in merger activity did markedly better afterwards than those that were involved. The reasons why firms merged, according to his analysis, were not those set out in the statements issued by the merchant banks to the Press and the shareholders. The catch-phrase 'industrial logic' and the vogue word 'synergy' (which has been defined *ad nauseam* as 'two plus two equals five') may have been the terms in which companies and their advisers wanted to express their desire for merging. But in reality, the motivations were far different. The main reason was that company managements wanted an easier life with a larger share of their markets under their control. This they could achieve quickly and decisively through a merger with a competitor. Newbould unearthed substantial evidence to show that the behaviour of companies in merger situations in a great many cases stemmed from a lack of any serious, lengthy analysis and was motivated by the narrow personal interests of the company's top management. Newbould found that in half the companies in his survey, it took eight weeks or less to make the preliminary analysis before entering into negotiations with either the victim firm or the merchant bank advisers. Another startling suggestion made by Newbould is that the directors of a victim firm who do not oppose a take-over bid may do so for reasons of personal security. And in doing so, they probably secure inferior terms for their shareholders than they would have done had they opposed the bid.

How much of the blame for this astoundingly irresponsible behaviour one apportions to the managements of companies involved in the merger boom and how much to their City advisers is a moot point. Both must share responsibility for activities which in the main paid scant regard for the interests of either the shareholders or the employees of the companies involved. Where the City as a whole was culpably negligent was more in the *how* than in the *why* of the merger boom. The fact of the matter is that a tenth of the non-nationalized assets of the country changed hands in an almost totally unregulated market place.

The City has long prided itself on its freedom from controls and regulations. Compared with most other financial centres, it is uncluttered with rules and regulations – which possibly explains why the Eurocurrency markets found a home in London in the late 1950s. Likewise the field of take-overs and mergers. The City has for years regarded with a feeling of dread the American Securities and Exchange Commission, better known by its awe-inspiring initials S.E.C. – the statutory body set up to regulate Wall Street after the scandals of the Great Crash.

Historically, restraints on City behaviour have essentially boiled down to what is implicit than what is explicit. The values of personal and collective integrity and honesty have been promoted as satisfactory alternatives to detailed regulation. Any rules, so far as they have been explicit, have tended to be *de minimis*. The City, like any business concern in the country, has to operate within the broad framework laid down by legislation. This includes three Companies Acts (two post-war ones), a Prevention of Fraud Act, a Protection of Depositors Act, and a body of other laws which in varying degrees impinges on the conduct of the financial community.

The City has frequently boasted that its own requirements go far beyond the requirements of the law. In particular, it can justifiably claim that the amount of information, for example, the Stock Exchange requires public companies to disclose is substantially more than the legal requirement (though by comparison with what the New York Stock Exchange demands, it has always been minimal). Apart from the Governor's ubiquity in the City, the main task of establishing discipline has traditionally devolved on the professional bodies. The Issuing Houses Association and the Accepting Houses Committee have been responsible for the merchant banks, the Stock Exchange for the stockbrokers and jobbers, the British Insurance Association for the insurance companies, the Committee of London Clearing Bankers for the clearing banks, the Institute of Chartered Accountants for the accountants, the Association of Unit Trust Managers for the unit trusts, the Association of Investment Trust Companies for the investment trusts, the National Association of Pension Funds for the pension funds – and there are others. These stand in relation to the Governor like the school prefects to the headmaster. As Christopher Marley has written: 'The point about City institutions is that their members' professional conduct is subject to the rules of their own professional clubs – in essence the City answers to itself for its own behaviour.'

It is in the broad field of take-overs and mergers that the City is at its most exposed. This is what attracts the public gaze. This is when the business press beams its searchlights through the windows of even the most secretive City building. As Anthony Sampson has somewhat indelicately put it: 'The City suddenly for a few days looks not like a Pall Mall club, but like a Western saloon bar, with bodies all over the place.' So it is not altogether surprising that the call for law and order, when it has come, has been in the take-over and merger arena. For if the City has one single notion to cherish it is that the Square Mile must be seen to be a place where fair play and integrity flourish. Against this, of course, must be balanced the delicate desire for *laissez faire*. All attempts so far to regulate the conduct of City institutions in take-over situations have to be seen as a compromise between, on the one hand, the desire for freedom and flexibility, and, on the other, the need to ensure that the ethics and reputation of the City as a whole are not seen to be questioned.

By the late 1950s questioning had begun in earnest. The Great Aluminium War (described in Chapter 3) had demonstrated to the outside world at large that when it came to a hard-fought battle there were few punches that could be pulled: and that the interests of some shareholders might be sacrificed, albeit unwittingly, in the name of victory. The Aluminium War was one of a series of take-over struggles at about that time which brought the propriety and ethics of the City under criticism – Charles Clore's bid for Watney Mann was another. Whichever was the last straw, the Governor of the Bank of England summoned the representative bodies of the merchant banks, the investment trusts, the insurance companies and the London clearing banks, together with the Stock Exchange elders, to form a working party.

What resulted were the first guide-lines – they were no more than that – on how to behave in take-overs. They were cautiously titled: 'Notes on Amalgamations of British Businesses'. The key principle they enshrined was that 'boards of directors must at all times bear in mind the interests of all the holders of all the respective classes of share and loan capital of their companies, according to their respective rights'. But there were no detailed points of procedure, no machinery to ensure that the principles were kept to and, above all, no sanctions for anyone who acted against the principles.

The day of reckoning for what became known as the

original 'Queensberry Rules' was not long in coming. In 1963, the Government-owned steel company, Richard Thomas & Baldwins, virtually guaranteed success in a bid for Whitehead Iron and Steel by agreeing to buy the shareholdings in Whitehead of the big investment institutions, at the same time undertaking to pay them the difference between the market price and any price R.T.B. may end up bidding for the company. The institutions could hardly go wrong, and accepted the terms, giving R.T.B., advised by Rothschild's, success against a rival bidder, Stewarts & Lloyds.

The working party of the various professional City clubs was reconvened, and their 'Revised Notes' contained an important modification to the old guide-lines. In future, a bidder who had published the terms of his bid, 'and who subsequently acquires effective control by buying, in the market or otherwise, should without delay revise his existing offer or make a formal offer to all uncommitted shareholders at a fair price having regard to the prices made in the market'. And, just as important, no bidder could attach conditions to one group of shareholders and not make these available to the others.

Three events in 1966–7 finally damaged the delicate fabric of the Queensberry Rules beyond repair. The first was the bitter fight between the Dutch electrical giant, Philips, and Sir Jules Thorn's Thorn Electrical Industries for control of Pye, an ailing Cambridge-based radio and electronics firm. Philips fired the first shot by acquiring five per cent of the Pye equity and by the end of November announced a takeover bid of 8s. a share. Thorn entered the fray a few weeks later with a bid of 10s. 9d. Meanwhile, though, the ingenious stockbroker, Edgar Astaire, at the head of his own broking firm, was mounting a massive buying spree, picking up as many Pye shares as he could lay his hands on at the right price. The point at issue was that Philips ended up with control of Pye by buying the holding built up by Astaire and his associates. A large part of this holding had been amassed at prices considerably above Philips' original price – its final bid was 12s. Some shareholders could justifiably have felt aggrieved at having sold out at the original bid price when at the same time Philips, through its agents, was buying in the market place at a higher price.

The second episode involved the redoubtable Sir Frank (now Lord) Kearton, chairman of Courtaulds, the textile giant, and at that time also chairman of the state-backed Industrial Reorganization Corporation. Kearton was known for his less than respectful views about what the City did and stood for – although he is now a director of Hill Samuel. This was no more clearly demonstrated than during a series of battles to gain control of a substantial slice of Britain's textile wholesaling industry. The battle around which most of the controversy centred began in May 1967, when Courtaulds bid 11s. 6d. for the wholesaling business of Wilkinson & Riddell. Within a week of Courtaulds' opening shot, another bidder appeared on the scene in the form of Rodo Investment Trust, a financial outfit run by a controversial operator called John Gommes Senior who was later to fall from City grace. During just over a month of frantic bidding and counterbidding, Courtaulds raised its price on no less than four occasions; Rodo three times. And then on 19 June, Courtaulds closed their formal offer with less than thirty per cent of W. & R. shares in their control, and went into the stock market to buy more shares. By the end of June, the battle, which was then focussed entirely on a slogging match between Kearton and Gommes in the stock market, reached a giddy climax. W. & R. shares went up to 66s. at one stage, compared with Courtaulds' final formal bid of 15s. 3d. Gommes, who was in fact buying on behalf of another wholesaler, Macanie, claimed victory. The matter was only finally resolved when Macanie agreed to sell out to Courtaulds a month later.

Courtaulds' antics did a fair amount to destroy the credibility of the Queensberry Rules and the whole system of voluntary guide-lines. The *coup de grâce* was delivered at about the same time in an extraordinary contest involving an electrical company, Metal Industries, and its merchant bankers, Kleinwort Benson. There were two suitors for the hand of

M.I. – Thorn Electrical Industries (again) and another electrical group, Aberdare Holdings. By the middle of July 1967, Aberdare, advised by Robert Fleming, had bought control of M.I., largely through the good services of friendly merchant bankers, Morgan Grenfell. Angered though the other camp were (they complained fiercely that at least the spirit of the City rules had been breached), they were not to be outdone. In a masterly defiant stroke, they pulled off a deal with Metal Industries by which M.I. issued a whole bunch of new shares to Thorn in exchange for part of Thorn's business. It was a 'now we have you, now we don't' situation. Aberdare's holding in M.I. was at once watered down from fifty-three to thirty-two per cent.

This was the last straw. *The Times* fulminated and more or less suggested an S.E.C.-type body to regulate the stock market. The Prime Minister referred to 'a power struggle (in the City) which has reached spectacular proportions', but declined to take the ball into the political arena. And the Stock Exchange, with the backing of the Governor, asked the merchant banks to reconvene the working party, this time with the Confederation of British Industry in tow. By the autumn the groundwork was laid for a revised Code on Amalgamations and Mergers and, more importantly, for the setting up of a Panel, under Sir Humphrey Mynors, a former deputy governor of the Bank of England, to 'supervise the operation of the Code'.

The Code when it appeared in March 1968 was essentially the work of four professionals at the take-over game: Michael Bucks of Rothschild's; Robert Clark of Hill Samuel; Ken Barrington of Morgan Grenfell; and Peter Cannon, whose finance house, Minster Trust, is not among the prestigious inner circle of merchant banks. All four men had seen either at first hand or else at close quarters the devious devices which City institutions had proved themselves capable of applying in the financial battlefield. The words of the Code, as the quartet drafted them, were not minced. In the preamble was a carefully worded justification for self-imposed regulation. 'It is generally accepted that the choice before the City in the conduct of Take-overs and Mergers is either a system of voluntary self-discipline based on the Code and administered by the City's own representatives or regulation by law enforced by officials appointed by Government. The City Working Party is firmly of the opinion that the voluntary system is more practicable and more effective.' Self-imposed discipline, they argued, would be speedier and more flexible than any legalistic procedures with the time-consuming and rigid paraphernalia of the courts to fall back on.

The Code went considerably further than its predecessor, the Queensberry Rules. Perhaps the most arresting passage was the recognition that 'the ensuing rules will impinge on the freedom of action of Board and persons involved in such transactions (take-over and mergers)'. The Code was not only addressed to the bidders, defenders and their advisers but also to their associates. Associates were defined in the wide sense as 'all parties (whether or not acting in concert with the offeror or offeree company or with one another) who directly or indirectly own or deal in the shares of the offeror or offeree company in a bid situation and who have (in addition to their normal interest as shareholders) an interest or potential interest, whether commercial, financial or personal, in the outcome of the offer'. In practice an associate could be a bank, a stockbroker, the pension fund of the bidder or the defender, an associated company of one of the parties involved, or an investment company or unit trust used to acting on the instructions of one or other of the participants.

The Code included principles and rules, roughly corresponding to the spirit and the letter of the new regulations. The principles enunciated the new theme of fair play. Companies defending against a bid could not do anything without shareholder approval which 'could effectively result in any *bona fide* offer being frustrated or in the shareholders of the offeree company being denied an opportunity to decide on its merits'. All shareholders of the same class had to be treated the same – no group of shareholders should receive less favourable terms than the rest once a bid was actually conceived. The interests of shareholders, employees and creditors had to be considered as a whole. The creation of rigged share markets was explicitly outlawed. Finally, scrupulous care had to be taken with the preparation of all documents in a bid situation, particularly those connected with profit forecasts. The rules went on to elaborate in detail how the game was to be played in future, at the same time blocking up most of the loopholes which had been deployed so skilfully in the past – like a defender disposing of assets or entering into material contracts without shareholder approval (Metal Industries and British Aluminium), or a bidder closing an offer with less than fifty per cent of the target company's equity then buying control afterwards in the market (Courtaulds/Wilkinson & Riddell). Perhaps the most controversial area the Code endeavoured to regulate was share dealing in the stock market before and after a bid is announced. Before an offer is announced, no one privy to the preliminary take-over or merger discussion was allowed to deal in the shares of either the bidding or the target company. And once an offer is announced the share transactions in the companies involved by all parties to a merger or take-over deal had to be reported to the Stock Exchange, the Panel and the Press. If the bidder secures shares in the target company after the bid is announced at above the bid price, then it had to offer a higher price to all those who had accepted the offer at 'such price being not less than the weighted average price . . . of the shares so acquired during the offer period'. Finally, where an associate buys shares in the market and frustrates an offer, then he 'must be prepared to satisfy the Panel that his action was not prejudicial to the interests of shareholders generally'. This was designed to put paid to the type of activities in the stock market engaged in during the Pye/Philips affair. In effect, the drafters of the Code were treading a dangerous path between control and *laissez faire*. On the one hand, they admitted that it was 'undesirable to fetter the market'. On the other hand, they wanted to eliminate the market abuses which in the recent past had clearly been to the disadvantage of a minority of shareholders. It was a dilemma of which this was not the final resolution.

The nicety, and toughness for that matter, of the new City take-over rules were impressive at first sight. The fundamental flaw in the new system consisted simply in that the body vested with the authority to supervise the rules – the Panel – was itself virtually powerless. It was an astonishing oversight – or stroke of wishful thinking, depending how one cares to consider it – that an impotent body should be asked to referee a game which in the recent past had shown so many signs of degenerating into a disorderly brawl.

The Panel, which set to work in March 1968, had a 'pretty rugged first year', to use the pardonable understatement of the Governor of the Bank of England. Those two gladiators of the previous year, Sir Frank Kearton and John Gommes, reappeared as rivals on the take-over scene in a contest for control of International Paints. Again there were points which seemed to stretch the City rules up to, and arguably beyond, their limits. Gommes' company, Dufay, a paint company and a heavily promoted 'go-go' stock at the time, produced some highly questionable profit forecasts: while Courtaulds angered the City by saying it intended to bid for International Paints without mentioning terms before Dufay's offer for I.P. was due to expire. I.P. shareholders were left in the impossible position of not having the facts before them to decide. As it turned out, Courtaulds won the day, but not without being censured by the Panel for breaching the Code.

For the Panel, there was far worse to come that year. The real test of strength came from two of the most established bastions of the City – there are very few bluer-blooded institutions in the country than Cazenove, the stockbrokers, and Morgan Grenfell, the merchant bankers (the latter in fact look after a sizable part of the Queen's private fortune). Both were firmly on the side of the City establishment during the Aluminium War. The act of provocation was a bid by Philip Morris, the American tobacco giant, for half the shares in Gallaher, the British tobacco company. There was an irony in that Philip Morris was advised by Warburg's, the arch-opponent of the City establishment in the Aluminium War. It was quite like old times.

The bid from Philip Morris came just a month after Gallaher had been heavily involved in the City. Tobacco companies have long been almost incestuously connected with each other, and Gallaher was no exception. Thirty-six per cent of its shares were held by its major British competitor, Imperial Tobacco, and thirteen per cent by Philip Morris's U.S. rival, American Tobacco. By the summer of 1968, Imperial Tobacco was resolved to rid itself of its stake in Gallaher and arranged with its friends and advisers in the City to offer it to the public. Morgan Grenfell headed the underwriters, and at an offer price of 20s. a share the Imperial Tobacco holding aroused little interest among the investing public at large – in fact a substantial part of it was left with the underwriters. Surprising then that when the Philip Morris offer of 25s. a share came a few weeks later, Gallaher's chairman, Mark Norman, should have dismissed it out of court as unacceptable.

The next move came from American Tobacco itself. Advised by Morgan Grenfell, it announced a bid on 16 July of 35s. a share for half the Gallaher equity. Each shareholder, in other words, was offered this price for half his holding. Unfortunately, he was not given the chance to sell. No sooner had the Morgan/American Tobacco team made their bid when they plunged into the stock market and through the good services of Cazenove bought over twelve million shares. Cazenove was able to get in touch directly with those institutions who had unhappily bought Gallaher shares at the time of the Imperial Tobacco offer, and relieve them of their entire holding at 35s., 15s. above the offer price a month before. The main bulk of the shareholders was not allowed so much as a sniff of the action.

There was outrage in the City. If equal rights for shareholders meant anything – and this principle had been clearly expounded in the Code – then Morgan's and Cazenove had to be taken to task. Their respective patrician heads, Lord Harcourt and Sir Antony Hornby, were summoned before the Panel to explain their behaviour. And then followed an astonishing defiance of authority. The Panel censured both Morgan's and Cazenove, but the two established City houses answered back with the view that they had not breached the Code. At the same time they refused to answer Press inquiries.

The Panel appeared to have been intimidated. It weakly agreed that both Cazenove and Morgan's had acted in good faith 'in their belief that such dealings were within the letter and the spirit of the Code'. At the same time it referred both City houses to their respective representative organizations: the Issuing Houses Association and the Stock Exchange. The Stock Exchange cleared Cazenove on the grounds that the stockbrokers could not have known about the possibility of breaching the Code in 'the confused and competitive bid situation'. Lord Harcourt publicly apologized to the I.H.A. after they had rapped Morgan's sharply over the knuckles.

Meanwhile the Governor intervened. He dispatched three letters to the Stock Exchange, the I.H.A. and the Panel saying that the results of the Panel's censures had been 'less than satisfactory'. Explicit in the Governor's letter was the menacing suggestion of Government action. 'If the present arrangements prove inadequate, no doubt some form of statutory control will be considered.' 'Sanctions against wilful infringements of the Code,' he added, should not be ruled out in ensuring that the Panel in future did its job. In effect, this was tantamount to admitting that no one really cared enough in the City about what the Panel thought. The Panel's censure was a dubious dishonour just as the freedom of an obscure American town in the mid-west may be a dubious distinction.

The pressure for more effective regulation had been turned on. It is an academic point how long the Panel in its old form would have lasted had it not experienced another terrible trauma in the same year. What finally proved the inadequacy of the Panel was a contest which turned out to be just as much a hot potato as the American Tobacco/Gallaher affair.

Opportunism is a vitally important ingredient of the takeover business. By autumn of 1968, there was one of those happy coincidences which go into the making of so many take-overs and mergers. On the one hand, there was Mr

Robert Maxwell, the tireless and controversial Czech-born publisher, who was determined to become the proprietor of a national newspaper. On the other hand, there was Professor Derek Jackson, an eccentric professor, former steeplechase rider, Swiss resident, and owner of over twenty-five per cent of the shares in the *News of the World*, the salacious Sunday newspaper. Maxwell already controlled a very substantial publishing empire centred on the public company he controlled, Pergamon Press, and had in the process of building it up aroused the hostility and suspicion of both the City and the publishing trade. His business methods were thought to be eccentric, to say the least.

Professor Jackson had no great affection for the family newspaper – his cousins, the Carrs, ran it. For a variety of personal reasons he decided to sell his twenty-five per cent stake in the *News of the World*. One of Jackson's family trustees was Jacob Rothschild, who was put in charge of disposing of the Professor's holding. It was to Rothschild that Maxwell went, on hearing that Professor Jackson's holding was up for sale. In the face of a lower offer from Sir William Carr, chairman of *News of the World*, and his merchant bankers, Hambros, Jackson decided to accept Robert Maxwell's offer of 37s. a share if Pergamon gained control of *News of the World*.

Maxwell announced his £27 million bid for *News of the World* on 16 October, and as things stood then the battle lines looked fairly evenly drawn up – Maxwell with twenty-six per cent and the Carr family with thirty per cent. The *status quo* was soon to be shaken. Hambros went into the stock market and within a week of the bid had mopped up over ten per cent of the voting shares. Meanwhile Maxwell raised his bid to £34 million. The odds already looked loaded against Maxwell. But the death blow was still to come.

By this stage the Panel was already in a tangle. The activities of Hambros in the stock market were fairly clearly designed to frustrate Maxwell's offer – though the merchant bank claimed they were buying on their own behalf not for the company, *News of the World*. This was hardly in line with both the letter and spirit of the Code. In any event, the arithmetic of the bid by that stage was such that Maxwell needed at least twenty-four per cent of the voting shares to win, while there were only just over thirty per cent still left in uncommitted hands.

All this time, events were being closely watched in Australia by Mr Rupert Murdoch, a youthful publishing tycoon, the son of an eminent newspaper proprietor. Murdoch, who had already enlarged the publishing group he had taken over from his father, had designs on the British newspaper industry. Murdoch hurriedly approached Morgan Grenfell and asked them whether anything could be arranged between his company, News Ltd, and *News of the World*. Morgan's entered the market on Murdoch's behalf and bought 3½ per cent of the *N.o.W.* voting shares. It was only left for Murdoch and Sir William Carr to clinch a deal giving News Ltd virtual control of *News of the World* in exchange for certain assets, and Maxwell's hopes were well and truly dished.

The Panel by now was in a hopeless position. The News Ltd/*News of the World* deal was a blatant breach of the principle that anything done to thwart a bid should be done with shareholders' approval. The shareholders had not been consulted. The Panel's actions, in the circumstances, had scarcely any effect. It got the agreement of all three parties to withdraw from the market, asked the Stock Exchange to suspend dealings and secured pledges from the three merchant banks involved not to vote the shares they had bought since Maxwell's original offer at an extraordinary general meeting which was being convened to decide on the News Ltd/*News of the World* deal. Even this made Maxwell's task almost impossible. The meeting took place at the beginning of January. The Carrs extolled the virtues of the deal with Murdoch, and played on the loyalties of shareholders and employees of their company, while Maxwell was booed and derided in an appalling outburst of xenophobia. The vote went in favour of the Carrs, and *News of the World* was saved from the hands of Robert Maxwell.

The feebleness of the Panel needed no further proof. Reform there had to be. And to make the need for reform that much more urgent, there were already disquieting noises being made at political levels. The President of the Board of Trade, Mr Anthony Crosland, told the House of Commons that if the proposals for reform proved inadequate, he would 'not hesitate to take statutory power'. This was strong stuff, later toned down somewhat by Harold Wilson in a speech at the Lord Mayor's banquet. Time was clearly running out.

The Governor, meanwhile, had his own very definite ideas about what needed to be done, which he had in fact discussed with the Government. The Panel, in his view, needed a full-time head with a full-time secretariat – Sir Humphrey Mynors was thought to be too nice a man for the job, and, with a string of directorships to his name, could clearly not devote enough time to it. Furthermore, in the Governor's mind, the Panel needed sanctions.

By the end of February, after a long delay (spent mostly trying to find the right man to head it), the new revamped Panel was almost ready to move into action. The chairman was to be Lord Shawcross, a Cabinet minister in the first post-war Labour Government, a formidable lawyer in his time and now a professional non-executive director (on the boards of Shell and E.M.I.). Ian Fraser, an ex-Reuter journalist who had made his way into the City and on to the board of Warburg's, was appointed the full-time director-general. The Stock Exchange provided his deputy in the form of Wilfred Wareham, head of the S.E.'s important Quotations Department, one of whose jobs it is to vet information released by public companies to their shareholders. And a handful of other full-time officials were drafted in.

There were more than new faces behind the City's watchdog. The Code was redrafted. Most of the changes were minor modifications. But there were significant alterations in the rules affecting bids for less than the entire share capital of a company. All so-called partial bids (for fifty per cent or less of a company) could only be made after prior approval from the Panel and neither the bidder nor its associates could deal in the shares of a target company during a partial bid – a change designed to avoid a repetition of the American Tobacco/Gallaher affair.

More importantly, there were to be sanctions. These caused some soul-searching among the major City groups. One idea was that the representative bodies should impose fines on any member who broke the rules. This was abandoned because of the legal difficulties – what would happen if a member refused to pay? In the end, sanctions turned out to be more of a mouse. The professional City clubs were to discipline their errant members and they were to be backed by the Board of Trade, which agreed, if necessary, to suspend privileges and licences granted under the law to bankers and dealers in securities. The Stock Exchange would stand ready to suspend a company's quotation on the stock market if the occasion required it to. Finally, of course, there was the wrath of the Panel. As Lord Shawcross summed up the situation: 'The Panel may sometimes have to bark, and barking is usually enough. But we are now showing that we have teeth as well.' *The Times* hit the nail on the head with its headline: 'Teeth at last – but how will they bite?'

There was one important concession to the doves in the City who were fearful that the Panel might overreach itself and act too tough. An appeal committee was to be established under Lord Pearce, the law lord of Rhodesia fame. Decisions of the Panel were to be made subject to appeal.

The new Panel had a shorter honeymoon than even the pessimists had dared hope for. Within weeks it was faced with its real test. As Christopher Marley has remarked: 'In the corporate and merchant banking worlds, attacker and attacked, aggressor and victim, change their roles with almost baffling speeds.' Robert Maxwell, who had been the injured party in the *News of the World* affair, was to become the challenger of the voice of authority.

Maxwell's failure to take over the *News of the World* did nothing to damp down his restlessness. For someone of his resilience, a set-back like that was to be shrugged off in a matter of no time. Early in 1969 Maxwell came in contact in New York with Saul Steinberg, an American self-made millionaire in his late twenties who was the leading light behind the high-flying computer leasing company, Leasco Data Processing Equipment Corporation. Steinberg was every bit a match for Maxwell – they are both supremely self-confident go-getters. By June, the two had hammered out a deal whereby Leasco, advised by Rothschild's, was to take over Pergamon at 37s. a share. Maxwell undertook to secure the support of his family which owned thirty-one per cent of the Pergamon equity, and the deal was announced to a somewhat startled financial press on 18 June.

During the course of July, Leasco reaffirmed its faith in the deal by agreeing to purchase £9 million worth of Pergamon shares – they were mostly bought from investment trusts managed by Robert Fleming, Maxwell's merchant bankers. But by the end of the month, Leasco's confidence was beginning to evaporate. There were a number of problems. In the first place, Maxwell was unhappy with the terms of the deal – he wanted the terms renegotiated on the grounds that his family interests would not agree on certain aspects of the deal. Secondly, Leasco was having difficulty obtaining financial information about Pergamon. Steinberg had set his accountants, Touche Ross, on to ferreting out financial data and they had met with little cooperation at Pergamon. There were also problems over the precise nature of Maxwell's family shareholdings in Pergamon.

In the first two weeks of August, Leasco's doubts were reinforced. By this stage, Leasco had become deeply worried about what it later described as the 'quantum and quality of Pergamon's profits'. Pergamon had made a profit forecast of £2·5 million for 1969, but it was becoming increasingly apparent that within the conventional limits of accounting this would be unattainable. There were a number of things nagging Leasco about the Pergamon profits. One was the question of profits resulting from the sale of properties by Pergamon. Another was the relationship between Pergamon and a private Maxwell family company. The point was that a significant part of Pergamon's forecasted profits was to come from profits on dealings with the private company,

Maxwell Scientific International, owned by Maxwell and his family. As Leasco saw it, the relationship between Pergamon and M.S.I. was essentially that of 'sale or return' – Pergamon by agreement sold back numbers of journals to M.S.I. at a profit but by the same agreement M.S.I. could require Pergamon to buy back unsold copies. The fact was that on Leasco's reckoning M.S.I. would have £1 million worth of unsold stocks by the end of 1969 which Pergamon could be asked to buy back. The £200,000 worth of profits which Pergamon expected to make in 1969 from its dealings with M.S.I. did not make much financial sense to Leasco.

Secondly, there was the question of International Learning Systems Corporation, a joint company owned by Pergamon and the British Printing Corporation set up to sell encyclopaedias. Leasco was originally led to believe that I.L.S.C. was making pre-tax profits at the rate of £500,000 a year. But when the draft accounts for the company's first eighteen-month trading period appeared on 12 August, it appeared there would be a net loss of around £431,000.

The time for a showdown with Maxwell had come. At a meeting in New York on 14 August, Maxwell agreed that his family should initially be paid only half for their shareholdings – the other half would be paid after Pergamon had met its profit forecasts. The next day, Maxwell astoundingly revoked his offer. Over the next five days there was a frantic series of meetings in London to patch up the differences, ending up in an all-night session at the flat of the ubiquitous Lord Goodman, at which a desperate compromise was hammered out. The compromise was to be short-lived. As Leasco explained, 'nothing had been said at that meeting which allayed their growing concern over the information which they had been given and the soundness of any conclusions which might be reached from it as to the fundamental earning power of Pergamon's business'. The bubble finally burst on 20 August, when Leasco was informed by Pergamon that considerably more of Maxwell's family holdings had been sold to the former than had previously been disclosed. The sales had taken place at the end of July and beginning of August and had been disguised through the use of an intermediary – the shares were sold first to a nominee company and then to Rothschild's acting on behalf of Leasco. The Take-over Panel had not been informed.

For Leasco, this was the last straw. Steinberg called off the whole deal. Over the next few days the whole affair gathered a frenzied momentum. At the Panel's request, the Stock Exchange suspended dealings in Pergamon shares. Recriminations flowed thick and fast. First, Robert Fleming, which had already guided their investment trusts out of Pergamon, abandoned Maxwell. And then Maxwell lost his stockbrokers, Panmure Gordon, which had been brokers to Pergamon Press ever since the company was floated in 1964 – Michael Richardson, the Panmure partner who was most closely associated with Maxwell, had happily joined rival brokers, Cazenove, four months previously.

The Panel was faced with its biggest challenge. The Code stated quite unambiguously that 'if any offeror who has announced his intention to make an offer does not proceed with the formal offer within a reasonable time, he must be prepared to justify the circumstances of the case to the Panel'. And then there was the question of all shareholders having the right to equal treatment – Leasco had already secured thirty-eight per cent of Pergamon shares in the stock market at 36s. a share, so the remaining shareholders should be offered a similar price. The Panel set to work fast. Lord Shawcross cut short his holiday in the Adriatic. All the various participants in the drama were paraded before the Panel to give their version of what had happened. In the early hours of 28 August, the Panel revealed its hand.

A new formula had been agreed by which the bid could be renewed. The bid would be made after a leading firm of chartered accountants had completed a report on Pergamon's profits for 1968 and 1969. The nub of the Panel's lengthy statement centred on the question of whether Pergamon shareholders had been given enough information about their company – the affairs of I.L.S.C. and the dealings between Pergamon and the Maxwell family private companies were at the forefront of their mind. The Panel decided to ask the Board of Trade to institute its own inquiry into this aspect of the affair – effectively admitting that the City's own powers were decidedly limited. Finally, worried about the City's questioning of the ethics behind Fleming's sale of Pergamon shares to Leasco, the Panel set up its own investigation into whether it was appropriate for a merchant bank at the same time to manage investment funds and advise companies in take-over situations. The dangers of what the City calls 'insider trading' could not be ruled out.

The omens for the Panel's bid formula were not good. Within a short time a squabble broke out about how the agreement was to be interpreted. The argument centred on who was to be boss of Pergamon: Maxwell or someone appointed by Leasco. Maxwell meanwhile had appealed against the Panel's findings.

Leasco's position had now hardened to the point that they wanted nothing more to do with Maxwell. Rallying the support of other big shareholders, the so-called 'third force' who were advised by Schroder Wagg, Leasco went on to sack Maxwell from the board of Pergamon at a stormy extraordinary general meeting in October, only paralleled in recent years by the meeting which concluded the *News of the World* battle. 'It began like a political rally,' said *The Times*, 'and ended with the conjuror pulling a surprise rabbit out of the hat.' The conjuror, of course, was Robert Maxwell; the rabbit: another offer, this time from him, for Pergamon shares; it never came.

The Pergamon affair continued to rumble on with occasional climaxes – indeed the shares have still not been requoted and Leasco has still not bid for the remaining Pergamon shares. Maxwell lost his appeal before Lord Pearce whose committee felt that the Panel was well within its brief and did not stray beyond its sphere in referring the affair to the Board of Trade.

The two further shocks were spaced at yearly intervals. The first was the report on Pergamon by the independent accountants appointed to investigate the profit situation – Price

Waterhouse. Their report showed that Pergamon in fact made a loss in 1968 of £495,000 compared with the profit reported to shareholders of £2·1 million. And in the first nine months of 1969, the year when Maxwell was forecasting profits of £2·5 million, there was a loss of nearly £2 million. From the sidelines Maxwell commented: 'Accounting is not the exact science which some of us once thought it was.'

A year later in 1971, the Department of Trade and Industry published its first report on the Pergamon affair, which looked in detail at I.L.S.C. Nor was this any more flattering than the Price Waterhouse report. Maxwell was found to be not 'a person who can be relied on to exercise proper stewardship of a publicly quoted company'. And directors of B.P.C., Pergamon's partner in I.L.S.C., were accused of negligence. Both Maxwell and B.P.C. immediately took legal action to clear their names. There was an irony in the fact that Maxwell had meanwhile reinstated himself on the board of Pergamon – a position from which he showed no sign of wanting to budge in spite of the strictures of the report's authors, Sir Ronald Leach, senior partner of the accountants Peat, Marwick, Mitchell (by the end there seemed to be few leading City accountants not in on the act) and Owen Stable, an eminent company lawyer.

The Pergamon affair has left terrible scars on the City. In the first place, it did little credit to the merchant banking fraternity. The Panel's report on merchant banks and insider trading (Chapter 3) by no means silenced the critics – 'Is all really well in the City of London?' asked *The Times*. Secondly, the effect on the accountancy profession was traumatic. One firm audited accounts showing a £2·1 million profit; another, a £495,000 loss over the same period. Nor was this the only recent piece of evidence to support Maxwell's suggestion that accountancy was no longer such an exact science. During the heat of the G.E.C. battle with A.E.I., the latter had made a profit forecast of £10 million, which later turned into a £4·5 million loss. The Pergamon fiasco was the last straw. The accountancy profession as a whole was jolted sharply into recognizing that some reform of their standards was urgently needed. This has since begun in a desultory sort of way.

As far as the City as a whole was concerned, the Pergamon episode seemed to show that a determined entrepreneur could win friends and support in the City when he was making money. When the danger signals appeared he could quickly find himself isolated.

If the Panel had emerged from the affair in the best light, its victory had been pyrrhic. If Leasco ever mounts a bid for the remaining shares in Pergamon it is almost bound to be at less than the price it paid other shareholders – leaving the principle of equal treatment for all shareholders in tatters. If the shareholders owe anything to the Panel, it is this. One day they may end up getting something for their shares from Leasco. In the meantime, thanks to the Panel, they must be considerably more aware of the affairs of their company than they were.

The Panel's baptism of fire certainly strengthened it and reinforced what appeared to be a tenable framework for law and order in the City. Certainly, no crisis of the order of the Pergamon/Leasco affair has recurred. By 1971, Lord Shawcross was able to look back with a sigh of relief: 'The Panel has been rather less "in the news" during the past year (that following the Pergamon drama): a welcome circumstance, not, as I think, solely attributable to the fact that few major problems have had to be dealt with, but also resulting from a general acceptance of the Panel's activity as part of the normal machinery of the City. Certainly the cooperation of the City community, sometimes in cases with significant financial implications, has continued to be very high.' The last sentence was a guarded reference to the fact that Kleinwort Benson, acting for Nigel Broackes' property and construction group, Trafalgar House, had agreed to stump up cash in a bid for Cementation, a building company – an act of generosity heralded as a triumph for the Panel. Trafalgar had originally offered its own shares and 'paper', but during the course of the bid had bought for cash a key Cementation shareholding from a rival bidder, Bovis. The Panel insisted on cash for all.

It is perhaps a sign of the times in the City that the problems the Panel has faced since the Pergamon/Leasco battle have come not from the grand old City houses which had caused so much trouble earlier. It was the young financial operator who was giving Lord Shawcross, Mr Fraser and their colleagues the headaches.

First a look at the type of creature who had sprung into the Panel's sights. By the first half of 1970, his habits were well enough known to Ian Fraser. 'It is noteworthy,' he wrote, 'that in recent months the bids and deals section of the market has often only been kept alive by the relatively high number of relatively small transactions that have had their origins in asset situations. The last year has seen a heavy crop of new finance companies and young, financially-orientated entrepreneurs entering into this field, in many cases with considerable initial success. It is necessary to use the word "initial" because most of them are still too recent to be able to substantiate the lofty claims which their share prices seem to be stating for them. It will be necessary to cast a retrospective glance in, say, 1975 or 1980, before a more mature judgement can be given. These entrepreneurs, some of them offshoots of established financial undertakings, have developed a remarkable similarity of style, possibly in imitation of a certain notably successful financial entrepreneur who made his debut in the mid-1960s (a reference presumably to Mr Jim Slater). The basic elements are those of a financial conglomerate with interests in unit trusts and investment trusts, property investment and dealing, some commodity trading maybe and perhaps an interest in pop products, leisure or retailing; seldom do these groups become involved in serious manufacturing or anything involving advanced technology. The group, once established, operates very much under the leadership of its founder and has as one of its main objects the unlocking of potentially rich asset situations to the benefit of its members.

'The objects are laudable, just as the methods adopted are fraught with danger from the market regulator's point of view. The London Stock Exchange Daily Official List (listing all shares quoted on the London Stock Exchange and their prices) is still sprinkled with companies whose asset values are twice their share prices and whose boards are themselves not disposed to take any steps to put the assets to more profitable use; the lists of the provincial stock exchanges are even more so. This, of course, was the combination of circumstances which, after ten years of dividend freeze, gave rise to the first asset-inspired take-over bids in the mid-1950s. The operators of those days were prepared to break up the companies they acquired if no better way of realizing the true value showed itself. However, after those first buccaneering days a fashion of greater delicacy prevailed, and acquiring companies voluntarily impeded their freedom by the liberal gift of undertakings "to maintain the business as a going concern" or "not to interfere with the present management of the company" even in cases where there was a crying need for the contrary. The new generation of financial crusaders are, it seems, less encumbered with the social and political inhibitions of their immediate predecessors and make a virtue of a declared policy to concentrate, close down and sell off.'

The preliminaries to this financial chess game,* in which the assets acquired – be they brick factories in the Midlands or asbestos mines in Southern Africa – are moved around like pawns, are fairly straightforward. The first thing to do, quite obviously, is to isolate the target – which is done usually not by exhaustive industrial knowledge but by simply combing through cards produced by Extel, a service providing detailed financial knowledge of all publicly quoted companies. The target is isolated; the share buying must begin. The strength of the financial operators is their share purchasing power. They have a wide range of investment companies, unit trusts, funds which they manage or simply friendly associates, into which the shares of an unsuspecting victim can be almost literally stuffed. This part of the operation is known as 'warehousing'. The law is to a large extent

* Jim Slater, incidentally, is a masterly player at the real game of chess – that played with a board.

on the side of the financial operator. Under the 1967 Companies Act, anyone acquiring ten per cent of a public company must reveal himself within a fortnight and thereafter must announce any changes in his shareholdings.

The new-style financial entrepreneur can neatly side-step this impediment by arranging for each of his dealing vehicles to buy up to 9·9 per cent of the target company. In this way, he is under no obligation to reveal his hand. Nor, if he disguises his share buying with the use of nominee names, need the victim, however diligent, suspect that anything untoward is going on. Only a rise in the victim's share price might give the game away.

Seldom can the financial operator go wrong in this way. By the time he announces a bid for the victim company he and his associates will have built up a substantial shareholding at below the average price of his bid. If his bid succeeds, he will have bought the company for an average of less than the bid price. If it doesn't, he will almost certainly be able to sell out and make a tidy dealing profit – either another bidder will have appeared on the scene or else the victim company will have convinced its shareholders that its own management can do much better than the bidder. From the Panel's point of view, this type of activity drives a coach and horses through the Code's Rule 30: 'No dealings of any kind . . . in the shares of the offeror and offeree companies by any person who is privy to the preliminary take-over or merger discussions or to an intention to make an offer may take place between the time (a) when the initial approach is made or intimated or (b) when there is reason to suppose that an approach or an offer will be made . . .' To which the young entrepreneur argues that he bought the shares initially only as an investment and only later decided to make a bid.

The Panel, representing the traditionally entrenched forces in the City, is probably at its weakest in dealing with the new generation of financial entrepreneur. Many of the financial manipulators have risen to prominence motivated by a strong contempt for the traditional City establishment. To them the Panel is not so much an authority whose voice of censure is to be dreaded but an inconvenient encumbrance which could conceivably be brushed aside if it stood firmly in the way of their ambitions. How the Panel dealt with two errant entrepreneurs in recent years is worth recalling.

> *'Mr David Rowland, it could be said,'* reported *The Times* at the end of 1971, *'has already contributed more than his fair share to stimulating discussion and change on the take-over front this year.'*

David Rowland is in many ways typical of the new breed of financial operator in the City: born in Morden, Surrey, the son of a scrap-metal dealer, he began his apprenticeship in the mysteries of finance at the age of sixteen in a City stock-broking office. By the age of eighteen, his attention was focussed on small-scale property dealing, buying and refurbishing old houses using a surveyor's office, where he worked, as his base. By the time he was twenty-three, the *Sunday Mirror* had already described him as 'a boy from the suburbs who has suddenly and dramatically moved into the big time'. He was the comprehensive school boy who had made good, in spite of being too stupid to pass his G.C.E. exams.

The 'big time' for Rowland was property. By the end of 1968, though still in his early twenties, he had managed to put together a property company which when it was floated in November was valued by eager investor supporters, including the I.C.I. Pension Fund, at around £1·5 million in the stock market. From then on the shares of Fordham, as his company* was called (after his mother's maiden name), were to go for a giddy ride, taking young Rowland well into the millionaire league. By the beginning of February the shares were worth 36s. each, nearly three times the value at which they had been launched. Rowland's confidence seemed to know no bounds. 'The trouble with too many property

* Like so many operations of its kind, it had originally been a dormant 'shell' rubber plantation company, until Rowland moved in.

men,' he was heard to say cockily, 'is they like beautiful buildings.' His mind was already set on acquiring a merchant bank – that almost indispensable vehicle for aspiring young financial operators.

Neither Rowland's public utterances nor his business methods were calculated to endear him to the more staid and established parts of the financial community. By the end of 1969, the voices of his detractors were being heard in no uncertain terms. 'At twenty-four and only a year after bringing his company to the stock market,' said the *Daily Express*, 'David Rowland has generated enough criticism, incredulity and rumour to last a lifetime.' The *Express* accused him of having done deals with 'those from the shadowy fringe of the property world' – and mentioned the names of Rachman and Craddock.

Credibility is vital for the rapid success of an operation such as Rowland was undertaking. Shareholder loyalty is conditional on one thing: that share values increase, and increase rapidly. During the course of 1969, the price of Fordham shares had plunged by almost two-thirds and was below the launching price. Investor loyalty in Rowland was fast waning.

From Rowland's point of view, the frustrations were obvious. The currency, with which he could expand the company by acquisitions, was the 'paper' of Fordham. The lower the share price of Fordham, the more his currency became devalued. By March 1970, Rowland decided he had had enough. In a deal which outraged the City, he sold his own 18½ per cent stake in Fordham for £2·4 million to a namesake's company, International Securities run by Reg Rowland (no relation). The price David Rowland got for his shares was way above the price on the stock market. To add insult to injury, he arranged for the deal to be carried out through a Bahamas-based company, avoiding nearly £1 million worth of U.K. capital gains tax. 'David behaved like a barrow boy,' one stockbroker remarked at the time. The ingenuity of the young man only later came to light when International Securities ridded themselves of their interest in Fordham, making a loss of £1 million on the deal. One of Jim Slater's offshoots, Ralli International, picked up the bits.

Having established himself 'offshore', young Rowland was not one to sit back and enjoy the £2·4 million he had made himself at the expense of his shareholders. In March, after a three-month round the world holiday, 'he intends,' reported the *Observer*, 'to challenge the American millionaire, Mr Bernie Cornfeld, for a slice of the large European investment market'. It all seemed too good to be true. Was there no question of 'once bitten, twice shy'?

Rowland's plans for emulating Cornfeld may have been promptly shelved after the demise of the latter's reign at I.O.S. Nevertheless, his 'skill for sniffing out a profit' and his 'appetite for doing deals' was reportedly not affected. By the beginning of 1971, he had taken up residence in Paris, with a plan to set up an international holding company with multifarious interests and a share quotation in London and New York. He had already bought control of a vehicle in Britain for taking over asset situations – Adepton, a public company which until he acquired it in 1970, simply ran a chain of garages based on Oxford.

Two take-over deals in swift succession brought Rowland headlong into collision with the City authorities. In the first, Rowland had isolated Williams Hudson, a sleepy wharfage and fuel distribution company rich in property and other assets. His first move was to buy one million shares in the company. Next he announced a bid for the company in the currency of Adepton paper, and this he followed with massive purchases of Williams Hudson shares in the stock market, until he had bought effective control of the company. Once he had effectively won the battle, he adjusted his 'paper' offer upwards to flush out those shareholders who had not sold. Williams Hudson hardly had time even to consider Rowland's 'paper' offer, let alone advise its shareholders what to do, by the time Rowland had won control.

The Panel was in a quandary. The Code, after all, said that all shareholders must be treated alike. The 'paper' currency Rowland was using in his bid was not quite as appealing, not to mention rock-sure, as that of, say, I.C.I. Yet many lucky shareholders had been paid in cash for their shares by selling out in the stock market. On the other hand, the Code also said that it was 'undesirable to fetter the market'. The Panel's way out of this predicament was, perhaps inevitably, a compromise. Rowland, it judged, had not broken the rules. But because Adepton was such a young (and presumably unpredictable) company, it had to offer cash to all remaining Williams Hudson shareholders as an alternative to the 'paper' offer. National and Grindlays Bank, the parent company of Adepton's merchant bankers, William Brandt, obligingly stepped in with a £5·3 million loan to finance the cash offer.

Rowland's second brush with the authorities took place in the last two months of the year. This time he had his eye on Venesta, a packaging and timber company run by Ronald Plumley, erstwhile boss of the tobacco group, Carreras. With a chequered profit record, Venesta had attracted a bid from another company called Ozalid. Rowland immediately saw the possibility of a battle developing and bought, through a public company he had acquired earlier in the year called Consolidated Signal, a fourteen per cent stake in Venesta. The seller was the silent financier, Sir Isaac Wolfson, with whom Rowland had struck up something of a financial relationship. Another bidder shortly appeared on the scene in the form of Norcros, a conglomerate company which was staging a comeback after falling from City grace. Rowland was not satisfied with the bids of either Norcros or Ozalid and proceeded to 'protect' his investment by buying control of Venesta in the stock market. Was Rowland frustrating 'a bona fide "offer" '? Were the Venesta shareholders being given equal treatment (Rowland did not bid for the holdings of a sizable minority once he had bought control)? The Panel was again in difficulties. Again it had to admit that Rowland was acting within the rules.

The rules had to be changed. When the Panel published its new Code at the beginning of 1972, the 'Rowland' amendments were two of the most important modifications to the

City charter. One was that anyone who bought fifteen per cent or more of a target company in the twelve months after a bid was required to offer remaining shareholders a cash alternative. The other stipulated that anyone who bought more than forty per cent of the voting rights of a company had to bid for the remainder. The youngster from Morden had run rings round the City authorities.

A Matter for Censure

Titled aristocrats and men with a distinguished record of public service can provide a shining façade of respectability in business life. The unhappy saga of the Norbury Insulation Group is perhaps a case in point. There were three main characters involved in the episode which unfolded in the first half of 1971: the sixth Earl of Norbury, nicknamed 'roly poly' ('At school I was as fat as a tub of lard'), an encyclopaedia salesman turned stockbroker; Sir Edward Beetham, a former Governor of Trinidad and Tobago who had taken to business life in his retirement from public service; and Robert Woods, every story-hungry financial journalist's idea of a whiz-kid.

In October 1969, with the familiar bonfire of publicity that normally accompanies this sort of occasion, Norbury Insulation, through the good services of the long-established merchant bank of Arbuthnot Latham, for the first time offered its shares to the public. The company was essentially the product of one man, Robert Woods, a twenty-seven-year-old who had started it a mere six years previously to supply the chemical and oil industries with insulation for their tortuous hardware.

The Press, like a herd of Gadarene swine, were not slow to make the most of the opportunity offered them. 'There is no company quite like it quoted on the exchange,' said the *Evening Standard* with a touch of unintended irony. The *Observer*'s man described Norbury Insulation as the 'king pin of the fast expanding thermal insulation industry'. Woods was quoted as saying: 'Nothing can stop us. We can only go from strength to strength.' 'In the current year,' the Sunday newspaper continued, 'Woods is expected to show a near 100 per cent leap in pre-tax profits to £180,000, and a return on net capital employed of 120 per cent, statistics that put him among Britain's most successful companies.' Woods at his tender age confessed to realizing £200,000 from the sale of part of his shareholding to the public, while the stock market would be putting a value of a further £1 million on the rest of his holding. With some of his new-found wealth, Woods had bought himself a Rolls-Royce and was planning to celebrate his company's flotation by buying a stud farm ('It's marvellous for impressing our American clients,' he said, referring to his motor car). Woods was the managing director of Norbury Insulation: Sir Edward Beetham the Chairman.

As the public oversubscribed twenty-six times to Norbury Insulation's share offering, the hubris of Woods seemed almost overbearing. 'It's nice to see the City club taking an interest,' he chuckled.

It is fairly predictable that a company which has been given such a rousing welcome to corporate public life as this will before long be heading along the take-over trail. A year after it had gone public, Norbury already had one unsuccessful take-over bid to its credit, and was planning its next manoeuvre. This time it was for a company called Hayeshaw, a Manchester-based building group. On 19 November, Norbury Insulation announced its £740,000 bid for Hayeshaw to the public for the first time. But before that date there had been mysterious goings-on in the market place. Norbury Insulation had decided to make a bid for Hayeshaw a good ten days beforehand. But in the intervening time, Woods, with the help of stockbroker Lord Norbury – it was entirely a coincidence that his name should have been the same as that of the company – decided to capitalize on the advance information he had at his disposal.

Woods' family trusts were held under the name of a Virgin Islands investment company called Wiltshire Investments. Lord Norbury, working for the firm of stockbrokers, Stoop Vigne, was charged with managing the Woods family fortunes in the form of Wiltshire Investments, and during the fortnight up until the take-over bid was made public bought 56,500 Hayeshaw shares (and sold 17,500). Between 30 October and 20 November the price of Hayeshaw shares rose from 4s. to 6s. 3d.

There was more to come. By the middle of December, Woods was intent on withdrawing the bid for Hayeshaw. The Manchester company's results had proved abysmal for the first half of its financial year. Having taken the decision to withdraw the bid (but not having announced the fact) Woods instructed Lord Norbury to sell the entire holding of Wiltshire in Hayeshaw immediately. The same day that his Lordship disposed of the holding, Woods was informed that the Take-over Panel would not countenance Norbury Insulation's withdrawing its bid. The bid was to go on, but meanwhile Woods in desperation told Lord Norbury to have the share sales cancelled and to purchase more Hayeshaw shares on behalf of Wiltshire.

The full extent of Woods' and Lord Norbury's share dealings (which also included substantial purchases of Norbury Insulation's shares) were not fully disclosed until the formal offer document setting out the terms of the bid for Hayeshaw was dispatched by Norbury Insulation's merchant bankers, Arbuthnot Latham. Before then, the game was up. The Stock Exchange carried out its own investigations following market rumours suggesting a leak and the Stock Exchange referred the matter to the Take-over Panel.

It is difficult to say which of the two – Woods or Lord Norbury – emerged from the Panel's report on this unsavoury affair in the more unfavourable light (the other two directors of Norbury Insulation, including Sir Edward Beetham, were found to be innocent by virtue of their ignorance). Both Woods and Norbury should have seen that all the share dealings that took place after 9 November and before the bid was announced took place in a take-over situation and ought therefore never to have been undertaken. The same was true of the dealings that took place around 16 December, when the future of the bid in Woods' mind was in doubt. What is more, both Woods and Lord Norbury had lied to the Panel. At different times, both claimed that the latter had acted independently of the former, whereas in fact Lord Norbury had acted on Woods' instructions. Woods in the view of the Panel was unfit to remain as managing director of the company. He resigned from the board (but was, oddly, reappointed managing director not long afterwards). Lord Norbury's behaviour was reported to the Stock Exchange. He was subsequently banned from dealing on the Stock Exchange for six months: at the same time four partners in his firm, Stoop Vigne, were censured by the Stock Exchange Council.

The Take-over Panel in its report took scrupulous care not to give the impression that the Norbury affair was commonplace in the City. 'It is sometimes thought,' said the Panel's delicately worded report, 'that directors of companies, brokers and others "in the know" have a great advantage over ordinary shareholders because of their inside knowledge and that this enables them to deal secretly in securities to their great personal profit. While it is true that this possibility does sometimes exist, we believe that, in general, advantage is very rarely taken of it. It is, or ought to be, very well known to directors, for the law and ethics of the matter have been constantly publicized and it is axiomatic in the City that inside information must never be used for personal gain.' It seemed more like a pious hope than a statement of fact.

Autonomy or Control

The Take-over Panel, under its new director-general, John Hull, a lawyer who built up Schroder Wagg's corporate finance department, resides symbolically high above the City on the twentieth floor of the new Stock Exchange building. The Panel itself consists of nine City elders – representing the City's principal professional clubs – and two nominees of the Governor, Lord Shawcross and Sir Alexander Johnston, the former head of the Inland Revenue. The Panel's full-time staff runs to five officials, which, as critics have pointed out, is small beer compared with the American S.E.C.'s 1400.

Sitting uneasily on the shoulders of the Panel and its staff are the functions of legislator, judge, jury and policeman.

The voices in favour of statutory controls, for the time being, are few and far between. There seems to be a general consensus that the City is capable of regulating its own affairs. There are, however, those who feel that in the long term the City cannot escape something along the lines of the American S.E.C. David Montagu, the prominent merchant banker, is one. He has argued that once Britain has joined the Common Market, 'the integration of financial markets will mean totally new legislation to eliminate anomalies as between different financial markets. . . . I believe that, in the second half of the twentieth century in this country, there are too many institutions managed by part-time councils instead of by highly qualified technical experts.' Others, including the great City pluralist, Sir Charles Hardie, have argued that the Take-over Panel is too limited in its scope of operations; that it should cover the entire behaviour of companies, not just when they are engaged in take-overs. The Pergamon/Leasco affair provided a strong case for widening the Panel's horizons to cover the entire financial system, by throwing up a whole series of complex issues not exclusively related to the question of the take-over bid.

If the Panel's powers were extended, it is difficult to see how it could be maintained as a voluntary body with no statutory foundation. The Government, through the Department of Trade and Industry, already has the function of supervising the corporate sector. It would be nonsense if the Panel to a large extent duplicated the D.T.I.'s functions. If the Panel's powers were extended, it would clearly have to come closer under the shadow of Whitehall.

Suggestions have been made, not least by Lord Shawcross, that the Panel should have some legal powers. 'There would in some ways,' he has said, 'be an advantage to having legal powers up one's sleeve, but there would be disadvantages as well. Once you have legal powers you also have legal duties and all the paraphernalia of the law is introduced and the informality and flexibility and expedition would be lost to a certain extent. I am not proposing at present that the City Panel should seek legal powers to *subpoena* witnesses or order the production of documents. We have not really been held up by the absence of legal powers so far. I would prefer to wait until we have a case, and perhaps we will, in which we are held up by absence of legal powers. If that happens, the City Take-over Panel will not be pusillanimous about it.'

Lord Shawcross looks enviously at the General Medical Council, a statutory body with the right to question witnesses. The Panel, he feels, could well use this right to elicit information, particularly in investigating share dealings by company directors and insider trading generally.

The fact that the City authorities had to rewrite the Code three times in five years – admittedly, most of the modifications have been minor – underlines the weakness of the Panel's authority. Most of the rules remain vaguely worded, in which possibly lies an advantage. It makes for plenty of gateways for the Panel to avoid having to impose its authority too often. On the other hand, it provides a favourable climate in which the fringe financial operator can flourish.

In the pragmatic environment of the City, it is hardly surprising that no one really cares to think too hard about the unthinkable – how the Panel would cope with another really serious bout of aggression.

'Many thousands of people had suffered misery and loss because of the irresponsible activities of certain so-called brokers and a few unsound companies. The majority of the public had, however, no cause whatsoever for concern because they could rely completely on the security and service unfailingly given by members of the B.I.A. (British Insurance Association) and by Lloyd's.'

Mr Francis Sandilands, Chairman of the B.I.A., 20 January, 1967

8. INSURANCE

Accountability has a particular significance in relation to the insurance industry. Its sheer size alone is enough to raise important questions about the industry's functioning in the economy. Insurance companies dispose of vast sums of money. Giant companies like the Royal, the Prudential, the Commercial Union and the Legal and General, each have more than £1 million worth of premium income a week to invest – in the course of a year the combined premium income of the insurance industry (nearly £5000 million) would be enough to finance several mammoth industrial undertakings from scratch. More than twelve per cent of all vote-carrying shares held in public British companies are controlled by the insurance industry. And that accounts for less than a third of the industry's total assets. The rest is spread far and wide, across property, unquoted companies and fixed interest stocks. In recent years, there has been a marked tendency for the decision-making process, controlling these gargantuan resources, to become more concentrated. No more than five companies account for half the total business in each of the two main sectors of the insurance industry. The decade following 1958 saw no fewer than twenty-four major mergers and take-overs among insurance companies. 1968 was the high point when the Guardian merged with the Royal Exchange, and the Commercial Union swallowed the Northern Employers (itself a merger a few years back between the Northern and the Employers Liability). With concentration on this scale, the dangers of abusing financial power become proportionately greater.

In terms of decision-making power, the insurance industry as an investment agency cannot be seen in isolation. The industry forms part of the complicated investment nexus of the City, alongside the pension funds, the investment and unit trusts and the banks. Add this lot together and one finds an arsenal with financial firepower equivalent to some thirty or forty per cent of the publicly quoted shares of British companies.

The significance of the insurance industry as investors has already been examined in Chapter 2. The other way of looking at the industry is in relation to the service it provides. The industry is conveniently divided into two main sectors: one going under the name 'life' (meaning 'death'); the 'non-life' called 'general'. As there is nothing more certain in life than death, the 'life' sector of the industry with macabre exactitude is usually referred to as assurance, and the big companies in this field, like the Prudential, the Legal and General, the Standard Life and the Guardian Royal Exchange, have the word 'Assurance' in their titles. The only uncertainty in life assurance is the length of time before death, but even this can be predicted with frightening precision by the technicians in this awesomely cold-blooded industry – the actuaries.

The other section of the insurance industry is no less preoccupied with disaster and misfortune. But here the so-called 'risks' are not so much the lives of people as the possibility of accidents – of nuclear power plants blowing up, of giant oil tankers sinking or of motor cars colliding with one another. In life insurance the only uncertainty is 'when': in general insurance, the uncertainty is 'whether'. Another important difference consists in the length of time insurance contracts in the two sectors run for. Life policies go on for as long as the insured is still alive – if they are not surrendered before then, that is: accident policies are renewed annually. This is reflected in the sums of money which insurers in each type of business have at their disposal. The life assurance companies have huge accumulated funds to dispose of because their policyholders get their benefit after years' worth of premium payments. Life assurance is basically a form of savings and in recent years has become a more actively competitive part of the savings industry – it is reckoned to account for around half of the country's entire personal savings (*i.e.* non-Government and non-company).

In 1971, British life companies collected around £1800 million in premiums, but, more significantly, had £14,800 million worth of accumulated funds invested. By contrast, non-life insurers had around £3000 million worth of premiums but less than £3500 worth of funds invested, reflecting the short-term nature of their business.

The dividing line between who conducts which type of business has become increasingly blurred. Many of the big companies, like the Commercial Union, the Royal, the Eagle Star, the Guardian Royal Exchange and the Legal and General, have both life and general insurance businesses, and are known as 'composites'. Companies doing both types of business have to keep the two separate in their balance sheets. In recent years they have done a lot better out of life assurance than accident insurance.

It was largely this reason that recently prompted Lloyd's to abandon its long-practised abstinence from life assurance. With a premium income now exceeding £600 million a year, Lloyd's has long been the biggest entity in the general insurance market, priding itself on its tradition – over 300 years old – the diversity of its business – insuring anything from Marlene Dietrich's legs to North Sea oil rigs and from the possibility of monsters in Loch Ness to jumbo jets – and on its foreign trade – threequarters of its business comes from overseas. Another strong selling point is its unlimited liability. Lloyd's is not a company but a collection of 6000 or more rich individuals (some, thanks to a recent easing of the membership rules, women and foreigners), most of whom are sleeping partners, there for the elasticity of their financial resources (as far as eligibility is concerned, £75,000 is the starting limit for British citizens; £100,000 for foreigners) rather than their insurance know-how. The real work is done by the underwriters grouped into about 260 syndicates. Behind each syndicate are the 'names' or members, each accepting unlimited liability, which in recent years, as the scale of risk-taking has escalated (jumbo jets and 500,000 ton tankers replacing the smaller more conventional aircraft and ships), had become far from a meaningless undertaking – Lloyd's made agonizing losses of over £20 million in the six years 1965 to 1970.

As the liability of Lloyd's is only unlimited in theory as long as the lives of its members, the traditional belief has been that it cannot collectively undertake the long-term business of life-assurance – for some years it has had a comparatively small but thriving short-term assurance business, such as limited length endowment policies. The way round the problem was found by setting up a liability company with members indirectly participating in the new business.

Traumatic is about the most appropriate word to describe the recent history of the insurance industry. As in most of the major traditional sectors of the City, change has tended to be forced on the industry. The industry has been largely responsive to change rather than an agent of change. In such a tradition-bound and rigidly conservative industry as insurance this could not easily have been otherwise.

For evidence of the traumas, one need go little further than the balance sheets of the industry. The agonies of Lloyd's have just been mentioned. The rest of the industry also showed a staggering facility for losing money. In 1972, the British Insurance Association, representing well over ninety per cent of the country's insurance companies, breathed a sigh of relief as it revealed that in 1971 'for the first time since 1967, there was an overall underwriting profit, albeit only minimal, on fire, accident and motor classes of £124 million, or approximately 0·6 per cent of premiums'. Motor insurance had proved the heaviest loss maker – B.I.A. members mismanaged their affairs in this sector to the extent of losing £130 million in the four years 1968 to 1971. Since 1951, no fewer than twenty car insurance companies have gone bust, with a total of more than two million motorists on their books at the moment of failure.

These agonies have been emphasized by the difficulties which the industry has found in adapting itself to change. For years the blood has been hardening in its organizational arteries. The result has been a general insensitivity to the changing environment within which the industry found itself having to operate.

The industry's attitudes had long become ossified, brittle and inflexible because of a number of factors. In the first place, most of the conventional insurers shared the dogmatic belief that there is something intrinsically different between running an insurance business and running any other form of business. The power was therefore firmly entrusted into the hands of the technicians – the underwriters and the actuaries. And it was clearly in the interests of these men to preserve the distinction for as long as possible. So when the firm of American management consultants, McKinsey, were called in the mid-1960s by the B.I.A. to recommend a programme of action for improving motor insurance, some of their most important recommendations – the abolition of the 'knock-for-knock' agreement for claims above £100 and of the 'no claims' bonus – were never implemented.

The other important factor which tended to ossify attitudes in the industry was the almost total absence of real competition in major sectors of the industry. In this respect, insurance has shared the same stultifying influence of other important sectors of the City. The two most notorious manifestations of this have been the Accident Offices' Association and the Fire Offices' Committee, two cartels fixing minimum premium rates in motor and fire insurance respectively. Only one survives – the Fire Offices' Committee* and in a somewhat modified form (it no longer applies to household fire insur-

* It is to be disbanded following a ruling by the Monopolies Commission that it operates against the public interest.

ance). The A.O.A. collapsed in 1968 under the pressure of competition from non-tariff insurers when ten of its largest members asked for the agreement to be abandoned. Nevertheless, over half a century's lack of effective competition had left its mark in terms of inflexibility of attitudes.

The forces that have dictated change to the insurance industry have been about as diverse as they have been numerous. The single most dominant agent of change has been the competitive challenge which the old-established insurers have found themselves increasingly having to face. In motor insurance, this has consisted of the rush of new companies entering the market – many of which, as we have seen, have since disappeared. This had the twin effects of causing the abandonment of the cartel and the cutting of rates to suicidal levels. In life assurance, the competition has largely come from the unit trust movement. The success of the unit trust movement has been largely based in the last fifteen years or so on a trick in life assurance, whose significance in commercial terms the slumbering giants of the industry had long failed to realize. The trick was simply this: the bulk of a life assurance policy is essentially an investment and not insurance cover: link life assurance in the most overt way possible with that great 'inflation-proof' investment medium, the equity, and, hey presto, one of the great business success stories of our time is born. Alan Parker of *The Economist* has explained the phenomenon. 'In its essence the equity-linked policy was no different from any other sort of policy. What it had really done was to expose the economics of the life office to public view. It was like a sort of clock with sides made of glass. You could see how it worked. And this new insight allowed you to infer much of how ordinary clocks worked too. Thus for the first time would-be policyholders could see that over ninety per cent of the premium on a typical with-profits endowment policy represented the investment element in the premium, while no more than ten per cent constituted the cost of cover against dying before the end of the term. In other words the typical endowment policy was overwhelmingly an investment contract.'

The more commercially agile unit trust groups were able to run rings round the established insurers. Variations on the theme have included linking life assurance to property instead of equities. The success of the whole movement can be gauged from the success of South African born Mark Weinberg. In less than a decade he built up from scratch one of the leading unit-linked assurance companies, Abbey Life. In 1970, he left to form another similar company, Hambro Life, which within a short time was already bringing in as much business as Weinberg's former company at the time. Predictably, the insurance industry's traditional heavyweights, like the 'Pru' and the Equity and Law, followed suit and started their own unit trust linked policies.

Another major uncontrollable force which has confronted insurers has been the rapidly escalating size of risks. The scale of industrial technology has in recent years far outstripped the insurance industry's expectations. Jets have become jumbo, marine tankers more and more super, and individual operating units in industry far larger. Inflation too has had its effect on magnifying the sort of liabilities insurers have been faced with.

These factors, combined with some shattering disasters – like the American hurricanes and race riots and the sinking of some of the first supertankers – have caused the industry deep concern about whether it has enough capacity to go on taking on these sort of risks: its business, in terms of premiums, has grown far faster than its capital. This has caused particular headaches at Lloyd's, which because of its unlimited liability does not have the same access to capital markets as the insurance companies. In effect, the only way for Lloyd's to become larger and to extend its capacity is to acquire new members. But as it was losing money heavily during the latter half of the 1960s finding new members was not easy. In 1968, Lloyd's asked Lord Cromer to look into the whole question of future capital requirements and the organization of the insurance centre. Cromer came up with a scheme for increasing Lloyd's capacity by an extra £100 million worth of premium income a year. None of the Cromer proposals individually was epoch-making. His committee played on the side of caution on the most controversial issue: whether Lloyd's should abandon its unlimited liability. The combined effect of the Cromer Committee's proposals, the decisions to admit foreigners and women, and the more favourable business climate has been to add more than 1000 new members over the last four years.

No less important are the changes that have gradually begun to manifest themselves in the way the industry is organized. Traditionally, insurance companies have been organized on fairly feudal lines. Like the clearing banks, they have preserved a separation of powers and responsibilities between the 'gentlemen and the players'. Their boards of directors have been distinguished more by the number of City pluralists and titled aristocrats than by their insurance expertise. The hardened professionals – most of them insurance men since leaving school – with their baffling conglomeration of titles such as chief general manager, assistant deputy general manager or chief assistant general manager, have increasingly become, like their banking counterparts, the people who effectively control the levers of power. Once the managerial hierarchy peters out, there are left the legions of clerks – more than 200,000 of them – which represent the engine room of the insurance machine. There was a time when insurance provided an attractive career for school-leavers – the pay was good by comparison with other comparable forms of employment and it was a solid respectable thing to be in. Over the years, these advantages have been progressively eroded.

Faced with ever more exiguous returns on their insurance business, the companies have increasingly turned their attention to saving costs by reorganizing the whole pattern of work in their vast processing departments. Consultants, stop-watch in hand, were brought in to assess what was needed and make their recommendations – which inevitably meant fewer men and women. More dramatic has been the introduction of computers, replacing masses of paperwork (and not a few jobs) with their spools, tapes and punch cards. The nature of work has been fundamentally changed.

It was into this situation that stepped the fiery Welsh democrat, Mr Clive Jenkins, secretary of the Association of Scientific,

Technical and Managerial Staffs. Denouncing the insurance companies as occupying 'skyscrapers about to be depopulated by the twin pestilences of the computer and the consultant' and with an advertising campaign proclaiming 'My tragedy was that I picked up a pen instead of a shovel', Mr Jenkins systematically set about extending his and his union's influence in the insurance industry.

Jenkins' first big success was the biggest insurance bastion of them all: the 'Pru', where in 1970 the staff associations voted to join A.S.T.M.S. A few months later, the Union of Insurance Staffs, with its modest 15,000 membership, voted to amalgamate with A.S.T.M.S. The white collar trade union movement in the insurance industry had begun in earnest. Not everything has been plain sailing for the A.S.T.M.S. evangelists. Some of the staff associations in the industry – which found themselves more sympathetic with the feudal conservatism of the insurance companies than with Mr Jenkins' new brand of militancy – have put up a strong fight to keep out A.S.T.M.S. The Commercial Union and the Guardian Royal Exchange have proved particularly tough nuts to crack. After two years of hard battling, Jenkins' hot gospel won over 45,000 converts to A.S.T.M.S.

This has been the framework within which change has taken place in the insurance industry in recent years. The industry has essentially been the victim of change: rather than the vehicle of change.

Throughout this period, hanging like menacing stormclouds over the industry has been the critical question of accountability. Who is really responsible for the affairs of the insurance industry? The fact of the matter is that the industry lies at the interstices between the public and private sectors. The industry, of course, is part of the private sector. That is for sure, although the Labour Party has tentatively committed itself in opposition to bringing the industry under state ownership. But insurance is subject to Government scrutiny and regulation far beyond that which almost all other private sector industries are. The reasons are quite clear. The services which the industry provides are vital to the community at large. In the case of motor insurance, they are not only vital but legally necessary – 'third party' insurance has been a statutory requirement since the Road Traffic Act of 1930. In relation to the economy, insurance not only acts as an enormous channel through which personal savings flow: it also makes a substantial contribution to the balance of payments. To an unusual extent, the industry has been built up on the confidence and credibility it has generated. The San Francisco earthquake of 1906, when all the British insurers paid up and the Americans failed to, lies deep in the mythology of British insurance. But confidence and credibility tend to be fragile. Once the credibility of one part is called into question, the credibility of the whole tends to come under suspicion.

This is the philosophy of Governmental control. The burning questions are how much control is needed: and who should exercise it. These are not questions to which the City likes to address its collective self too openly. Self-policing is generally preferred to outside regulation. When the Vehicle and General Insurance Company crashed in March 1971, leaving its 800,000 policy-holders uninsured and losing its shareholders and policyholders up to £20 million, these questions could hardly be avoided.

The rise and fall of Vehicle and General is essentially the story of how three men came to challenge the conservative institutionalism of the insurance industry and failed. Numerous insurance companies failed before they did: one or two have done so since. The drama of V and G consists in the heights which the company attained in the insurance world, and, therefore, the depths to which it plummeted. At one time, it was the second biggest motor insurer in the country, with roughly ten per cent of the motoring public on its books. More significantly, it became the first member of the British Insurance Association to fail.

The story began in the early 1960s with a restless entrepreneur, Reggie Burr, who had made around £80,000 running his own spaghetti and macaroni factory in Oldham. Manufacturing tends to have less attractions than financial services for the aspiring millionaire. Burr was no exception. At roughly the same time, he selected the two corporate launching pads which were to send him and his colleagues into the City's stratosphere. The first was Liverpool and County Discount, the company whose name was later changed to First Finsbury Trust and which later became a unit trust, insurance broking, property and financial wheeling and dealing outfit. The other was Vehicle and General, a tiny Liverpool company insuring bicycles.

At first, Burr and his accountant friend, Laurie Kershaw, with whom he had teamed up, were going to turn V and G into an investment trust – the company had a useful £100,000 share portfolio and a quotation on the Liverpool stock exchange. But it was another friend, Tony Hunt, who concentrated their thinking in another direction. Hunt claimed to be an insurance expert. He had previously been associated with an American insurance group, which shortly after he left it collapsed and whose U.K. activities were later investigated by the Board of Trade. The two other young turks were not to know that.

Hunt's idea quite simply was to convert V and G into a motor insurance business. His formula was deceptively simple. It was to base premiums on the experience and claims record of the motorist. This involved paying huge 'no claims' bonuses – as much as fifty per cent of the premium after four years without a claim – and refusing to collaborate in the 'knock-for-knock' agreement by which each insurer paid the claims of its own client motorists. By doing this, Hunt hoped to attract only above average motorists. All risks above £2500 were to be laid off. Insurance brokers were offered well above average commissions to bring in business for V and G.

With this package the V and G triumvirate were to confront the full might of the established motor insurance cartel, which competed not on premiums but on service and advertising. And for a few glorious years it really looked as if it was working. The formula had an explosive effect on V and G's business. Premiums went ahead in leaps and bounds: from

£300,000 in 1961 to £800,000 in 1962, to £1·4 million in 1963, to £2·1 million in 1964, to £2·7 million in 1965, to £4·1 million in 1966, to £11·4 million in 1967, £11·8 million in 1968, and £11·7 million in 1969. Shareholders in the company were buoyed along by its apparent successes. By 1964, a share stake in the company was worth more than ten times its original value in 1961. At one stage, the shares were so high that their yield was less than one per cent.

The giddy rise of V and G was watched with more than a detached interest in two important quarters: the Board of Trade and the British Insurance Association. The Board of Trade (now merged into the Department of Trade and Industry) has a particular interest in the affairs of insurance companies, stemming from a succession of Acts of Parliament, whose essential philosophy was best summarized by Sir Stafford Cripps, a former President of the Board of Trade. The object of the legislature, he explained, was 'to ensure the maintenance of an adequate standard of solvency with the minimum of outside control' by introducing 'standards of overall solvency with which insurers must comply'. Legislation over the last twenty-five years has tended to be more or less in line with this philosophy. Insurance companies have been required to lodge financial data about their affairs regularly with the Board of Trade, solvency has been more closely defined, and the Government has been given greater powers to intervene in a suspect company. The 'minimum of outside control' could hardly be said to have been increased to oppressive levels.

The B.I.A. has also long had an interest in the good health of its members – it has around 290 members which do about ninety-five per cent of the world-wide business of British insurance companies. The affairs of all new members of the Association are supposedly subjected to the most rigorous scrutiny. And the Association in general has prided itself on the high standards of its members. In the latter half of the 1960s, when cut-price insurers (who were not members of the B.I.A.) were collapsing like ill-prepared soufflés, the Association embarked on an advertising and public relations programme with the slogan: 'Get the strength of the insurance companies around you.' At the beginning of 1967, shortly after the failure of two non-member companies, the Association announced that 'motorists have been strongly warned by the B.I.A. to insure with members of the B.I.A. or Lloyd's'.

Right from the start, V and G was suspect in the eyes of the Board of Trade and the B.I.A. The trouble was that the solvency requirements of the Board of Trade could be interpreted in a fairly elastic way. Officially, the assets of an insurance company have to exceed its liabilities by more than ten per cent of its premium income. The difficulty arises over how one defines assets and liability. From the outset, V and G decided to use about the least conservative definition conceivable. Huge lumps of 'goodwill' and shares in associated companies loomed large in the V and G balance sheet. In 1963, for example, the company had an official solvency margin, expressed in its balance sheet, of £730,000. But nearly £450,000 of this represented 'goodwill' and shares in its associated company, Liverpool and County Discount. Both of these assets would have been difficult to realize suddenly if the need arose. On the other side of the balance sheet there was the question of providing for claims. All motor insurance companies have outstanding claims at the end of their financial years, and these claims have to be provided for in the balance sheet. All the evidence pointed to V and G not setting enough aside for future claims. What in effect the company was doing was living off its premium income and paying out a substantial part of its claims from the huge increases in its premiums – an age-old recipe for disaster.

The irony of the V and G saga is that the faster the company grew, the unsafer it became: yet the larger it became, the more difficult it was for the Government to stop it. It was one thing to crush the odd handful of insurance minnows. The second biggest motor insurer was quite another thing. By 1966, the Board of Trade had more or less missed its chance. Though there were ample grounds later for calling a halt to V and G, the cautious civil servants in the Board of Trade were not prepared to chance their arm and stage a full-scale confrontation with all the publicity that would have implied.

In the early years of the company's growth, there was no shortage of eyebrow-raising. Back in May 1964, concern about the company percolated through to the Secretary of State at the Board of Trade, Edward Heath, but nothing was done. A few months later, Thomas Smeddles, a persistent critic of V and G, wrote on behalf of the B.I.A. to the Board of Trade setting out his own gloomy analysis of the company. In the following year, the Board of Trade commissioned a study of V and G from Cooper Brothers, the accountants. All this pointed towards the shakiness of the company. But the Board of Trade preferred to accept the explanation of the insurance maverick, Tony Hunt. Hunt argued that V and G was a special case. It insured predominantly good risks, it reinsured everything over £2500, it paid its claims promptly, and its high 'no claims' bonuses encouraged its clients to pay for small claims out of their own pockets.

Hunt's arguments evidently carried some conviction. But if there was any reason for fear on the part of the civil servants it seemed to be cleared up in November 1966, when V and G was admitted into the lap of the establishment, the B.I.A. The B.I.A. was not altogether happy about allowing this unorthodox intruder into its membership. But, as Francis Sandilands of the Commercial Union and chairman of the B.I.A. at the time, concluded: 'While there is no doubt that the company were at one time sailing pretty near the wind, there now appears to be a genuine desire to go "respectable".' He reckoned that V and G were better in the B.I.A. than out. And the company had just received a fresh injection of capital from an American insurance group.

In 1967, the ground-rules governing the Board of Trade's regulation of the insurance industry shifted significantly. The 1967 Companies Act for the first time gave civil servants powers to take action against the possible *future* insolvency of an insurance company. Previously, they could only act if they had 'substantial' doubts about the *current* insolvency of an insurance company.

Admission to the B.I.A. had no moderating influence on the way V and G ran its business. Nearly £4 million was splashed out on acquiring two insurance companies. When the motor insurance cartel was abandoned, the company, against the advice of some of its experts, decided to cut its premiums at a time when inflation was progressively swelling the size of individual claims and should have dictated a rise in premiums. In the memorable words of the Government-appointed Tribunal, set up to investigate the V and G saga after the crash, 'The company was conducting its affairs with the panache and imprudence of a gambler, and with a risk of future insolvency if the gamble did not succeed'.

Opinion among the civil servants was divided between the injudicious caution of the doves and the unprevaricating attitudes of the hawks. Among the latter was Mr H. H. Knight, an insurance senior executive officer in the Board of Trade, who said he 'would not insure a cat, let alone a car, with the company'. In spite of its newly acquired powers and in spite of anxious representations by leaders of the B.I.A., the Board of Trade failed to act. The civil servants repeatedly asked for information from the company which was either inadequate or not forthcoming.

By the summer of 1970, the V and G story was beginning its sudden and dramatic crescendo. The precarious financial structure of the company had begun to totter. Losses on its underwriting were bigger than the profits on its share dealings, its solvency margin was dangerously insubstantial and the company had resorted to the outrageous course of borrowing money from its life assurance companies to make good its liquidity problems. In November, a confrontation was staged between Kershaw and Burr, their solicitor, and a team of civil servants at the Department of Trade and Industry – Hunt had resigned from V and G at this stage on the grounds of ill health: a move hardly calculated to inspire confidence in the company. The V and G directors told the civil servants that steps were being taken to improve the company's financial

15

health – including selling off two subsidiaries. At the same time, they let off a smoke bomb which neatly clouded the issue. To the civil servants' astonishment they revealed that secret information about V and G had been leaked from the Department. The effect was to delay any action on the part of the Department for another three months. At the end of February, V and G was given notice by the Department that it would be stopped trading. A few days later, the B.I.A. dispatched Cooper Brothers to carry out an urgent review of the company. It took Cooper Brothers only a weekend's work to discover that V and G was 'irretrievably insolvent'. On 1 March, V and G declared itself insolvent – it had lost £10 million in fourteen months.

The immediate aftermath of the V and G collapse had all the ingredients of a tragi-comedy. The B.I.A. was at pains to conceal its embarrassment about the whole affair. 'We have made a mistake,' admitted its chairman, Kenneth Bevins of the Royal. 'Our public relations has been too effective. Our campaign, "Get the strength of the insurance companies around you", has given some people the wrong impression.'

In the same breath, he announced that there would be 'no general rescue' of V and G policyholders – only a fund of last resort to help passengers injured in crashes while being driven by V and G policyholders. Third party liability claims were to be met through the insurance industry's collective emergency fund, the Motor Insurers' Bureau. There was to be no compensation for anyone who had lost his premium.

The Government's predicament was no less awkward. Within a few weeks, the leak of information from the Department of Trade and Industry was public knowledge. Into this aspect of the affair the Prime Minister ordered a judicial inquiry under Sir Arthur James, the High Court Judge distinguished among other things for his prosecution of the Great Train Robbers. Three other inquiries were mounted into various aspects of the V and G affair.

The Tribunal's enquiry, which was widened to include not only the leak but also the question of misconduct and negligence on the part of civil servants or Ministers and whether shareholders or policyholders of V and G had suffered from 'impropriety, negligence or misconduct found to have occurred', sat for fifty-six days and delivered its report early in 1971. A scapegoat was found in the hapless Christopher Jardine, the Under Secretary of the Department of Trade and Industry in charge of the insurance division; an unfortunate photo-copier in the Department, Mrs Rose Norgan, was found guilty of misconduct; and that was about the extent of the blame laid. Neither the Department nor any Minister was held 'liable for any loss suffered by any policyholder or shareholder of the Company or any other company in the group, or by any member of the public'. It is worth adding that V and G's merchant bankers, Keyser Ullmann, carried out some deft manoeuvres in the shares of V and G for their investment clients. But they too were exonerated from any impropriety.

The Tribunal's findings left the really critical questions unanswered. Some of these issues were posed in the report itself. 'Is the staff of the Insurance Branch of the Department adequate in numbers, training, qualifications and capacity to deal with the work with which it is charged?' There were 'large, fundamental and controversial' problems, said the Tribunal, 'concerning the relationship between the Department on the one hand and the insurance industry on the other hand'. Should the Department alone supervise the insurance industry? Or should supervision be the role of a joint organization composed of civil servants and executives from the insurance industry?

Since the Tribunal's report was published, the B.I.A. has more or less discarded the notion of collective responsibility. Its chairman, Kenneth Bevins, has told the Association's members that 'effective supervision can only be exercised by a body that has the ultimate power over the ability of a company to trade. It is only with such power that effective investigation, and hence effective supervision, can be exercised. It follows that without any such supervision any voluntary system of mutual guarantees is quite impracticable. ... We take no pleasure in having come to these conclusions for had it been practicable to have concluded otherwise this might have been preferable to the imposition of more onerous legislation. We would, however, be deceiving ourselves to imagine that self-supervision is a practical proposition for the industry.' Once bitten twice shy.

As it turned out, the Government took up the running. In 1973, it introduced an Insurance Companies Bill giving Whitehall virtually unlimited powers to intervene in the insurance industry.

9. HOW TO MAKE A MILLION OUT OF THE CITY

Mr Oliver Jessel has, by his own admission, suffered from a 'terrible contortion' in his life. Of all the contortions people tend to have in their lives, Mr Jessel's one must be among the least common. 'I've always been financially independent,' he goes on to explain. 'It is a terrible thing to inherit a lot of money. It confuses the young terribly. But it is something that happened – it cannot be helped – and I have to live it down as best I can.'

Jessel has played a vitally important part in the City phenomenon which has become more and more pronounced over the last fifteen years – the emergence of young financial entrepreneurs. Jessel's significance is important for two reasons. In the first place, he has been at the game rather longer than almost all his contemporaries – he antedates Jim Slater by several years (Jessel had already established himself with a sizable financial empire before Slater left Leyland for the pursuit of greater pleasures, not to mention riches, in the City). Secondly, he has coached a number of other operators, the most notable being Mr Christopher Selmes, who in different ways have sought to emulate the achievements of their mentor. He is said to foster 'financial talent in young people with almost paternal pride'.

On the face of it, Jessel, now in his early forties, is untypical of his generation of financial peers. He not only started off in life with a very large inheritance – to his great embarrassment; he also happens to have come from the heart of the City establishment. One of his great-grandfathers (on his mother's side) was Marcus Samuel, the founder of Shell and M. Samuel, the merchant bank which later merged to form Hill Samuel. Today his family connections extend into the financial, commercial and political communities of the country. One cousin is David Montagu of merchant bankers Samuel Montagu; another heads the discount house Jessel Toynbee. His brother, Toby, is a Conservative member of Parliament.

Whether or not all this really was a serious handicap, the fact remains that Oliver Jessel is now at the head of a company, Jessel Securities, controlling assets worth over £400 million, and making profits of more than £6·2 million a year. The company is sprawled across a wide variety of industries from unit trust management and insurance to sugar plantations, engineering and shipping.

Jessel started off his business life in a modest enough way – insofar as any rich man can have modest beginnings. 'I am an absolutely hopeless case really,' he says in a moment of typical false modesty. 'I passed a few Bar exams, got married (his wife, Gloria, until recently was a director of Jessel Securities), got fed up with law and decided to go into business on my own account.' Jessel first tried his hand at running a chain of grocery shops, but by the time he was twenty-seven got bored – his mind was already focused on the richer pastures of the City. 'I simply wanted at that time to get started in the City running investment portfolios and so on, which has continued to be an absorbing interest of mine.'

Jessel's rise to prominence in the City was not the result of any blinding vision of a rich, hitherto unexploited business idea. 'I was one of the people crawling out of the chrysalis at this stage (the late 1950s) who simply didn't believe that the sort of thing that has happened in recent years was possible. I must say that anything like the present sequence of events was completely beyond my contemplation.'

Jessel's early business beginnings have been described as 'deplorably dilettante'. He started in the City, investing part of his family's not inconsiderable fortunes and buying up 'shell' companies – neglected businesses which had quotations on the stock markets but whose share values did not reflect the true value of the companies. One 'shell' owned tea estates in Ceylon; another, an asbestos mine in Rhodesia; another, a greyhound stadium in Salford, Manchester, where Jessel now lands his helicopter on visits to his northern satrapies. There were six in all.

The key to Jessel's career has always been the stock market. In 1960 when he first opened an office in the City (as his entry in *Who's Who* baldly states), the stock market was riding high. There were a number of related circumstances at work. In the first place, the economy was gathering momentum as the controls imposed upon it during the war and sustained by the first post-war Labour Government were progressively lifted. The Macmillan Government had been returned to power after the Suez fiasco with the pledge to maximize economic growth. As far as companies and their share prices were concerned, there were two important long-term factors. One was the dismantling of dividend restraint. For part of the post-war period, companies had been restricted in the amount of profits they could pay to their shareholders in the form of dividends. And as it was the dividend which largely determined a share price, the values of many companies in the stock market were artificially low. The second thing was inflation. This particularly affected property values, which had increased rather faster than the cost of living generally. The fact was that many companies had a large proportion of their assets in the form of land and property which they were valuing in their balance sheets at, or not much more than, the cost at which those assets had been bought, probably thirty or forty years previously. The opportunities for the astute financial operator were manifest. Charles

Clore, in particular, had mastered the technique of exploiting 'asset situations' with devastating success. His only really major failure had been his bid for brewers Watney Mann in the late 1950s.

Young Jessel had watched the activities of Clore and other take-over practitioners with an eagle eye. 'The build-up of asset situations,' says Jessel, 'started in 1935 and went on till 1955 without any interruption. I think companies got into a rut. Dividend restraint was only a minor factor. The main thing was that the idea of getting a return on their assets wasn't in people's minds. They were all concerned with rationing and taxation and wartime conditions.'

The first investment delicacy Oliver Jessel served up to the public at large was an investment trust whose *raison d'être* was trading in the shares of newly quoted companies. 'I had an idea in 1961,' he explains, 'to form a company to invest in new issues. Everyone said it would just be a "public stag". We called it New Issue Permanent, an investment trust with £100,000 issued capital. We had an appalling job to find the money but we just about managed to find it between us all. Then it was reported in the Press. I was amazed nobody said it was a fraud. On the contrary, one was treated as a celebrity straight away.'

Meanwhile, Jessel had become attracted by the idea of wider share-ownership, a movement which gathered pace in the City about this time and on which the development of unit trusts was based. Jessel talked of causing 'equity investment to stretch its tentacles to the weekly wage-earner, who has so far resisted all overtures from Throgmorton Street'. It was a philanthropic justification for an activity which had other attractions for the financial operator than introducing the delicacies of the stock market to the man in the street. Not long after New Issue Permanent had been launched, Jessel introduced a unit trust with much the same sort of investment brief.

Looking back on his City career, Jessel now considers that he was 'sidetracked' through building up his unit trusts (even though his company now looks after unit trusts valued at over

£40 million). The real heart of the action was to be in developing and exploiting asset situations. Jessel has set about this task with an almost missionary zeal. 'There is no doubt,' he says, 'that this is the only way we can liberate our national capital resources. What is deplorable is that so much of the country's resources is stuck in these frightful old companies of which we see hundreds here.' And like a Borstal head discussing his juvenile delinquents, he adds: 'We just reorganize as many as we can. But we can't, of course, scratch the surface of them.'

'Such companies,' he has told his shareholders, 'commonplace in industry, shipping and commodities, have normally been built up to a position of strength by one or two people, now long dead. Few companies succeed in developing management which survives and expands through slumps and wars. The majority of long-established public companies, in which much of our national wealth reposes, are drifting respectably out of the industrial revolution into the common market era with no true understanding of corporate development. If they are 'lame ducks' (a significantly latter-day Tory phrase), a wheel-chair usually exists in the form of rising property values, which disguises, often for many years, the futile nature of large parts of the companies' efforts. ...' Jessel, like many of his financial peers, justifies what he is doing not only in terms of the benefit he is doing for himself and his shareholders, but also in terms of the good he is doing the country.

By the middle of the 1960s, Jessel was already a financial operator of some substance in the City, but his company lacked assets. In 1966, for every share in Jessel Securities whose nominal value was 25p, there was only 39p worth of assets: but by 1971 assets per share had climbed to 175p. Jessel evolved a comparatively simple trick for buying in assets.

It worked like this. At around that time the shares of his investment trusts were standing at well below their real asset value: that is, the value of the shares in their investment portfolios. Jessel arranged for the master company, Jessel

Securities, to buy up in the stock market the shares of the investment trusts and these in turn were buying companies whose share prices were below their real asset values. 'We decided to go back to first principles,' says Jessel. 'We collected in our own investment trusts. We bought, for example, New Issue Permanent at 3s. – their assets were 6s. – and they in turn were buying France Fenwick (the insurance broking and shipping group which Jessel Securities eventually acquired) at 7s. 6d. when their assets were 15s. So you got a quadrupling effect in the asset value. We were buying in the investment trusts and the investment trusts were buying asset situations.' It was in effect no more complicated than buying pound notes with couples of half-crowns.

Jessel's ruthless logic is never slow to show itself once asset-rich companies are under his control. Anything not earning its proper return is seldom spared the axe. In a couple of hectic years, he took over France Fenwick; Demerara, a sugar company; Stevinson Hardy, a shipping and oil merchanting outfit; and Falks, the lighting and gas cooker manufacturer. All in all, he paid £19·4 million for this quartet, and was able quickly to realise £8 million by selling off properties and businesses within these companies. Some of Jessel's descriptions of how his companies are reorganized (to use the euphemism) read like notes of a corporate undertaker. 'It was evident that Switchgear & Equipment Ltd. had limited prospects, and it has now been sold for £770,000. . . . The wholesale lighting division was placed in voluntary liquidation . . . the New Zealand subsidiary was making losses and its assets have been sold for approximately £100,000.' On a more constructive vein, there are regroupings. Bits of one company are removed and added to bits of another. No wonder the name of Jessel is to be dreaded in the industrial backwaters of the country. One company on learning that Jessel had bought a significant amount of its shares doubled its dividend and issued more shares to encourage Jessel to sell out his shares at a profit. Jessel's take-over bid for Staveley, the ailing machine tool giant, caused a similar rumpus.

Not surprisingly, Jessel's belief in the stock market as being the best method for distributing the wealth of the country is almost supreme. 'The rationale of this group,' he says, 'is its quoted investment base. Everything here is quoted (on the stock market), or can be quoted. Practically everything we buy as an investment is through the stock market.' The main quoted associates, Leeds Assets (involved in heavy engineering), Richard Johnson and Nephew (wire manufacture) and Eastern Produce (commodities), orbit round the master company like satellites. Each satellite is encouraged to make its own acquisitions and through its share quotation to offer its managers incentive schemes based on cut price share offers. 'It is impossible to exaggerate the importance of having one foot in the City and one in industry,' says Jessel. 'Introducing the services of the City to industry' is how he euphemistically describes his activities; that includes, among other things, descending on inefficient companies 'like an avenging angel'.

'It is essential that we should inflate share prices,' says Jessel. 'That is what people cannot understand. Otherwise you cannot issue more shares. And if you cannot issue more shares you cannot raise money for expansion.' This simplistic view of capitalism is based on two fallacies. One is that companies rely on the stock market predominantly for finance. They don't. Secondly, it assumes that the stock market is the best mechanism for distributing the wealth of the country. It isn't. It completely ignores the majority of social and economic values. The value of a company on the stock market can, and often does, have very little relation to the intrinsic value of that business. Stock market values only reflect the opinions of a comparatively small, and not always the best informed, group of people.

Oliver Jessel has always been something of an outsider in the City. He has never enjoyed the continued popularity of Jim Slater, with whom he is almost inevitably compared in the City.* One reason for this may be that Slater has tended to be more open in his dealings with the Press than Jessel. Some

* This is reflected in the way the stock market has rated the two companies.

critics have described Jessel Securities as a conglomerate lacking in rationale. Others remember the embarrassing moment in 1966 when one of his fellow directors, David Shaw, was named by the Stock Exchange in the bond-washing scandal – Jessel, himself, denied any involvement in the affair and Shaw left the board of Jessel Securities as a result (though he stayed on as a director of Constellation Investments, the former Jessel satellite which provides a tax avoidance service for show business people).

'The Press are rarely kind to him,' said the *Investor's Review*. 'The gossip that appears in the columns and is repeated in the wine bars has always been that he is lucky. He is accused of not producing increased earnings per share. He is accused of warehousing in his unit trust portfolios shares of companies he will later bid for (with some justification, one should add).'

Jessel also suffers from the image of being a one-man band. Critics make the suggestion that Jessel Securities has made the transition from an entrepreneurial outfit to a sizable corporation while Jessel himself still supervises too wide a range and depth of detail: that his lieutenants, most of them still not much older than thirty, could not carry the load if their master was tomorrow run over by a bus. Jessel naturally has no doubts about the qualities of his underlings. 'I have no personal ambitions for myself any more,' he says. 'I am only carrying on building up through force of habit and for the benefit of the younger generation here who are a magnificent crowd.'

Oliver Jessel has already made well over £1 million for himself and his family. Where does he go from here? 'Making money,' he says, 'is not my principal objective: it never has been. If I simply came in here to make money, I would be very much better off than I am. My principal objective is simply to build up a first-class share.' City opinion is divided on how far he has to go to achieve that ambition.

*

Hardly a month went by without Mr John Bentley buying or selling bits, or the whole, of a company. In three hectic years, he converted a tiny, 150-year-old, Brighton-based firm of wholesale chemists into one of the biggest European toy manufacturers, the largest U.K. force in outdoor advertising and one of the country's leading pharmaceutical wholesaling businesses. The almost forgotten business of Barclay & Sons, earning in 1968 profits before tax of £63,000, became Barclay Securities, a company whose profits by 1971 had increased more than twenty times, whose turnover had risen by more than eight times and whose earnings per share had gone up more than three times. In the process, Bentley had made himself a millionaire two and a half times over.

Bentley had many things in common with the new breed of financial entrepreneurs. Youth was one of them. Still in his early thirties, he had an obsessive belief that beyond the age of forty-five there is not much left for the businessman except the golf-course or the crematorium. 'One of the things we need in Britain,' he was once quoted as saying, 'is a generally accepted salary structure by which your earnings rise from twenty to thirty-five, then stay on a plateau until you're forty-five, and then gradually decline until retirement. This would encourage initiative earlier and achieve maximum earnings for the average executive when he most needs it, to educate and have his children and so on. . . .' 'I really haven't got anything against age,' he told me, 'except that I believe that people in their thirties have the right degree of energy and dynamism, aggressiveness and a certain amount of built-in caution. I think that's a pretty good balance.'

He also shared many of his financial peers' contempt for parts of the traditional City establishment. In his early days, stockbrokers and merchant banks did not respond favourably to the ideas for making money he brought to them. His lack of respect for traditional tycoonery was thinly disguised. 'When I was nineteen or twenty, tycoons were all men of fifty to sixty puffing large cigars. People thought that they had to live for forty years in order to acquire the ability to become a tycoon.' Not young Bentley.

If John Bentley owed his success to anyone but himself, it was to Jim Slater, whom Bentley describes as 'a business friend, a personal friend and a very good person to have around'.* 'The best thing Jim ever did for me,' he says, 'was to give me confidence in my age. I've an enormous admiration for him. I think he's doing a fantastic thing for British industry – just the fact that he exists frightens people into action. He's the best thing to happen to British industry in decades really.'

The relationship between Bentley and Slater went back to 1965. Before that, Bentley had savoured employment in some of the traditional quarters of the City without any real enthusiasm. He had left Harrow at the age of seventeen with a relatively modest income from a family trust and what he regards as a radical attitude towards the *status quo*. Public school radicalism being what it is, he entered Throgmorton Street to serve an apprenticeship in a firm of City stockbrokers – first as a messenger boy, then an arbitrage clerk, and, finally, an investment analyst. This was not enough to satisfy Bentley's energies, and after a short spell he set off to Australia, returning after fifteen months, with more capital than he took with him, to join another firm of London stockbrokers. Again he felt frustrated and within three years decided to move on. 'I stopped working for people when I was twenty-three. I can't work for people any more. I hate working for people. I just don't have the temperament for it.'

Bentley's early days as a lone entrepreneur were spent dabbling in small businesses – a launderette here, and a property or two there. But his heart was nearer the stock market. By this time, he had a pretty good insight into the tricks of the financial operators' trade. He knew about asset situations and had identified not a few of them, having thumbed through Extel cards during his brief and unhappy career in stock-

* Relations between the two were never all that plain sailing. Bentley was reportedly not a little upset when Slater attempted to reduce his shareholding in Barclay Securities, and thus induced a sellers' raid on Barclay shares.

broking. 'I'd been hawking deals around the City for a long time,' he explains. 'I was in and out of merchant banks. I met Jim in 1965 when I was twenty-five. I took this one deal to him and it worked out very well. So I then did another joint deal with him a few months later which again worked out very well. I did another one and that worked out immensely well.' Bentley claimed to have given Slater the biggest deal the latter had done up to that point of time. It was a Scottish life insurance company capitalized in the stock market at less than £5 million and with funds of over £40 million, which Bentley had located through his meticulous searches. The two buccaneers bought a large slice of the company's shares, the company got involved in a take-over battle with two rival bidders, and Bentley and Slater, smiling on the sidelines, sold their shares at just about double what they paid for them.

After this Slater adopted Bentley as a free-lance henchman to sort out companies in which they both took investments – Newman Holdings, a shoe manufacturer, was one; Barrow Hepburn and Gale, a firm of tanners, was another. All the time, Bentley was building up enough capital resources to get himself on to the corporate launching pad. The break finally came. 'I had lunch with Jim one day,' he explains. It was at the time when Slater was fast trying to rid his company of its conglomerate image. Conglomerates had had an appalling ride on Wall Street and Slater saw the same thing happening in Britain. He therefore set out to convert Slater Walker from a hotchpotch industrial holding company into an investment bank, providing finance and advice to client companies, many of which the master company was to continue to have an interest in. He did so by acquiring from Sir Isaac Wolfson the Ralli Brothers banking house. Concealed in the web of Ralli when he took it over was the tiny independently quoted concern, Barclay & Sons.

At lunch, Slater asked Bentley what he was proposing to do with himself. 'I said that I was going to go round the world or something. So he said: "You must do some work; come and work at Slater's." It was something I had always refused to do.' Slater then offered him the chance to buy Barclay, but

Bentley again refused. After the lunch, says Bentley, 'he rang again and said: "It would give you something to do."' Bentley explained why he decided to take it. 'I had looked at all sorts of rubber plantation companies and had not been attracted at all. I'd looked at quite a lot really. Barclay was a good size and I liked what it was in. I liked the pharmaceutical distribution industry because of its liquidity and because of its spread of customers.' Bentley agreed to buy half of Ralli's sixty per cent stake in Barclay. Slater, through his various interests, still controls around thirty per cent of Barclay.

Bentley's business philosophy contained the familiar theme of patriotism. 'It's quite obvious, the theory of what we're doing here. It is to release half the cash, half the assets and half the number of people employed. If you put them into a new factory in a new industry with money to back them and retrain them, then theoretically you'd double the gross national product. It must be doing a useful thing. It must be good that we are getting rid of outmoded, old-fashioned management. It must be good that we're releasing assets which don't have a worth unless they're used the way that we use them.' But he added significantly: 'We're not in business just from a patriotic viewpoint.'

From the discreet opulence of Barclay's London headquarters in Curzon Street, Bentley and his team of young accountants, lawyers and investment analysts set the sights on the next take-over target – sifting through balance sheets, keeping an eagle eye on the stock market, tracking down properties and waiting for the right moment to jump. Anything up to 100 different industries at a time were being combed through to see if they would throw up the right candidates.

Bentley tended to take on single industries, rather than companies, at a time. They had to fit a certain pattern. That meant, he explained, an industry 'must be fragmented and outmoded in the way it conducts its affairs. It must have family-type management, and under-utilized and undervalued assets.' He steered clear of anything involving a lot of technology and disliked industries where there were big risks resulting from large contracts. Toys, outdoor advertising and pharmaceutical wholesaling all fitted the pattern nicely.

Once the take-over victims had been safely taken into the fold, the treatment was fairly straightforward. Sometimes an acquisition was made to see if the industrial blueprint sketched out in Curzon Street was the right one. Among Bentley's earlier acquisitions were a retail jewellery business and a West Country department store company. Neither proved satisfactory and were promptly disposed of. Those that remained within the fold went through three phases of Bentley treatment.

The first was the familiar ritual of instant rationalization; or asset stripping, to use the less delicate term. Properties were sold off, and, in some cases, leased back again – the 'sale and leaseback' formula is a popular device of the financial operator. Stock levels were reduced, whole bits of businesses were sold off, and, inevitably, heads rolled. The second phase consisted of finding other companies to buy to slot in with the companies already under Barclay control. By combining like with like, big savings could be made, particularly in purchasing.

In one of his pharmaceutical businesses, Bentley was able to increase profits by fifty per cent simply by trimming $1\frac{1}{2}$ per cent off all purchases – a statistical quirk possible in a business with low profit margins and high turnover. Profits were doubled in one of the toy businesses by shrewder, and more centralized, buying tactics. Finally, in the third stage, new management ideas were introduced. New products were developed to fit in alongside existing ones. New services were added to the existing range. This was the creative act.

Not surprisingly, Bentley's calculated industrial blueprints did not receive universal support. In 1971, he stormed the advertising industry like a bull in a china shop and left a wake of unpopularity behind him. Through the kind services of Slater, he laid his hands on Dorland, a sleepy advertising agency which for years had paid more attention to servicing clients and conjuring up slogans than to making money. No sooner had Bentley laid his hands on Dorland for £2·3 million than four of its subsidiaries plus a range of properties were sold off at a profit before the Dorland management could say 'Madison Avenue'. It was no way to win friends in the advertising industry.

Bentley has one or two firm inhibitions about making money. The second mortgage business – lending money to old age pensioners at interest rates of thirty-five per cent, as he calls it, and inertia selling, are two industries he feels he would like to keep out of. 'It's very difficult to moralize as a businessman,' he says, 'because all businesses are tricking somebody more than he can trick you. That's a cynical comment, but it is what it boils down to – tricking them to the extent that you're asking for a higher price for your product. The cleverer you are at it the more successful you are as a businessman.'

Bentley's ambitions seemed to know no bounds. He had been reported as saying that if Barclay's growth continued at its present rate it would be 'bigger than I.C.I. well before another decade were up'. Before then, he hoped to float off parts of his empire into separately quoted companies, creating, if you like, satellites of a satellite. Mr Bentley's laws of corporate astronomy were hardly given time to be put to the test. In 1973, Barclay Securities was taken over by J. H. Vavasseur, another wheeler-dealing company, and Bentley left the company. A case of the stripper stripped.

Percy – invariably known as 'Pat' – Matthews is a man of several parts. He is president of Aston Villa Football Club, whose financial fortunes he revived in the late 1960s. He is an honorary fellow of St Peter's College, Oxford, which has a building named after and financed by him. He owns a brass foundry (for sculptors) near Basingstoke and a nine-hole golf course which he created on his Thames-side estate near Henley. But in the City, he has one manifestation, and one manifestation only; as deputy chairman, managing director and leading light of First National Finance Corporation. As such, he is at the head of a financial empire which extends across merchant banking, property and hire purchase and whose shares are valued in the stock market at over £100 million. Of this no less than £8·5 million belong to Matthews himself and his family.

Pat Matthews has risen to financial glory in the City in a matter of fifteen years or so against all the odds. In almost every sense of the word, he is an outsider. He is the son of a Polish/Jewish immigrant, who had been a furniture worker in the East End of London. He never went to a public school – he ended his schooldays, in fact, at the age of fourteen. His mind never turned towards the City until the comparatively ripe age of thirty-six. And when it did, he chose a route which had never earned anyone much respect among, let alone admission to, the traditional heights of the City – hire purchase. 'I liked fighting,' he says, 'I liked going slightly outside the conventional forms of business.' 'I enjoy a challenge,' he adds, 'I like creating operations and situations.'

Matthews started off in life in the aircraft industry as a jig and tool draughtsman for de Havilland at Hatfield near where his family were living. He stayed there during the whole course of the war, working on the production of Mosquito planes and ending up as a planning engineer. 'I learned a great many things about production,' he says, 'labour relations and being associated with big company technology and big company techniques. I learned about the political asides that go on in a big company, the structure of a big company and how a big company thinks, if it ever does think.'

But being attached to an industrial juggernaut was not the life for him. In 1964, he decided to join his father in recreating the furniture business which the latter had been running in a small way before the war. 'I wanted to apply the same techniques,' he says, 'which I had been applying as a planning engineer at de Havilland.' So for fourteen years, he, his father and his brother developed an antique reproduction furniture business which, according to Matthews, eventually became one of the biggest of its kind in Europe.

Even this had its limitations for Pat Matthews. By 1957, his father wanted to retire and his brother was not quite sure what he wanted to do. This was the cue to change. The Matthews family furniture business was sold for £150,000. Pat Matthews stayed on as an employee of its new owners. But for such a restless entrepreneur as he, this was no future. 'Their methods of doing business,' he says, 'were not compatible with mine.' When he quit the furniture trade he personally had around £150,000, a little more than his share of what the family business was sold for.

Pat Matthews claims he never made a conscious decision to enter the City. He simply moved progressively nearer it once he had left behind him the furniture trade. The first step was an office in Holborn, which he rented at 30s. a week from his solicitor. From there he set about collecting a rag-bag of small businesses. 'I went a little erratic,' he explains. 'I started and bought a string of small businesses in eighteen months.' He started a company running a chain of do-it-yourself shops in the City called 'The House that Jack Built'. There was a bicycle company, a perambulator business and a wholesaling firm. Then there were tankers for delivering paraffin. When he moved to an office in Moorgate, he says, 'I was in the City unconsciously with a series of industrial companies. I didn't even know what the City was. I was going to be an industrialist and build the companies up.'

Matthews' knowledge of how the City worked was understandably sketchy. It was to the Lord Mayor of London, Sir Seymour Howard, a stockbroker, that he looked for advice. His advice was that Matthews should divide his fortune into three parts: putting a third into equities; a third into gilt-edged securities; and another third into the business. On the strength of the securities, Matthews raised a loan from one of the big clearing banks of £300,000 which he sunk into his business, at that time called Smasons Associated Companies (after the company's telegraphic address).

Matthews' first involvement in the hire purchase business was in a small enough way. One of his paraffin lorry drivers told him that he could sell a lot of paraffin heaters and that he could sell even more if he provided credit terms as well.

Matthews was attracted by the idea but found the going tough at first.

'We started supplying credit for small domestic units, including oil heaters,' he explains, 'and then expanded into motor vehicles and plant and machinery financing. That's where the trouble started because we didn't have enough money. It was all out for longer periods of time. The cash flow was all up a gum tree. There I was, sitting in Moorgate with various companies, with a £300,000 overdraft and £150,000 of my own money – with a family to provide for and money going out of the back door like nobody's business in hire purchase. The time had come for a reappraisal.'

What Matthews decided he needed was a rich partner to finance him. He started looking for a wealthy businessman and ended up with a bank. His association with the Ionian Bank, at the time a tiny, recently revamped merchant bank, came about through a complicated personal introduction and really set Matthews on his feet. 'They were thirsty for a client,' he says, 'and I was thirsty for a bank.'

The Ionian Bank lent Matthews £1 million and at the same time took a twenty-five per cent share stake in his master company. Now at last he was on the launching pad. 'It was then that I took a conscious decision,' he explains, 'of really going into the hire purchase business in a big way, and I bought a small hire purchase company. I said to my partners: "I'm going to sell everything other than the hire purchase company. Do you mind?" And they replied: "Do what you like." So I did. I made money on some and lost money on others. I eventually came out making £50,000 profits.'

So Matthews' attention was concentrated on the 'never never' business at a time when hire purchase restrictions were being released. But although he was dealing in fairly small items – never more than £30 each – he found that the company's appetite for money was almost insatiable. The Ionian Bank lent him another £1 million and took another large chunk – this time twenty-four per cent – of the shares of the company. On top of this, another clearing bank, through an associated company, lent a further £1½ million.

By this stage, Matthews' financially tuned mind was scanning across a horizon wider than that of hire purchase. Through his ties with the Ionian Bank he had developed an interest, not to say flair, for merchant banking and property dealing. 'They handed me all sorts of things,' he says, 'industrial companies, property companies. And they asked me what I thought of this and that. I had always been interested in property because I had never made a bad acquisition when I was in the furniture business. Privately, I worked on one or two things on the basis that I got a small percentage of the equity. There was no capital gains tax in those days. So it was pretty easy to make money. I did this apart from running my own business.' Separate though these other activities were, some of them had their side-effects on the hire purchase business. Through one property venture, Matthews came into contact with Jocelyn Hambro. 'Jocelyn liked me and I liked him. He said: "What about putting up some money for your Smasons thing?" So Hambros Bank lent me £1 million and took an option on ten per cent of the shares of the company exercisable fourteen days either side of a flotation.' On the strength of this, Matthews bought himself another hire purchase company – the Berkshire Finance Company, which had run into trouble.

By 1960, Pat Matthews had become concerned about having too many of his business eggs concentrated in one basket – hire purchase. Around that time there had been a number of frauds in the hire purchase industry and these reflected ill even on the more respectable names in the business. Matthews decided he wanted to become a money-lender, so went to a lawyer friend, Morris Finer, to discuss how he should set about it. 'I'd like to lend money, I told him, but I don't want to operate through a money-lender's licence (which involves all sorts of red tape and scrutiny by the authorities). So he said: "Why don't you buy yourself a bank?" I put an advertisement in the paper saying: "Gentleman in the hire purchase business would like to buy a bank."'

Before long, a firm of chartered accountants had helped him out of his difficulties. They had a client which had a banking subsidiary called Cassel Arenz for sale. Matthews paid £40,000 for it. There was £30,000 in cash in the kitty, so in effect he acquired it for £10,000 net.

'So I had two hire purchase companies and a bank,' he explains. 'I didn't know how to run a bank, so the Ionian Bank provided me with two bankers. They went on the board along with myself. To build up the current accounts of the bank I had to get all my friends to open accounts with a few pounds. A bank must have 200 accounts to have bank status. The bank was really just a name with 200 of my friends as depositors.'

Meanwhile, Matthews' relations with the Ionian Bank were reaching a climactic point. Around 1961, the Ionian Bank had acquired a substantial shareholding in the Birmingham Railway Carriage and Wagon Company, an ailing rolling stock manufacturer based in Smethwick. Under the chairmanship of Sir Bernard Docker, it was losing money at the rate of £300,000 a year. But more important, it owned fifty-seven acres of land in the heart of the industrial Midlands. There were 54s. worth of assets for every share in the company which was valued at 17s. in the stock market. It was a plum ripe for any financial operator to pick.

The Ionian Bank had built a share stake of thirty per cent in Birmingham Railway Carriage and Wagon and by 1961 prepared to launch an attack on its incompetent management. It commissioned Cooper Brothers, the chartered accountants, to make a report on the company and their findings turned out to be a solid indictment of the company's management. The management was persuaded to hand over control and Pat Matthews, with the promise of ten per cent of the Ionian Bank's share of the profits in the company, was sent in to help sort it out. It was eventually decided to shut the industrial operations down and to sack all the men (some 7500 in all). The company was run down to the point where it virtually had cash of £1·5 million and a very large vacant property of fifty-seven acres.

Birmingham Railway Carriage and Wagon had become a shell company. The question was, what to do with it. Here, opinion was divided. Ionian and Hambros Banks wanted to inject Pat Matthews' three companies into it. The chairman of the company wanted to make it into an industrial holding company. Negotiations between all the parties concerned were getting nowhere when Matthews decided to take himself off to the South of France for a holiday. 'I went away on 1 August,' he says, 'and on 3 August they said to me: "Come back; the deal is on." I said "No. If you want to sign up, you come out here." They came and signed in the South of France on my dining-room table.'

The deal effectively made Matthews' hire purchase and banking businesses into a public company. Ionian Bank ended up with forty-four per cent of it; Hambros Bank with six per cent; and Matthews himself with sixteen per cent. The name of the company was soon changed to the American-sounding First National Finance Corporation – a television programme gave Matthews the inspiration. But it was not a situation with which Matthews was happy to live.

The Ionian Bank came to be a sword of Damocles hanging over the company. The problem was that the dominant holding of the Ionian Bank was too large a percentage of the company for comfort – any time the Ionian Bank could have unloaded its share with disastrous effect on the company's share price. Matthews realized that the only thing to do was to persuade the Ionian Bank to dispose of the majority of their shares. They agreed to do this, provided it could be done at a suitable price and fairly rapidly. Matthews went straight round to Jocelyn Hambro and with his assistance, together with that of Joseph Sebag, arrangements were lined up to place most of these shares, within a matter of hours, with a variety of institutions. Hambros and Phoenix Assurance emerged as the main shareholders.

Nothing is more likely to arouse the hostility of the City establishment than a successful outsider. Pat Matthews was no exception. He has had no shortage of detractors who have been prepared to write him off as an overnight success story. In 1969, First National launched a £29 million take-over bid for Bowmaker, one of the established hire purchase giants. The bid aroused furious resentment in the City. Bowmaker's chairman, Sir John Cowley, claimed that Matthews had discussed a merger on a previous occasion and had made an assurance that he would not make a take-over bid for Bowmaker. Matthews replied that his assurance no longer held good because circumstances had changed. As it turned out, Bowmaker flopped into the arms of a favoured suitor, the equally established City company, C. T. Bowring.

Pat Matthews seems to have taken the hostility of the City establishment more to heart than have many other new financial entrepreneurs. 'Once I knew what the City was about,' he says, 'I wanted to be part of it, not outside. I don't like being a maverick.' Matthews' desire to conform has had many manifestations.

In the first place, it is significant that the chairman of First National Finance Corporation is Lord De L'Isle, a former Governor of Australia. Secondly, Matthews has made strenuous efforts to attract institutional investors to become shareholders of his company – the hallmark of respectability in the City. F.N.F.C. shareholders include several of the biggest insurance companies and pension funds in the country. Some of them acquired shares in F.N.F.C. as a result of a deal of amazing ingenuity which Matthews engineered when his company took over (and promptly sold again) the financial rump of Charles Gordon's ailing empire, Spey Investments (see Chapter 2). Shares in F.N.F.C. were issued to Gordon's institutional backers in exchange for three banking businesses which had been acquired by Gordon at inflated prices. Thirdly, Matthews himself is a director of Phoenix Assurance, one of the country's largest insurance companies – a distinction, which, as he points out, has not been bestowed on most of the other new breed of financial entrepreneurs in the City. Finally, F.N.F.C. has been awarded the full status of a bank* by the Department of Trade and Indus-

* The only legal definition of a British bank is laughably that of 'a body of persons . . . who carry on the business of banking' or 'any person *bona fide* carrying on the business of banking'. Official recognition as a bank by the authorities, however, does carry with it certain privileges and exemptions under the law.

try – an accolade not lightly given to financial newcomers.

'Today,' says Matthews, 'I like to play the game. I've always played the game. But I like to play the game their way – maybe in a better way – but I still like playing the game the right way.'

First National Finance Corporation is substantially similar to many of the other financial empires in the City built up over the last decade or so. It buys and sells property, an activity for which in the recent property boom the company has been harshly criticized (to Matthews' dismay); it launches businesses on the stock market; it lends money; and it builds up shareholdings in companies cheaply and sells them off later more expensively. Under the last group of activities, F.N.F.C. has bought its way into a bizarre range of businesses from a crematorium and a mint in Birmingham to the publishers of Mrs Beeton.

Matthews rewards his employees with generous share incentive schemes and hopes they will stay with his company. He has not always been successful. Like Jim Slater and Oliver Jessel, he has a reputation for providing a nursery and training ground for aspiring financial operators. Once the doors of the temple of Mammon are opened to them, young entrepreneurs usually prefer to run their own activities. Christopher Selmes, the millionaire in his late twenties, was one of Matthews' protégés.

Matthews is still, ironically, striving towards further acceptance in the City. He remains excessively sensitive when criticisms are made of him and his financial activities. The fact of the matter is that he remains, to an important extent, an outsider in the City. As for the future, he says, 'I'd like to build up a very interesting company that would be there for many years to come, a solidly based financial institution in the City of London which keeps its word and plays the game with a very straight bat.'

EPILOGUE

The power, or potential power, of the City has increased, is increasing, and will almost certainly continue to increase. This power has a variety of manifestations, just as the City itself is no single homogeneous entity In money terms, the power lies in the mammoth investment resources which are controlled from within the City. These resources have increased in recent years, both absolutely and proportionately. The most recent survey of the Department of Applied Economics at Cambridge University shows that the percentage of shares held by private individuals, their executors and trustees fell between 1957 and 1960 from 65·8 to 47·4 per cent. Investment institutions in all their various forms now account for over half the shares of quoted U.K. companies – a stake in money terms worth something approaching £20,000 million.

At the same time, the control of this money power, or potential power, has tended to become more concentrated as the institutional forces which wield it have become more concentrated. Fewer institutional investors account for a larger proportion of investing power, as insurance companies and investment trusts have become more concentrated, as large industrial companies have merged and in the same process pooled their pension funds, and as unit trusts have proliferated to channel the savings of small investors.

In recent years, the potential power – expressed in terms of the voting rights which an equity stake in a company carries with it – has tended to be translated more and more into real power. Institutional investors have become concerned about 'making their investments work'. It has become established dogma in the City that investors should exert their proprietorial influence on the managements of companies in which their vast funds repose. The Governor of the Bank of England has discreetly talked of 'improving the means whereby institutional investors can collaborate with industrial management to secure increased efficiency', and in 1972 set up a working party to look at the problem.

The power structure in the City, of course, is not confined to the investing institutions. The mammoth bodies, in which such a huge proportion of the country's wealth lies, confer indirectly a succession of powers on other parts of the City nexus. The merchant banks, for example, have an enormous influence which is almost wholly vicarious. They have powers quite disproportionate to their economic significance – as entrepreneurs or go-betweens: intermediaries between the providers of capital and those in need of it. The destinies of many giant industrial companies have at some stage been largely determined by the pressures of merchant bankers. What would P & O's future be without the guiding hand of Lord Poole of Lazard's? Where Bowater's without Hill Samuel's Mr Robert Clark and Mr Jim Slater? Merchant bankers, in short, can make industrial things happen, and on a giant scale, even though they themselves may not directly command the means with which to do so.

The means can usually be found. Investment banking is an euphemistic cloak for a peculiarly brutish form of activity which has become prominent in the City in recent years. It effectively means deploying the bullying power that can be used with a sizable equity stake in a company to force that company, often against the will of its own management, into merging with another company, disposing of its assets or some other major departure from its normal course of action. Mr Peter Parker, chairman of Rockware Group, an industrial company which at one stage became the object of financial wheeler-dealing, has adequately summarized this form of activity. 'There are some merger manoeuvres,' he said, 'nothing to do with industrial logic, which must leave a bitter taste in the mouths of many whose livelihoods are literally at stake. The manipulation of shareholdings, a deft and often devious disregard of codes, and then the raid for the control of a company and its assets – this is not attractive to the industrial community with a growing sense of its social standards and values which are under challenge. . . . The jiggery poker playing of some wheeler-dealing could develop a dangerous sense of alienation at a time when industry is trying with painful self-restraints to grapple with the concept of public interest as a central social responsibility.'

What safeguards are there that this mammoth power is not abused? As members of a democratic society have the British public not assigned to the City the privilege of immunity – an immunity which no other power structure in the country of any comparable size enjoys? In a democratic system, power must at some stage engender commensurate responsibility.

There are two fundamental questions which must be asked of the City. Does the City collectively or individually exercise its responsibilities in a way that could be reasonably expected of such a vast power structure in a democratic society? And is there adequate machinery built into the City's whole organizational structure to ensure satisfactory accountability? The answer to both questions must surely be 'no'.

It is difficult to escape the conclusion that the City interprets its responsibilities in the narrowest sense. The name of the game for bankers and institutional investors is maximizing the financial efficiency of the funds at their disposal. Profits are profits. Social consciences do not belong in the City. The Church of England cannot have won themselves much admiration from the hard-core institutional investor when they decided to sell their shares in Rio Tinto-Zinc because they disagreed with RT-Z's policies in southern Africa. The ethical investor, who puts his money where his conscience is, is an eccentric creature in the City. Yet asset strippers, closing down factories with apparent scant regard for their employees, are idolized within the Square Mile. There are a few people who see a new social consciousness emerging in the City at some stage. Lord Seebohm of Barclays Bank, which incidentally ran into deep political waters over its support for the Cabora Bassa dam in Portuguese East Africa, is one. 'I believe that in the future,' he said, 'the City as a whole would be wise to study the problem of the direction of investment in the light of the overall social and economic long-term needs of the country. In particular, I do not see how financial advisers, and the major financial institutions and funds, can ignore entirely the social consequences of making available capital (which is always a scarce commodity) for purposes that may have in the long term an adverse effect on the environment or on society.'

The machinery, such as it exists, for making the City accountable is plainly inadequate. Government control is *de minimis*. And there is little, if any, independence in the mechanisms within the City – they exist essentially to preserve and sustain the City's self-confidence and self-respect. In regulating the securities market, the Take-over Panel suffers from manifest inadequacies. It covers only a limited area of the securities market – the realm of take-overs and mergers – and it has no legal or statutory powers to support it. Even its chairman, Lord Shawcross, has admitted the Panel's shortcomings. Commenting on the Panel's promised tougher action on insider trading (share deals based on privileged information for personal gain), he confessed that 'there is no fully effective machinery for identifying suspicious deals' and added that he could not 'help feeling . . . that we sometimes catch the smaller fry whilst the big fish get away'. The London Stock Exchange and the professional clubs, representing the forces of institutional investment, are weak companions to the Panel in trying to establish order and equity in share markets. In its regulation of the insurance industry, the British

Insurance Association has amply displayed its inadequacies over the failure of Vehicle and General.

What is self-evidently needed is a powerful single body, bringing together many of the diffuse responsibilities of the professional clubs, with strong, independent, highly paid membership (qualified lawyers and accountants) and statutory powers to back them up. Without such a body, there will always be bolt holes for the perpetrators of skulduggery to hide in: investors will always be able to disguise their misdemeanours behind nominee holding companies; and secrecy generally will always be preferred to openness as a style of life in the City.

As industry begins to view its responsibilities in a much wider perspective, the City becomes increasingly isolated. It is a tragedy that in a democratic society so much power resides in the hands of individuals with such myopic vision.

BIBLIOGRAPHY

MAGAZINES AND NEWSPAPERS

Financial Times, The Times, The Economist, Investor's Chronicle, Investors Review, Money Management, Observer, Sunday Times, The Banker, Investment Analyst, Euromoney.

GOVERNMENT AND OFFICIAL PUBLICATIONS

Committee on the working of the monetary system (Radcliffe Report), published by H.M.S.O.

Report of the Company Law Committee (Jenkins Report), published by H.M.S.O.

Report of the Tribunal appointed to inquire into certain issues in relation to the circumstances leading up to the cessation of trading by the Vehicle and General Insurance Company Limited (James Tribunal Report), published by H.M.S.O.

First report from the Select Committee on nationalized industries, session 1969–70, Bank of England, published by H.M.S.O.

Consumer Credit, report of the committee under Lord Crowther, published by H.M.S.O.

Report of the Tribunal appointed to inquire into allegations of improper disclosure of information relating to the raising of Bank Rate (Parker Tribunal Report), published by H.M.S.O.

Bank Charges, Report Number 34 of the National Board for Prices and Incomes, published by H.M.S.O.

Barclays Bank Ltd, Lloyds Bank Ltd and Martins Bank Ltd, a report on the proposed merger by the Monopolies Commission, published by H.M.S.O.

Bank of England Quarterly Bulletin.

BOOKS

An Economic Study of the City of London by the Economists Advisory Group, published by George Allen and Unwin Ltd.

Accounting Principles and the City Code, by Edward Stamp and Christopher Marley, published by Butterworth & Co. Ltd.

The City in the World Economy, by William M. Clarke, published by Penguin Books Ltd.

The City, by Paul Ferris, published by Penguin Books Ltd.

Men and Money, by Paul Ferris, published by Hutchinson Ltd.

The Merchant Bankers, by Joseph Wechsberg, published by Weidenfeld & Nicolson Ltd.

The New Anatomy of Britain, by Anthony Sampson, published by Hodder and Stoughton Ltd.

British Insurance, by G. Clayton, published by Elek Books Ltd.

The London Clearing Banks, by Edward Nevin and E. W. Davis, published by Elek Books Ltd.

Investment and Unit Trusts in Britain and America, by D. C. Horner and H. Burton, published by Elek Books Ltd.

A Banker's World, edited by Richard Fry, published by Hutchinson Ltd.

Montagu Norman, by Andrew Boyle, published by Cassell & Co Ltd.

The Management of Unit Trusts, by Oliver Stutchbury, published by Thomas Skinner & Co Ltd.

After the V. & G. Crash, by Ronald Beale, published by City Press and Compton Press.

The Multinationals, by Christopher Tugendhat, published by Eyre & Spottiswoode Ltd.

The Stock Exchange and Investment Analysis, by R. J. Briston, published by George Allen and Unwin Ltd.

Strictly Personal, by Cecil King, published by Weidenfeld & Nicolson Ltd.

Management and Merger Activity, by Gerald D. Newbould, published by Guthstead.

Takeovers and Mergers, by M. A. Weinberg and M. V. Blank and A. L. Greystroke, published by Sweet & Maxwell Ltd.

The Establishment, edited by Hugh Thomas, published by Anthony Blond Ltd.

Anatomy of a Merger, by Robert Jones and Oliver Marriott, published by Jonathan Cape Ltd.

INDEX

Abbey Life Assurance, 209
Aberdare Holdings, 174
Accepting Houses Committee, 64–5, 75, 92
Accident Office's Association, 207
Adepton, 195
Advertising, 22, 96
A.E.I., 48–9, 168, 118
Alcoa, 69
Allen, Sir Douglas, 143
Allen, Harvey and Ross, 160, 163
'Aluminium War', 69–70, 171, 176, 177
American banks in London, 83–101
American Securities and Exchange Commission (S.E.C.), 169, 174, 200
American Tobacco, 178–9, 183
Anatomy of a Merger (Jones and Marriott), 63
Anglo-Scottish Tea Investment Trust, 35
Ansbacher's, 82
Arbuthnot Latham, 65, 132, 197, 199
Armstrong Whitworth, 153
Associated Commercial Vehicles, 13
Association of Chart and Technical Analysts, 43
Association of Investment Trust Companies, 52–4, 170
Association of Scientific, Technical and Managerial Staffs (A.S.T.M.S.), 210–211
Association of Unit Trust Managers, 52, 170
Astaire, Edgar, 172
Aston Martin, 129
Austin (E. J.) and E. J. Austin International, 35–9

Bagehot, Walter, quoted, 1
Baker, Sir Herbert, 133
Baltic Exchange, 19
Banca Commerciale Italiana, 89
Banco di Napoli, 93
Bank for International Settlements, 144
Bank of America, 90
Bank of England, 2, 18, 21, 64, 80, 83, 90, 103, 107, 109, 110, 111, 112, 113, 115, 120, 133–66, 170, 171, 174, 244; and clearing banks, 149–50; and discount

market, 155–66; annual reports, 134, 139; Court of Directors, 134, 138, 148; Discount Office, 161, 165; duties and roles, 144–5, 149–51; Government White Paper (1971), 143; independence, 146–8; Quarterly Bulletins, 134, 139; rescue operations, 152–4
Bank of England Act 1946, 142, 147, 148, 150
Bank of Ireland, 113
Bank of London and South America, 80, 123
Bank of Scotland, 131
Bank Rate, 108, 135–7, 145–7
Bank Rate Tribunal (1957), 10–12, 136–7
Banker, 118, 121, 125
Bankers Trust International, 89, 90, 94
Banque de Paris et de Pays-Bas, 89
Banques d'affaires, 15
Barber, Anthony, 151
Barclay & Sons, and Barclay Securities, 229, 230n., 231, 232, 234
Barclays Bank, 84, 102, 105, 106, 109, 110, 111, 112–17, 123, 125, 126, 127; Barclaycards, 122; pension fund, 59
Barclays DCO (now Barclays International), 123
Baring Brothers, 61, 63, 65, 74–5, 89
Baring, Peter, 73
Barkshire, John, 163
Barrington, Ken, 174
Barrow Hepburn and Gale, 231
Barton, Hugh, 136
Beckman, Bob, 45–7
Beecham, 65, 88
Beetham, Sir Edward, 197–9
Bentley, John, 229–34
Berger and Gosschalk, 16
Berkshire Finance Company, 238
Berwin, Stanley, 72
Bevins, Kenneth, 218, 219
Bills of exchange and bill brokers, 158–60, 163, 165–6
Birmingham Railway Carriage and Wagon Company, 239
Blair-Cunynghame, James, 131
Blessing, Dr, 147
Blomquist, Robert, 90
Board of Trade, and V and G, 202–19
See also Department of Trade and Industry
Bolton, Sir George, 80, 155
Boots, 66
Bovis, 81
Bowater, 81, 244
Bowmaker hire purchase company, 240–41
Bowring (C. T.), 20, 241
Boyle, Andrew, 146, 153
B.P., *see* British Petroleum
Brandt (William), 16, 65, 79, 92, 196
Briston, Richard, 76, 79
British Aircraft Corporation, 73
British Aluminium, 11, 69, 176
British Insurance Association (B.I.A.), 22, 54–5, 170, 203, 206–7, 212, 214–19, 246–7; Protection Committee, 55
British Match Corporation, 137
British Petroleum (B.P.), 65; pension fund, 57
British Printing Corporation, 185, 188
British Steel Corporation, 3
British Sugar Corporation, 66
British Wagon, 106
Broackes, Nigel, 189
Brown, Sir David, and David Brown Corporation, 129
Brown Shipley, 3, 65, 82
Buchanan, Alastair, 163
Bucks, Michael, 174
Bundesbank (West Germany), 147
Burmah Oil, 50
Burr, Reggie, 212–20

Cabora Bassa, 246
Cadbury, Adrian, 138
Cadbury Schweppes, 65, 138
Cannon, Peter, 174
Carr, Sir William, and Carr family, 180–81
Carreras group, 196
Cassel, Arenz, 239
Cater Ryder, 162
Catto, Lord, 148
Cazenove, 20, 89, 177, 178–9, 186
Cementation building company, 189
Certificates of Deposit (C.D.), 165
Chalfont, Lord, 59
Chambers, Sir Paul, 59
Chambers, Wayne, 36–8
Charterhouse Japhet, 64, 65
Chartists, 43–6
Chemical Bank, 83
Church Commissioners, 49, 245
Churchill, Sir Winston, 147; quoted, 133
City Code, *see* Code on Amalgamations and Mergers
Clark, Robert, 72, 81, 174, 244
Clarke, William, 104
Clearing banks, 84, 102–32, 141, 150, 153, 154, 170, 171; and computers, 124–5; and management techniques, 124; and non-banking specialists, 124; cartel, 106, 110, 119; diversification, 122–4; employment of graduates, 127–8; expansion of branches, 109; P.I.B. report, 111–14
Clegg, Sir Cuthbert, 113
Clive Discount, 161, 163, 165
Clore, Sir Charles, 14, 71, 171, 223–4
Cobbold, Lord, 148
Code on Take-overs and Mergers, 167–202; 'Rowland' amendments, 196–7
Columbia Gramophones, 64
Colwyn Committee, 112
Commercial Bank of Australia, 92
Commercial Union of Insurance, 8, 17, 56, 203, 205, 211, 216
Commerzbank, 93
Committee of London Clearing Banks, 113, 170
Common Market, 86–7, 201
Companies Acts, 43, 108, 170, 192, 216
Competition and Credit Control (Bank of England pamphlet), 119, 151
Computers, 125, 162
Confederation of British Industry, 174
Conservative Party and Governments, 3–4, 119–20, 135, 148, 160, 222
Consolidated Signal, 196
Constellation Investments, 228
Consumer Council, 116
Cooper Brothers, 82, 114, 163, 216, 218, 239
Cooper, Pat, 163
Cornfeld, Bernard, 39, 82, 152, 195
Corporate finance, 61–82
Cotton, Jack, 58
Courtaulds, 65, 173, 176, 177
Coutts Bank, 112
Cowdray, Lord, 22, 73
Cowley, Sir John, 241
Credit cards, 96, 122
Crédit Suisse, 93
Cripps, Sir Stafford, 147, 214
Crittall-Hope, 14
Crocker Citizens National Bank, 84
Cromer, Lord, 2, 111, 140, 145, 148, 209
Crosland, Anthony, 70, 115, 182
Crown Cork, 53
Crowther, Lord, 120
Cundy, Geoffrey, 130

Daily Express, 194
Daily Mail, 75
Daily Mirror group, 72
Daniell, Sir Peter, 145
De Havilland, 235
De L'Isle, Lord, 241
Demerara sugar company, 226

Department of Trade and Industry, 211–20, 241–2; report on Pergamon, 188; and V and G, 219
De Stein, Edward, 64
Deutsche Bank, 89
Dibbs, Alex, 131
Discount houses and discount market, 18, 155–66
District Bank, 113
Docker, Sir Bernard, 239
Dollar drain, 89
Dorland advertising agency, 233
Dow Jones Industrial Averages, 46
Drayton, Harley, 36
Dresdner Bank, 89
Drucker, Peter, 124
Du Cann, Edward, 4, 33
Dufay paint company, 177
Duncan, Sir Val, 138

Eagle Star, 161, 205
Eastern Produce, 227
Economist, 4, 9, 17, 22, 35, 37, 49, 84, 107, 111, 121, 125, 138, 208
Eliot, T. S., quoted, 1
Ellinger, Allan, 44
El Sobrante Mining Corporation, 37–8
E.M.I., 59, 63, 73, 182
Employers Liability, *see* Northern Employers
English Electric, 63
Equity and Law, 209
Equity cult, 42, 47
Eurocurrency markets, 7, 11, 16, 83–90, 93, 146; Eurobonds, 86–8; Eurodeutsche Marks, 86; Eurodollars, 69, 85–6, 93, 99–101, 123, 164; European Monetary Units, 86; Euroyen, 86
Evening Standard, 197
Exchange Equalisation Account, 144
Extel, 191

Faith, Nicholas, 29
Faulkner, Eric, 117, 123, 131, 132
Federal Reserve (U.S.A.), 90
Ferris, Paul, 88, 136
Finance Act 1965, 52
Finance press and financial journalism, 22–4, 78, 141
Financial Times, 22, 37, 129; Ordinary Share Index, 1
Finer, Morris, 238
Fire Offices' Committee, 207
First Boston Corporation, 84
First Finsbury Trust, 213
First National Bank of Boston, 83
First National City Bank, 11n., 83, 88, 90, 91, 96–8, 100, 123
First National Finance Corporation, 35, 60, 234, 240–42
Fisher, Sir Henry, 72
Fleming (Robert) and Co., and Fleming family, 28–32, 43, 174, 184–7
Forbes, Sir Archibald, 131, 132
Fordham property company, 193–4
Foreign banks in London, 11, 12, 154
See also American banks
Fortune magazine, 84, 96
France Fenwick group, 226
Fraser, Hugh, 71
Fraser, Ian, 167, 182, 190–92
Fraser, Lionel, 70
Freshfields, 71
Friedman, Professor Milton, 146
Fry, Richard, 11

Gallaher tobacco company, 64, 73, 177–9, 185
Gammell, William, 52–3
G.E.C., 63, 65, 73, 138; take-over of A.E.I., 48, 49, 168, 188
Gerrard and National, 158, 161
Gibbs (Antony), 64, 65
Gillett Brothers, 161
Gillum, John, 71, 73
Gillray, James, 146
Gilt-edged market, 145
Gladstone, W. E., 146
Glyn Mills, 113, 115, 127, 129, 132
Gommes, John, 94, 173, 177

Goobey, Ross, 56–7
Goodman, Lord, 185
Gordon, Charles, 58–60
Gore Brown, Thomas, 145
Graduates in banks, 127
Great Portland Estates, 161
Greene, Sir Sidney, 138
Grierson, Ronald, 3
Guardian Royal Exchange, 204, 205, 211
Guinness Mahon, 2, 65, 82, 127
Guy Butler, 165

Haller, Gilbert, 46
Hambro, Jocelyn, 18, 238, 240
Hambro Life Assurance, 209
Hambros Bank, 18, 63, 65, 69, 180, 238, 239, 240
Harcourt, Lord, 178
Hardie, Sir Charles, 16, 201
Harland & Wolff, 66
Harris Trust and Savings Bank, 84
Harrods, 107
Hayeshaw building group, 198–200
Headquarters and General Supplies, 79
Heasman, Roy, 141
Heath, Edward, 3, 216
Helbert, Wagg, 70
Higginson & Co., 63
Hill, Samuel, 3, 8, 16–17, 20, 22, 50, 61, 65, 67, 72, 76, 81, 82, 88, 168, 173, 174, 222
Hire purchase, 107–108, 235–9
Hire Purchase Trade Association, 116
Hoare Govett, 20
Hoffman, John, 49–50
Hollom, Jasper, 143
Home Counties Newspapers, 74
Hornby, Sir Antony, 178
Horsman, Malcolm, 81
Howard, Sir Seymour, 236
Howarth, Kenneth, 36–8
Hudson's Bay Company, 132
Hull, John, 200
Hunt, Tony, 213, 216, 217

IBM, 162
I.C.I., 44, 59, 62, 165, 193, 196, 234; Pension Fund, 59, 193
Imperial Tobacco, 178; Pension Fund, 56–7
Industrial and Commercial Finance Corporation, 107
Industrial Reorganisation Corporation (I.R.C.), 2, 51, 127, 173
'Insider trading', 9, 187, 188, 246
Institute of Chartered Accountants, 170
Institute of Directors, 15
Institutional Investor, 29
Institutions and institutional investors, 47–60, 67, 243–4
Insurance and insurance companies, 27, 47–9, 170, 171, 203–20; and trade unions, 211; 'composites', 205; general insurance, 204–5; life assurance, 204–5, 208–9; motor insurance, 204, 206–7, 208, 212–19
Insurance Companies Bill, 220
Inter-bank market, 164–5
Inter-bank Research Organisation, 130
Interest Equalisation Tax (U.S.A.), 86
International Bank for Reconstruction and Development (World Bank), 144
International Bank of Washington, 108
International Learning Systems Corporation, 185–8
International Monetary Fund, 144
International Money Mobilisation, 98
International Paints, 177
International Securities, 194
International Telephone and Telegraph, 94
Investment analysis and analysts, 40–46
Investment banks, 15
Investment managers and management, 25–39, 55–6

Investment Research, 44
Investment trusts, 47–8, 52–4, 170, 171, 224, 225–6
Investors Bulletin, 46
Investor's Chronicle, 22, 58
Investors Overseas Services (I.O.S.), 34, 39, 82, 153, 195
Investors Review, 228
Ionian Bank, 237–40
Iraq Petroleum Company, 53
Issuing Houses Association (I.H.A.), 75, 170, 179

Jackson, Professor Derek, 180
James, Sir Arthur (Mr Justice James), 218
Japhet (S.), *see* Charterhouse Japhet
Jardine, Christopher, 219
Jardine, Matheson, 136–7
Jenkins, Clive, 210–11
Jenkins Committee on company law, 41
Jenkins, Roy, 142
Jessel, David, 161
Jessel, Oliver, 36, 221–8, 242
Jessel Securities, 222, 223, 225–8
Jessel, Toby, 222
Jessel Toynbee, 161, 222
Johnson (Richard) and Nephew, 227
Johnston, Sir Alexander, 200
Jones, Aubrey, 111, 113
Jones, Robert, 63

Kearton, Sir Frank (Lord Kearton), 173, 177
Keith, Sir Kenneth, 16, 20, 22
Kershaw, Laurie, 213, 217
Keswick, W. J., 137, 138
Keynes, Lord, 33
Keyser Ullman, 38, 49, 50, 219
Kindersley, Lord, 63, 137
King and Shaxson, 160
King, Cecil, 72
Kleinwort Benson, 3, 61, 65, 69, 71, 173, 189
Knight, H. H., 14, 217
Knight, Jasper, 59
Kuhn Loeb, 69

Labour Party and Labour Governments, 2–3, 12, 48, 139, 147–8, 160, 211, 223
Laing, Sir Maurice, 138
Laporte, chemical company, 50
Lazard Brothers, 22, 63, 65, 69, 70–71, 73, 77, 81, 137, 244
Lazard Frères, 71
Leach, Sir Ronald, 188
Leasco Data Processing Equipment Corporation, 31, 184–90, 201
Leasing and factoring, 122
Leeds Assets, 227
Legal and General Insurance, 204, 205
Leyland, 13–16, 221
Life assurance, 204–5, 208–9; link with equity, 209; link with unit trusts, 208–9
Linklaters and Paines, 71
Liverpool and County Discount, 213, 215
Lloyd, Richard, 128–9
Lloyd George, David, 146
Lloyd's, 6, 9, 19n., 205–6, 209–10, 215
Lloyds Bank, 16, 84, 102, 110, 112, 113, 114, 115–16, 117, 122, 123, 126, 127, 129, 131
Lloyds Bank Europe, 123
Lloyds Bolsa International, 124
Lockwood, Sir Joseph, 59
London Discount Market Association, 160
London Stock Exchange, *see* Stock Exchange
Lotery, H., 14
Lyons (J.), 59

Macanie, 173
Mackinnon, Duncan, 161
McKinsey and Co., 141, 207
MacMillan committee, 104, 107
MAIBL, *see* Midland and International banks

Management consultants, 141, 207, 210
Manufacturers Hanover Bank, 85, 94
Marine Midland Bank, 84
Marley, Christopher, 170, 183
Marmor, Boris (Bobby), 59
Marriott, Oliver, 63
Martins Bank, 110; merger, 113–17
Matador Ranch, 70–71
Matthews, Percy ('Pat'), 35, 234–42
Maudling, Reginald, 3
Maxwell, Robert, 30–31, 82, 179–81, 183–8
Maxwell Scientific International, 185
Medium-term finance, 92–4
Melchett, Lord, 3
Mellon National Bank and Trust Company, 83
Mellor, Sir John, 49
Mensforth, Sir Holberry, 63
Mercantile Credit, 64, 106
Merchant banks, 10, 12, 13, 16, 17, 20, 28–32, 48, 61–82, 153, 170, 188, 244
Mergers, 50, 80–81, 167–202
Mersey Docks and Harbour Board, 4
Metal Industries, 173–4, 176
Metropolitan Estate and Property Corporation, 8, 16–17, 50
Midland and International Banks (MAIBL), 92, 93, 109, 110
Midland Bank, 79, 84, 92, 102, 110, 119, 122, 126, 127, 131, 146, 153
Mikardo, Ian, 139, 140–41, 142, 143, 155, 166
Milligan, P. W., 20
Minster Trust, 161, 174
Moate, David, 3
Monopolies Commission, 207n.; report on clearing banks, 115–17
Montagu, David, 201, 222
Montagu (Samuel), 16, 65, 79, 109, 222; Montagu Trust, 79
Monthly Haller Theory Report, 46
Morgan et Cie, 89
Morgan Grenfell, 38, 65, 138, 174, 177–9
Morgan Guaranty Trust, 90
Morse, Jeremy, 127
Motor insurance, 18, 206–7, 208 212–19
Motor Insurers' Bureau, 218
Mullens and Co., 145, 147
Multi-national banks, 92–4
Multiple Shops Federation, 116
Murdoch, Rupert, 181
Murray, Angus, 49, 56
Mynors, Sir Humphrey, 174, 182

National and Commercial Banking Group, 115, 131
National and Grindlays Bank, 79, 92, 196
National Association of Pension Funds, 52–4, 170; Investment Protection Committee, 54–5
National Bank of Seattle, 84
National Car Parks, 59
National Chamber of Trade, 116
National Coal Board, 138
National Commercial Bank of Scotland, 113, 115
National debt, 145
National Discount, *see* Gerrard and National
National Provincial Bank, 110, 112–13; merger with Westminster Bank, 114–15
See also National Westminster Bank
National Union of Bank Employees, 127
National Union of Railwaymen, 138
National Westminster Bank, 80, 84, 102, 103, 117, 119, 126, 127, 131
Nelson of Stafford, First Lord, 63; Second Lord, 138
Nepotism, 18–19
New Issue Permanent, 224, 226
New issues, 8, 74–9

New York Stock Exchange, 170
Newbould, Gerald, 168–9
Newman Holdings, 231
News Ltd, 181
News of the World, 30–31, 180–81, 183
Norbury, Earl of, 197–200
Norbury Insulation Group, 197–200
Norcros, 196
Norman, Mark, 178
Norman, Montagu (Lord Norman), 146–7, 148, 153
North Central Wagon, 106
Northern Employers, 204
'Notes on Amalgamation of British Businesses', 171; 'Revised Notes', 172

O'Brien, Sir Leslie, 134, 141, 143–4, 148, 151, 152, 153, 166
Observer, 195, 197
Oceanic Growth unit trust, 34
Odhams, 72
Organisation for Economic Cooperation and Development, 144
Ormond, John, 34–5, 37–9
Ozalid, 196

P. and O., 73, 81, 244
Panel on Take-overs and Mergers, 31–2, 167, 174, 177–83, 186–90, 192–3, 195–6, 199–202, 246
Panmure Gordon, 82, 186
Parallel markets, 163–4
Park Royal vehicles, 13
Parker, Alan, 208
Parker, Sir Hubert (Lord Parker), 136, 137
Parker, Peter, 245
Parry, Ken, 53
Peake, Harald, 115
Pearce, Lord, 183, 187
Pearl Assurance, 49
Pearson (S.) and Son, 22, 73, 77
Peat Marwick Mitchell, 71, 82, 188
Penguin Books, 79
Pension funds, 47–8, 52–4, 56–7, 59, 170, 204, 244
Performance and performance cult, 33–40
Pergamon Press, 30–31, 82, 180, 181, 184–8, 201
Philip Morris, 177
Philips, 94, 172, 176
Phoenix Assurance, 240, 241
P.I.B., *see* Prices and Incomes Board
Pierson, Heldring and Pierson, 89
Pilkington, Lord, 138
Piper, B. H., 131
Plumley, Ronald, 196
Polwarth, Lord, 131
Poole, Lord, 244
Poseidon, 37, 44
Post Office Giro, 106
Powell Duffryn, 66
Powell, Enoch, 161
Press, the, 22–4, 43, 168, 176
Prevention of Fraud Act, 170
Price Waterhouse report on Pergamon, 187–8
Prices and Incomes Board (P.I.B.), 111–12, 117–8, 123, 161
Prideaux, John, 119, 131, 132
Protection of Depositors Act, 170
Prudential Assurance, 49, 56, 203, 204, 209, 211
Public relations firms, 24 and n.
Public Works Loan Board, 164
Pye, 172, 176

'Queensbury Rules', 172–3

Radcliffe Committee and Report, 57, 76, 102, 103, 108, 137–9, 147, 158, 166
Ralli Brothers and Ralli International, 15, 81, 231
Real Estate Fund of America, 3
Regulation Q (U.S.A.), 90
Republic National Bank of Dallas, 83
Research departments, 40
Reynolds Metals, 69–70

Richard Thomas and Baldwins, 172
Richardson, Gordon, 66, 134, 138
Richardson, Michael, 186
Rio Tinto-Zinc, 138, 245–6
Road Traffic Act 1930, 212
Robarts, David, 103, 108
Robens, Lord, 138
Rockware Group, 245
Rodo Investment Trust, 94, 173
Roll, Sir Eric, 22, 138
Rolls-Royce, 4, 45, 66, 97, 129, 153–4
Roskill, Sir Ashton, 115
Rothschild, Evelyn de, 22
Rothschild, Jacob, 180
Rothschild, Leopold, 138
Rothschild's, 17, 62, 66, 72, 93, 94, 110, 161, 172, 174, 184, 186; Intercontinental Bank, 93; Investment Trust, 161
Rowland, David, 193–7
Rowland, Reg, 194
Royal Bank of Scotland, 112, 115
Royal Exchange Assurance, 137, 203–4
Royal Insurance, 59, 73, 203–4, 205, 218
Rubner, Alex, 55
Rummel, Bob, 91

Salmon, Sir Julian, and Salmon family, 59
Sampson, Anthony, 102, 170
Samuel, Harold, 14
Samuel, Marcus, and M. Samuel, 222
Samuel, Peter, 76
Sandilands, Francis, 203, 216
Save and Prosper unit trust group, 29, 33
Scandinavian banks, 93
Scottish and Newcastle Breweries, 66
Scrimgeour, James, 17
Sebag, Joseph, 240
S.E.C., *see* American Securities and Exchange Commission
Seccombe, Hugh, and Seccombe, Marshall and Campion, 159
Security Pacific Bank, 85
Sedgwick Collins, 20
Seebohm, Lord, 246
Select Committee on Nationalised Industries, 139–44, 147, 150–52, 155
Seligman Brothers, 64
Selmes, Christopher, 221, 242
Shaw, David, 228
Shawcross, Lord, 167, 182, 183, 186, 189–90, 201–2, 246
Shelbourne, Philip, 72
Shell, 65, 182, 222
Shell Transport and Trading, 132
Singer sewing machines, 106
Skimming, Ian, 20
Slater, Jim, and Slater Walker Securities, 4, 13–16, 36, 43, 190, 191n., 195, 221, 227, 230–32. 233, 242, 244
Slaughter and May, 71, 72
Smasons Associated Companies 236, 238
Smeddles, Thomas, 216
Smith, Frank, 70, 73
Smith St Aubyn, 160
Soane, Sir John, 133
Special Buyer, the 159
Spence, Christopher, and Spence, Veitch, 38
Spey Investments, 59–60, 241
Spillers, 132
Stable, Owen, 188
Standard and Chartered Banking Group, 92
Standard Life Assurance, 204
Staveley machine tool company, 226
Steinberg, Saul, 31, 183–6
Sterling, Jeffrey, 70
Stevens, Sir John, 138
Stevinson Hardy, 226
Stewarts & Lloyds, 172
Stock Exchange, the, 5, 6, 8–11, 27, 37, 45, 71, 72, 141, 147, 154, 170–71, 174, 176, 179, 182, 183,

186, 199–200, 228; entry, 19; Council, 19; Daily Official List, 190–91
Stock Exchange outside London, 6
Stokes, Lord, 13, 15
Stoop Vigne, 198, 200
Strauss Turnbull, 89
Stutchbury, Oliver, 33
Sunday Mirror, 193
Sunday Times, 22, 128
Surinvest, 34, 39
Switchgear and Equipment Ltd, 226

Take-over Panel, *see* Panel on Take-overs and Mergers
Take-overs, 48–50, 68–70, 80–81, 153, 167–202
Tax avoidance, 9
Technical analysts, 43
See also Chartists
Term lending, 96–7
Thomson, Sir John, 111, 114, 119, 122, 131, 132
Thorn, Sir Jules, and Thorn Electrical Industries, 172, 174
Times, The, 8–9, 17, 22, 38–9, 60, 64, 115, 119, 120, 154, 174, 183, 187, 188, 193
Titmuss, Professor Richard, 25
'Tombstones', 88
Toronto Dominion Bank, 92
Touche Ross, 71, 184
Trade unions and insurance companies, 210–11
Trades Union Congress, 48
Trafalgar House Investments, 15, 17, 189
Transparent Paper, 161
Treasury, the, 109–12, 115, 120, 140–43, 147–9, 151
Tube Investments, 69
Tugendhat, Christopher, 87
Tuke, Anthony W., 102, 106, 108

Unemployment statistics, 1
Unicorn Securities, 34
Unigate, 66
Unilever, 59; pension fund, 59
Union Discount, 160–61
Union of Insurance Staffs, 211
Unit trusts, 9–10, 28–9, 33–5, 47–8, 52, 122, 170, 204, 208–9, 224, 228
United California Bank, 83–4
United Dominions Trust, 107
United International Bank, 93
Upper Clyde Shipbuilders, 97
U.S. Government, 85, 86

Vavasseur, J. H., 234
Vehicle and General Insurance Company (V and G), 18, 22, 212–19; Tribunal's enquiry, 216, 218–20
Venesta packaging and timber company, 196
Vickers, 67, 132, 138, 153
Villiers, Charles, 2–3, 51, 127
Vokey, Richard, 96

Walker Moate, 3
Walker, Peter, 3–4, 14
Warburg, Sir Siegmund, 69
Warburg (S. G.), 3, 22, 64, 66, 69, 72, 86, 89, 138, 182
Wardle (Bernard), 14
Wareham, Wilfred, 182
Watney Mann, 171, 224
Wedd Durlacher, 16
Weinberg, Mark, 209
Weinstock, Sir Arnold, 48, 63
Wells Fargo Bank, 84
Western Ground Rents, 57
Westminster Bank, 102, 113; merger with National Provincial, 114–15
See also National Westminster Bank
White, Weld, 89
Whitehead Iron and Steel, 172
Wilde, Derek, 105
Wilkinson and Riddell, 173
Williams Deacon's Bank, 112–13, 129
Williams and Glyn's Bank, 80, 84, 93, 128–9

Williams Hudson, 195–6
Willis, Derek, 71
Wilson, Harold, 2, 6, 51, 140, 148, 182
Wiltshire Investments, 198–9
Wimpey, 66
Wise, T. A., 70
Wolfson, Sir Isaac, 71, 100, 196, 231
Women in the City, 19
Woods, Robert, 197–200
Woolworths, 107
World Bank, 144

Zambonakis, Minos, 94

EUROPE: THE RADICAL CHALLENGE
Hugh Thomas

Does British membership of the EEC mean an end to a thousand years of history? Does it mean subordination to a large and clumsy organisation over which we can never have effective, or democratic, control? Professor Hugh Thomas thinks not, and in this provocative guide to and investigation of Britain's political, social and economic future in the EEC he presents lucid and cogent arguments as to why membership presents Britain with a massive opportunity to preserve and rejuvenate the liberal heritage within a creative, humane and outward-looking European community.

Wide-ranging and tersely written. It touches on most 'European" subjects and then moves on with an agreeable rapidity' – Roy Jenkins, *The Observer*

Hugh Thomas is Professor of History at Reading University, and is the author of *The Spanish Civil War* which has sold nearly a million copies and has become a classic of contemporary history.

Politics/World Affairs 50p

STATE IN CAPITALIST SOCIETY
The Analysis of the Western System of Power
Ralph Miliband

'A sustained essay in demystication; honest, taut and disciplined . . . It makes an effective contribution to that formidable and sophisticated restatement of Marxism which the English language until recently lacked' – *The Guardian*

'An important piece of contemporary social analysis . . . will help to dispel many myths' – *The Times Educational Supplement*

Politics/Economics 60p

HOAX

Stephen Fay, Lewis Chester and Magnus Linklater

'This almost incredible tale cannot help but make fascinating reading' – *The Economist*

Hoax tells the inside story of how a virtually unknown American novelist persuaded one of the biggest publishing companies in the world to part with three quarters of a million dollars for the forged 'autobiography' of America's richest and most notoriously eccentric hermit, Howard Hughes.

'Highly readable' – *Sunday Telegraph*

Current Events 50p

TO TAKE ARMS

Maria McGuire

An account of a year in the Provisional IRA from its first-ever defector.

'She was a devout Republican – she clearly still is – and her book is a valuable insight into Provisional thinking' – Simon Hoggart, *The Guardian*

'Real historical significance' – Conor Cruise O'Brien, *The Observer*

Autobiography 40p

These books are obtainable from booksellers and newsagents or can be ordered direct from the publishers. Send a cheque or postal order for the purchase price plus 6p postage and packing to Quartet Books Limited, P.O. Box 11, Falmouth, Cornwall TR10 9EN